Shrinking Economic Distance

SUSTAINABLE INFRASTRUCTURE SERIES

Shrinking Economic Distance

UNDERSTANDING HOW MARKETS AND PLACES CAN LOWER TRANSPORT COSTS IN DEVELOPING COUNTRIES

Matías Herrera Dappe, Mathilde Lebrand,
and Aiga Stokenberga

 WORLD BANK GROUP

ABOUT THE SERIES

Sustainable infrastructure is a key enabler of economic and social development, as well as environmental sustainability. Quality infrastructure enhances productivity and competitiveness, contributing to economic growth and employment, as well as to facilitating international trade. Broad coverage of infrastructure services promotes social inclusion and equity and supports the formation of human capital. Green infrastructure safeguards local environmental quality while contributing to the global decarbonization process. The challenge of delivering sustainable infrastructure services is a complex one that goes far beyond "bricks and mortar" to encompass good policy, sound planning, efficient procurement, smart regulation, transparent governance, affordable finance, and functional markets. The Sustainable Infrastructure Series covers a wide range of policy topics relating to network infrastructure services, including energy, multimodal transportation, information and communication technology and digital development, water and sanitation, and urban and rural infrastructure, as well as irrigation and flood management.

PREVIOUS TITLES IN THIS SERIES

Shrinking Economic Distance: Understanding How Markets and Places Can Lower Transport Costs in Developing Countries (2024) by Matías Herrera Dappe, Mathilde Lebrand, and Aiga Stokenberga

Advancing Cloud and Infrastructure Markets: Strategic Directions for Low- and Middle-Income Countries (2024) by Natalija Gelvanovska-Garcia, Vaiva Mačiulė, and Carlo Maria Rossotto

The Path to 5G in the Developing World: Planning Ahead for a Smooth Transition (2024) by World Bank

The Economics of Electric Vehicles for Passenger Transportation (2023) by Cecilia Briceno-Garmendia, Wenxin Qiao, and Vivien Foster

Off the Books: Understanding and Mitigating the Fiscal Risks of Infrastructure (2023) by Matías Herrera Dappe, Vivien Foster, Aldo Musacchio, Teresa Ter-Minassian, and Burak Turkgulu

Laying the Foundations: A Global Analysis of Regulatory Frameworks for the Safety of Dams and Downstream Communities (2020) by Marcus J. Wishart, Satoru Ueda, John D. Pisaniello, Joanne L. Tingey-Holyoak, Kimberly N. Lyon, and Esteban Boj García

Rethinking Power Sector Reform in the Developing World (2020) by Vivien Foster and Anshul Rana

Lifelines: The Resilient Infrastructure Opportunity (2019) by Stephane Hallegatte, Jun Rentschler, and Julie Rozenberg

Beyond the Gap: How Countries Can Afford the Infrastructure They Need while Protecting the Planet (2019) by Julie Rozenberg and Marianne Fay

All books in the Sustainable Infrastructure Series are available for free at http://hdl.handle.net/10986/31290

Contents

Boxes

Figures

Maps

Tables

Foreword

The world's first container ship, a converted World War II oil tanker called the *Ideal X*, departed the port of Newark, New Jersey, on April 26, 1956. On board were 58 truck-trailers bound for Houston, Texas.

Carrying mass amounts of cargo by maritime transport transformed global trade, and as a result, the global economy. Containerization enabled globalization, the dispersion of value chains between countries, and unprecedented economic growth.

Transport infrastructure has come a long way since the *Ideal X's* maiden voyage in 1956. Today, the world's largest container ships carry 24,000 containers or more, dwarfing those from half a century ago. As shipping capacity has increased, costs have declined by up to 39 percent by weight and 62 percent by value since the 1960s. Around 90 percent of the world's goods are shipped this way.

But even as transport costs have decreased and global shipping has become the norm, transport cost reductions have been uneven between countries. It is still 50 percent more expensive to export to the United States from a low-income country than from a high-income one. International transport prices, such as for dry bulk goods like grains and minerals, also remain highly volatile, mostly due to shipping demand shocks but also due to one-off events like the COVID-19 pandemic and the closure of the Suez Canal.

These inequities persist at the domestic level as well. For many developing countries, road transportation remains the main mode of shipment. As this report demonstrates, the cost of trading within developing countries is between 3 and 14 times higher than in the United States.

What is behind these disparities? Why does it cost so much more to ship goods from and within developing countries than in high-income countries? Some reasons are intuitive: distance, geography, and the quality of infrastructure all impact the amount of money required to move goods from point A to point B. But this is not the full story.

When transport is slow, it costs more. In developing countries, trade policies and procedures add time and money to routes that can already be onerous due to poor road conditions, treacherous topography, and unpredictable weather. Borders are major bottlenecks, with the average time to comply with export regulations often exceeding 4 days in low-income countries, compared to just 1 day in high-income countries. Sometimes, shipments spend 15 percent or more of the total export time simply waiting at ports. Both travel to the main port or border crossing and between cities tend to be slower in poor countries than in rich countries, with the speed on intercity roads in the latter being twice as high as in the former.

Market regulations are another often overlooked contributor to transport costs in developing countries. In some places, markets for trucking services are still not competitive. Price regulation, formal and informal entry barriers, high market concentration by a few players, and collusion all trigger higher transport costs. A lack of alternative routes, especially in land-locked countries, also plays a role.

This report demonstrates how different market frictions impact the cost of transporting goods worldwide. This is a crucial problem for policy makers to solve for many reasons, but paramount among them is that inefficient transport exacerbates food insecurity and geographic inequalities, as well as threatens climate resilience. In Sub-Saharan Africa, for example, transport costs can represent up to 50 percent of food prices, and about 40 percent of food is lost before it ever reaches people's plates—often due to poor logistics. Maritime transport comprises 3 percent of global emissions; 15 percent of this figure is generated by ships stalling at ports.

To compete in global markets, developing country governments need to keep transport costs down. Creating efficient markets and seamless connections between places is essential to addressing this challenge. This report offers a fresh perspective on transport connectivity by drawing on a wealth of new data and original research. In doing so, it provides a policy framework for the needed reforms that can make markets more efficient and the infrastructure investments that can make places better connected.

We hope the report's findings will help guide decision-makers in designing impactful reforms and look forward to working closely with our client country governments, development partners, and the private sector to deliver solutions that will help shrink the economic distance between and within countries and thus promote growth and sustainable development.

Nicolas Peltier-Thiberge
Global Director for Transport
Global Practice
World Bank

Binyam Reja
Practice Manager for Transport
Global Practice
World Bank

Acknowledgments

This report was prepared by a team led by Matías Herrera Dappe, Mathilde Lebrand, and Aiga Stokenberga. Its wide scope meant that a large team of experts, including World Bank and external researchers, undertook the underlying research. The team comprised Atsushi Iimi, Alejandro Molnar, Nino Pkhikidze, Forhad Shilpi, and Burak Turkgulu (World Bank); Prottoy A. Akbar (Aalto University); Treb Allen (Dartmouth College); Adina Ardelean (Santa Clara University); David Atkin (Massachusetts Institute of Technology); Santiago Cantillo-Cleves (University of California, San Diego); Kerem Coşar (University of Virginia); Victor Couture (University of British Columbia); Bernardo Díaz de Astarloa (Universidad de Buenos Aires and Universidad Nacional de La Plata); Gilles Duranton (University of Pennsylvania); Lin Fan (London School of Economics); Carlos Eduardo Hernández (Universidad de Los Andes); Volodymyr Lugovskyy (Indiana University); Nick Porée (Porée and Associates); Brock Rowberry (University of Michigan, Ann Arbor); Adam Storeygard (Tufts University); David Terner (Indiana University); and Ron Yang (University of British Columbia). Juan Ignacio Fulponi, Eigo Tateishi, and the World Bank's cartography unit provided support with maps and figures. Azeb Afework provided administrative support.

The team is thankful to Crickmay & Associates; Gael Raballand; the national statistics offices of Georgia, Kenya, Madagascar, Nigeria, Rwanda, and Tanzania; SATLOCK; and the World Food Programme for providing access to data for the underlying research.

The report's peer reviewers provided valuable guidance. They included Megersa Abate, Luis Blancas, Charles Kunaka, and Roman Zarate Vasquez (World Bank). Tomas Serebrisky (Inter-American Development Bank) and Tony Venables (University of Oxford) provided guidance at the inception stage. The report also benefited from comments from Muneeza Alam, Theophile Bougna, Leonardo Cañon, Vivien Foster, Martin Humphreys, Yin Yin Lam, Shomik Mehndiratta, Javier Morales Sarriera, Harris Selod, Stéphane Straub, and Felipe Targa (World Bank); Andrés Chaves Pinzón

(2BONEC); Jan Hoffmann (UNCTAD); and David Hummels (Purdue University). Pablo Fajnzylber, Nicolas Peltier, and Binyam Reja provided helpful guidance.

This report would not have been possible without generous funding by the Public-Private Infrastructure Advisory Facility (PPIAF).

We thank Jewel McFadden, acquisitions editor; Christina Davis, production editor; and Orlando Teofilo Mota, print coordinator (World Bank), for their work on this book. Barbara Karni edited the report, and Ann O'Malley proofread it. The cover was designed by Veronica Elena Gadea (World Bank), and the book was typeset by Datapage International Ltd.

About the Authors

Matías Herrera Dappe is a senior economist and the global lead on transport economics and policy at the World Bank, where he leads policy research programs on infrastructure with a focus on transport. He has published extensively on a wide range of topics, including infrastructure economics, economic development, trade and logistics, public-private partnerships, state-owned enterprises, competition, auctions, and fiscal policy. Before joining the World Bank, he worked for consulting firms and think tanks, advising governments and companies in Europe, Latin America, and North America. He holds a PhD in economics from the University of Maryland, College Park.

Mathilde Lebrand is a senior economist in the Prospects Group, a unit of the World Bank's Development Economics Vice Presidency. She is also a member of the team producing the 2024 *World Development Report* on economic growth in middle-income countries. Previously, she worked in the Infrastructure Chief Economist and the Europe and Central Asia Chief Economist units. Her research focuses on economic geography, transport, and trade. She has taught at the University of Montreal and worked at the World Trade Organization in Geneva. She holds a PhD in economics from the European University Institute.

Aiga Stokenberga is a senior transport economist at the World Bank, where she leads analytical work and investment and policy lending operations in urban mobility, regional economic corridors, and transport resilience in Latin America and the Caribbean and, previously, in Africa. She also co-leads global transport knowledge products and initiatives, including by leveraging Big Data–intensive approaches. Before joining the Transport Global Practice in 2016, she worked on electricity regulation and governance, energy policy, and trade and logistics at the World Bank and at the World Resources Institute Ross Center for Sustainable Cities. She holds a master's degree in international energy policy and international economics from the Johns Hopkins University School of Advanced International Studies and a PhD in urban economics and land use from Stanford University.

Main Messages

Despite the reduction in transport costs over the past decades, the world today is still far from being a single integrated economy. Developing countries face higher transport prices than developed countries, for both international and domestic shipments, and shipping times are longer and less reliable. Tackling the problems can increase both income and general welfare in these countries, improving the lives of the people who live there.

This report assesses the main determinants of the economic costs of freight transport in developing countries and identifies the frictions keeping transport prices above an efficient level, times high, and reliability low. It focuses on maritime and road transport, particularly road transport, as evidence in this area has been scarcer than it is for maritime transport. By deepening the understanding of the frictions driving the economic costs of freight transport, the report can help policy makers target reforms in areas in which reforms can be expected to have the greatest impact and avoid unintended consequences.

Three main findings stand out from the analysis:

- **Transport infrastructure can reduce the frictions of physical geography, but its ability to do so depends on the quality, service level, and operation of the infrastructure.** The transport price for a shipment increases with distance and topography; more direct routes can therefore reduce the cost of moving goods. Cutting the distance for the median shipment delivering food in low- and middle-income countries by 100 kilometers reduces the transport price by about 20 percent on average, for example. For a given distance, highways are associated with average transport prices that are about 20 percent lower than prices on lower categories of roads. Low-quality road infrastructure can also exacerbate the impact of extreme weather events. Shipments during the rainy season cost about 6 percent more than shipments during the dry season, and the premium is higher in countries in which the quality of the road infrastructure is lower.

Improving both the technical efficiency and the operational performance of container ports can significantly reduce transport costs. Raising performance—as measured by the World Bank's Container Port Performance Index, which is based on the time vessels spend at ports—from the bottom 25 percent to the top 25 percent could reduce shipping costs by 37 percent.

- **Increasing competition in the transport sector can increase the quality of service and lower prices.** Several countries deregulated their trucking sectors over the past few decades, creating competitive sectors. Elsewhere, however, markets for trucking services are not competitive. Deregulation and strong competition in trucking markets bring significant benefits for shippers and the economy as a whole. In Colombia, for example, a 10 percent decrease in a trucker's market share on a route yields a 0.57 percent decrease in the trucking price.

  Private sector involvement in port operations coupled with competition between and within ports are conducive to better port performance and lower maritime shipping costs. Consolidation and increased cooperation in the container shipping industry can reduce maritime shipping costs because of economies of scale and scope, but increased market power can lead to higher prices, potentially offsetting the benefits.

- **Market failures, government policies, and the distribution of economic activity across space can raise transport prices.** Empty running trucks and cargo vessels are common across the world. Regulations that forbid or limit the ability of trucks and vessels to pick up cargo at the destination and information frictions that limit the ability of shippers and carriers to find each other increase the probability of empty trips. The distribution of economic activity, particularly its heterogeneity, is an important determinant of transport demand and the incidence of empty trips. In countries facing food security issues, the trucking price to a destination with economic density in the top 25 percent is about 14 percent lower than the price to a destination whose economic density is in the bottom 25 percent.

Efficient, high-quality transport reduces economic distance, bringing people and firms closer to each other, fostering economic welfare, and reducing emissions. Crafting policies to reduce economic distance is complex, however, because of potential synergies and trade-offs, including heterogenous effects. Policy makers need to begin by understanding the main problem a policy aims to address and identifying the market failures and policy-driven frictions that warrant government intervention.

All countries are different, but any reform agenda to develop an efficient, high-quality freight transport and reduce economic distance should aim to foster efficient markets and places as follows:

- **Efficient markets** are markets in which service providers, workers, and suppliers have the incentive and ability to invest, innovate, increase productivity, and supply the best possible goods and services at the lowest possible prices and buyers can find the goods and services they need. Creating such markets requires tackling market failures and market frictions, including those caused by governments, along the transport supply chain. Measures include efforts to strengthen competition for and in the market, promote the development of efficient transport service providers, and improve demand aggregation and matching.

- **Efficient places** are places in the transport network—from the road, rail, and water links to the nodes of the transport network, such as ports and border posts—that are properly planned and function in a way that reduce the frictions associated with distance and topography (which climate change can exacerbate) and the costs of agglomeration. Measures include those aimed at developing adequate transport infrastructure, improving the efficiency of ports and border crossings, and managing urban congestion.

Without efficient markets, the full benefits of measures to ensure efficient places will not be realized. For this reason, efficient markets should be created first.

Abbreviations

CAREC	Central Asia Regional Economic Cooperation
CPPI	Container Port Performance Index
EMDEs	emerging markets and developing economies
EU	European Union
GDP	gross domestic product
GPS	Global Positioning Service
GIS	Geographic Information System
GVC	global value chain
HHI	Herfindahl-Hirschman Index
IBA	Indian Bank Association
ICC	Interstate Commerce Commission
km	kilometer
km/h	kilometer per hour
MTEF	medium-term expenditure framework
OECD	Organisation for Economic Co-Operation and Development
PPI	Private Participation in Infrastructure
PPP	public-private partnership
PPP	purchasing power parity
SOE	state-owned enterprise
TEU	20-foot equivalent unit
UNECE	United Nations Economic Commission for Europe
VOC	vehicle operating cost

All dollar amounts are US dollars unless otherwise indicated.

Overview

Declining freight transport costs over the past several decades have been an important contributor to the rapid growth of trade, a main driver of economic growth and economic convergence between developing and developed economies. Global transport costs declined by 33–39 percent by weight and by 48–62 percent by value between the mid-1960s and the mid-2010s (Ganapati and Wong 2023). As costs fell, the participation of emerging economies, especially China, in global trade increased, and the composition of trade shifted from natural resources toward more manufacturing products and intermediate goods. Manufacturers are no longer located close to their customers; firms have expanded and even fragmented their production supply chains, altering the geographic location of economic activity (Antras and Chor 2022; Redding 2022).

Despite the increasing globalization of production and trade, the world is still far from being a single integrated economy. Poorer countries face higher freight transport costs than wealthier countries. For example, it is 57 percent more expensive to export to the United States from a low-income country than from a high-income country, controlling for the distance, weight, and types of goods transported. Poorer countries face higher costs on both the international and the domestic legs of the journey. On average, within-country transport costs to export and import in high-income countries are half those in low-income countries (refer to figure O.1). In some African and Eastern European countries, the costs of trading within the countries are 3–14 times as large as in the United States (Atkin and Donaldson 2015; Díaz de Astarloa and Pkhikidze 2024).

1

FIGURE O.1 Domestic transport costs to import and export, by country income group

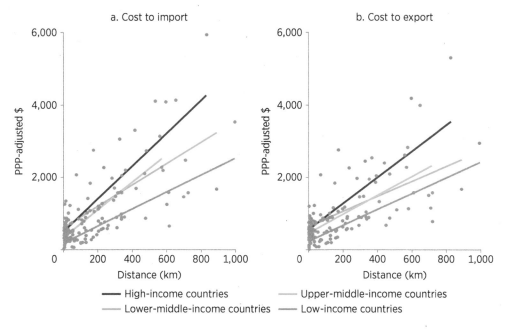

Source: Original figure for this publication using data from the 2020 Doing Business survey.
Note: Dots show observations by country. Lines are fitted lines per income group. PPP = purchasing power parity.

Transport prices have been volatile and the transport network vulnerable to unforeseen disruptions. In addition to the downward trends over the past decades, there have been abrupt movements of transport prices, in some instances nearly tripling on a year-to-year basis. The COVID-19 pandemic, for example, disrupted the transport network and had a much greater effect on transport prices on trade routes to developing regions than to developed regions.

It takes significantly longer to move goods within poorer countries, adding to the differences in the economic costs of transport between developing and developed countries. Shippers care not only about the transport price but also about the transport time and reliability, which affect inventory and hedging costs. Domestic times to export goods are much higher in developing countries, with a significant share of the time within the exporting country spent at the port. Both travel to the main port or border crossing and intercity travel tend to be slower in poorer countries (refer to figure O.2). Intercity road speed in a country in the top decile of intercity road speed is about twice as fast as it is in a country in the bottom decile.

FIGURE O.2 Correlation between travel speed and per capita income

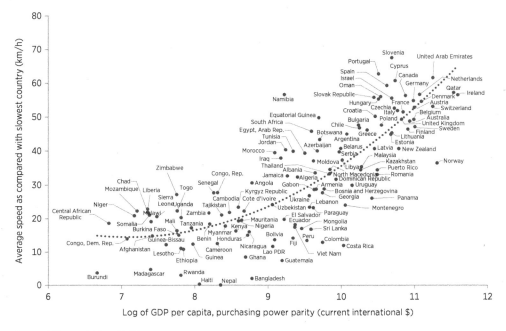

Source: Akbar and others 2024.
Note: Figure reports average speed in a country above the average speed in the slowest country in the sample (Nepal). The average speed is obtained as the country fixed effect in an ordinary least square regression, including speed measures for more than 36 million road segments covering all countries.

WHY SHOULD POLICY MAKERS CARE ABOUT THE COST OF MOVING GOODS?

Reductions in the cost and time of moving goods in and out of countries can increase trade volumes and influence the patterns of trade; high within-country transport costs and time can hinder the benefits of trade liberalization. Donaldson, Jinhage, and Verhoogen (2017) claim that the high cost of domestic transport in African countries is one of the main reasons the impact of trade liberalization has been limited and geographically unbalanced on the continent. Reducing domestic transport time and cost can promote international trade. Indeed, one study (Freund and Rocha 2011) finds that a one-day decrease in overland travel time is associated with a 7 percent increase in African exports.

Reductions in domestic transport costs and time affect not only international trade but also domestic trade, productivity, and investments. In India, for example, a 1 percent reduction in trucking unit costs is associated with a 2.8–3.9 percent increase in domestic trade flows (Lall, Sinha-Roy, and Shilpi 2022). Expansion of the railways in India increased interregional and international trade, with a 1 percent reduction in the distance between origin and destination associated with a 1.6 percent increase in trade (Donaldson 2018). A reduction in transport costs also increases productivity by promoting the clustering of activity; it may trigger investments as firms move into a cluster of activity, further increasing agglomeration and productivity (Duranton and Venables 2018).

Reductions in domestic transport costs and time can create jobs and shift labor away from the agricultural sector. In Mexico, a 10 percent increase in market access resulted in a 2.9–6.5 percent increase in employment (Blankespoor and others 2017). In Cameroon, Chad, Djibouti, Ethiopia, Kenya, Nigeria, and Somalia, reductions in land transport costs and electricity investments increased manufacturing and services employment at the expense of agricultural employment (Herrera Dappe and Lebrand 2024).

The increase in trade, investment, and productivity, and changes in employment can increase income and welfare—for the entire country and for specific locations. In China, the reduction in transport times and costs as a result of expansion of the highway system between the 1990s and 2000s increased intra-national trade, leading to an increase in aggregate real income (Roberts and others 2012), with a relocation of economic activity away from peripheral areas along the highways (Faber 2014). In Sub-Saharan African, a 10 percent reduction in transport costs led to a 2.8 percent increase in income for cities 500 kilometers from the port (Storeygard 2016).

Reductions in freight transport time and costs can also help reduce food insecurity. In 2022, over 258 million people experienced high levels of acute food insecurity (FSIN and Global Network Against Food Crises 2023). In Africa, improved road transportation improved household nutrition and reduced the number of stunted children (Blimpo, Harding, and Wantchekon 2013; Stifel and Minten 2017). In India, the railways played an important part in improving food security, dramatically reducing the ability of rainfall shocks to cause famines in the colonial era (Burgess and Donaldson 2010).

Reducing inefficiencies that keep transport costs high can also reduce emissions. The use of larger and more fuel-efficient trucks, reductions in empty and partly empty trips, more efficient driving practices, and good-quality roads that allow driving at speeds that minimize emissions can reduce both the private and social costs of transport (Collier and others 2019; Díaz-Ramirez and others 2017; Rizet, Cruz, and Mbacké 2012; Walnum and Simonsen 2015).

WHAT DOES THIS REPORT BRING?

Shrinking economic distance to bring people and firms closer to each other requires efficient, high-quality transport. Doing so requires reducing the frictions keeping transport prices above an efficient level, times high, and reliability low—that is, reducing the economic costs of transport.[1]

The goal is not to lower transport prices at all costs, which could lead to lower-quality transport with higher times and lower reliability, but to decrease the economic costs of transport.

This report assesses the main determinants of the economic costs of freight transport in developing countries and identifies the frictions keeping transport prices above an efficient level, times high, and reliability low. The report focuses on maritime and road transport, the dominant modes of transport in international, domestic, and regional trade. The emphasis is on road transport, an area in which evidence has been scarcer than it is in maritime transport. Drawing on important new sources of evidence (see box O.1 for a brief description of background papers and appendix A for a description of datasets used) and compiling many others, the report provides benchmarks and evidence to inform the design of policies to deepen the economic integration of developing countries.

BOX O.1

Background papers prepared for this report

Road transport

- Coşar (2022) reviews the literature on overland transport costs, particularly trucking, with a focus on the methodologies and data used to estimate costs.
- Allen and others (2024) develop a new spatial model to study the effect of imperfect competition in the transport sector on transport prices and the way in which investments in infrastructure cannot only reduce physical costs of shipping but also improve competition and induce better firms to enter the transport sector. The paper uses shipment-level data on nonagricultural shipments in Colombia between 2015 and 2021 (excluding 2018), covering a total of 50 million trips to confirm the model's predictions.
- Díaz de Astarloa and Pkhikidze (2024) estimate internal trade costs for six low- or middle-income countries (Georgia, Kenya, Madagascar, Nigeria, Rwanda, and Tanzania). The paper exploits unit-level price data collected by countries' national statistical offices for consumer price index calculation purposes and applies the price differential methodology.
- Iimi (2023) studies long-haul road shipments in seven countries in Eastern Europe and Central Asia (Azerbaijan, Georgia, Kazakhstan, the Kyrgyz Republic, Tajikistan, Turkmenistan, and Uzbekistan) to understand how carrier costs correlate with distance, average speed, freight volume, and topography.
- Yang (2024) conducts a meta-analysis of estimates of empty trips, empty miles, and backhaul probabilities covering 40 years and 27 countries.

(continued)

BOX O.1   **Background papers prepared for this report** *(continued)*

The paper also reviews the empirical evidence behind three potential mechanisms behind empty trips—geographic imbalances in freight demand, search and matching frictions, and regulatory barriers—and develops a stylized model to capture these sources and evaluate potential policies.

- Akbar and others (2024) investigate travel speed, reliability, and congestion of road travel between cities in 134 countries and analyze their association with road infrastructure availability and physical and human geography. Using a standard web-mapping platform, they collect data on the travel time of trips between cities that represent a large majority of cities with over 50,000 people, excluding China and the Korean peninsula.

- Herrera Dappe, Lebrand, and others (2024) study patterns and determinants of transport prices in 60 low- and middle-income countries in 2019–20, covering 53,106 shipments transported across 4,659 different routes, using a proprietary dataset of transport contracts to deliver food. The paper identifies the role of distance, quality, and availability of road infrastructure; seasonal rain patterns; conflict; economic geography; and border frictions associated with the ability of foreign shippers to access the market.

- Molnar and Shilpi (2024) use freight transaction data from a digital trucking platform in India that covers almost 480,000 freight transaction records for 2017–20. The paper examines the relationship between freight rates and a wide range of determinants, such as road infrastructure (including roads managed under public-private partnerships), urban congestion, topography, and truck characteristics.

Maritime transport

- Ardelean and others (2022) review the research on the determinants of maritime shipping, focusing on containerized and dry-bulk shipping and emphasizing recent trends and determinants of freight rates. The paper also presents several novel empirical exercises that draw insights from the literature.

- Herrera Dappe, Serebrisky, and others (2024) study the role of port performance as a determinant of maritime shipping costs across the globe, using various measures of performance, including the World Bank's Container Port Performance Index and a measure of technical efficiency estimated by the authors. The paper uses detailed data on over 250 container ports in 97 countries and close to 2 million observations on maritime shipping costs to the United States.

A deeper understanding of the frictions driving the economic costs of freight transport can help policy makers target reforms in areas in which they can be expected to have the greatest impact and avoid unintended consequences. **This report contributes to the debate on developing an efficient, high-quality freight transport sector by putting forward**

policy options to tackle the frictions keeping transport prices above an efficient level, times high, and reliability low and a framework for the design of country-specific reform agendas.

The report is organized as follows. Chapter 1 presents stylized facts and benchmarks on freight transport costs. Chapter 2 introduces a framework that links the factors that determine the economic costs of transports with their components and identifies the interactions among them. Chapter 3 provides new empirical evidence on the role of physical geography and infrastructure in determining transport costs. Chapter 4 identifies market failures and market frictions that affect transport times and prices. Chapters 5 and 6 present policy options and a framework that can help policy makers design country-specific reform agendas. Appendix A presents the main datasets used. Appendix B discusses methods for measuring overland transport costs. The rest of this overview presents the report's main findings and policy recommendations.

WHAT MATTERS IS ECONOMIC DISTANCE

The economic costs of transport depend on several factors, which interact with each other in complex ways to determine the price, time, and reliability of transport (refer to figure O.3). Through their impact on fixed and variable costs, the utilization of trucks and vessels, and the mark-ups charged by transport service providers, the physical and economic geography, infrastructure in place, inputs required to provide transport services,

FIGURE O.3 Economic costs of freight transport and its determinants

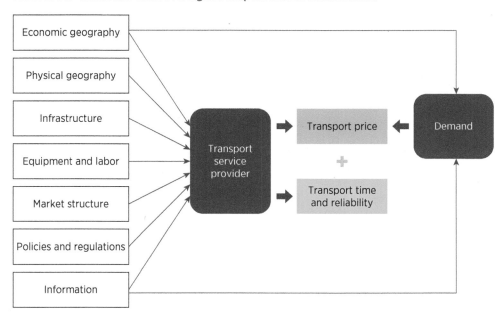

Source: Original figure for this publication.

structure of the transport market, policies and regulations, and the information on business opportunities affect the operation of transport service providers and hence the price they will have to receive to be willing to supply services. Economic geography and information on available services and prices are important determinants of the demand for transport services and the price shippers are willing to pay. All of these factors also play a role in determining the quality of the transport service in terms of time and reliability.

EFFICIENT, HIGH-QUALITY INFRASTRUCTURE CAN REDUCE THE FRICTION OF DISTANCE

Physical geography, particularly distance, is an important determinant of transport times and prices. The prices for trucking services increase with distance. The total transport price of a road shipment increases by about 3.1 percent for every 10 percent increase in trip distance (the increase is not proportional because of the fixed costs of shipping). In a sample of shipments in 60 low- and middle-income countries, moving from the 25th to the 75th percentile of travel distance for a representative shipment—that is, increasing from about 112 kilometers (km) to 420 km—is associated with a 43 percent decline in the transport unit price ($/ton-km) (Herrera Dappe, Lebrand, and others 2024). The topography of the terrain also increases transport costs, because of higher fuel consumption, longer travel times, and longer distance, as routes in mountainous areas are more tortuous.

Transport infrastructure can reduce the frictions of distance and topography, but the extent of the reduction depends on the quality and service level of the infrastructure. Removing 100 km from the trip distance for the median road shipment is associated with a total transport price saving of about 20 percent (Herrera Dappe, Lebrand, and others 2024). Compared with shipments traveling on routes that do not use highways at all, shipments that travel on highways for the entire length of their routes have 20 percent lower transport prices per ton-km on average (Herrera Dappe, Lebrand, and others 2024). Traveling along major highways in India reduces transport costs by 17.4–19.2 percent compared with traveling along roads with a lower service level (Molnar and Shilpi 2024). In Malawi, the trucking rates for bad roads are 9–15 percent higher than rates on all-weather roads (Ksoll and Kunaka 2016).

The capacity and quality of transport infrastructure are important determinants of time-related costs. Congestion is more important within than between cities. For intercity travel, the difference between the fastest time of day and the slowest time of day is only 2 km per hour relative to an average speed of about 70 km per hour—about 3 percent (Akbar and others 2024). In contrast, the slowest time of day in urban travel is 25 percent slower than the fastest across 1,119 cities (Akbar and others 2024). Road characteristics, such as the number of lanes, surface types, road lighting, and the quality of roads, are among the most important determinants of speed on interurban roads. Other potential important determinants are the quality of the vehicles and driver behavior.

The poor quality of transport infrastructure can increase the impact of extreme weather events by hindering the ability of the transport sector to move goods and keep the economy functioning during those events. Shipments during the rainy season pay a premium of about 6 percent on average. The effects are heterogeneous across countries, with the increase in transport price associated with the rainy season higher in countries in which road infrastructure quality is lower (refer to figure O.4).

The availability of good-quality infrastructure can affect the intensity of competition—and hence transport prices—across routes and regions within countries. On routes in Colombia that are more costly to serve because they are farther from economic activity and not well connected, fewer and smaller truckers provide services at higher prices (Allen and others 2024). The intensity of competition on a route also depends on the alternative transport modes available. In India, for example, trucking prices are higher on routes with weaker competition from rail (Molnar and Shilpi 2024).

The availability and quality of port infrastructure and the operation of ports are important determinants of maritime shipping costs. Policy makers can influence both. Raising efficiency in the use of container port facilities from the 25th to the 75th percentile reduces shipping costs by 3.2 percent (Herrera Dappe, Serebrisky, and others 2024). The country with the least efficient port sector in the sample could reduce maritime transport costs by 60 percent if it became as efficient as the most efficient country.

FIGURE O.4 Median transport price premium in the rainy season for median shipment, by quality of a country's road infrastructure

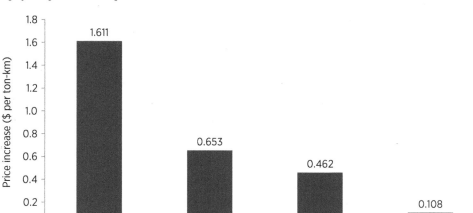

Source: Herrera Dappe, Lebrand and others 2024.
Note: The increase in transport price is relative to Türkiye (the benchmark country). Quality of road infrastructure is classified from 1 = lowest to 7 = highest.

Similar results are found when looking at the operational performance of container ports as measured by the World Bank's Container Port Performance Index, which is based on the time vessels spend at ports. Raising operational performance from the 25th to the 75th percentile reduces shipping costs by 37 percent. The country with the lowest average performance in the sample could reduce maritime transport costs by over 92 percent if it matched the performance of the best-performing country in the sample in 2021. Privately operated ports and those with good landside connectivity tend to have better performance and lower maritime transport costs.

THERE IS A LIMIT ON HOW MUCH INFRASTRUCTURE CAN REDUCE ECONOMIC DISTANCE

In competitive markets, service providers and consumers can freely enter and exit and agree on prices for their transactions. In such markets, the price for a service represents its marginal cost. Service providers that are faced with vigorous competition are continually pressed to become more efficient and productive, which drives innovation through investments in capital and new technologies and processes. Competition leads service providers to strive to offer higher-quality services and lower prices.

Several countries have deregulated their trucking sectors over the past few decades, creating competitive sectors. In other countries, markets for trucking services are still not competitive, because of price regulation, formal and informal entry barriers that lead to high concentration, and collusion. Eighteen out of 83 emerging markets and developing economies (EMDEs) for which data are available regulate trucking prices, mostly in response to pressure from trucking associations and unions. A common policy that softens competition is to restrict the entry of foreign trucking operators. Thirty-one of 94 (non-island) EMDEs do not allow cross-border delivery of cargo, and only 7 of 43 allow cabotage services (pickup and delivery of cargo inside the same country). In some countries, including Bangladesh and West and Central African countries, trucking unions and associations control access to loads and prices, the latter not just by influencing government regulation but through intermediaries who set prices and allocate jobs to carriers in noncompetitive ways. Imperfect competition on routes across Colombia means that prices are higher on routes with less intense competition. A 10 percent increase in a trucker's market share on a route yields a 0.57 percent increase in the average price on the route.

The evidence shows that regulation of trucking markets hurts shippers and the economy in general and that deregulation yields significant gains. Price floors for trucking services in Colombia led to about 50 percent higher prices on average and a 40 percent average reduction in shipped tonnage, reducing the efficiency of the market. This led to a loss to society of 8–12 percent of the market value of transportation services in a competitive market (Hernández and Cantillo-Cleves 2024). On average, shipping food across a border in low- and middle-income countries is about

70 percent more expensive than shipping within a country. The border premium is smaller when trucking companies from a richer neighboring country are allowed to compete in the local market (Herrera Dappe, Lebrand, and others 2024). The deregulation of the trucking sector in the Czech Republic, France, Hungary, Mexico, Poland, and the United States led to significant entry into the market, productivity gains, lower carrier costs, improvements in the quality of services, and reductions in the trucking prices paid by shippers (Combes and Lafourcade 2005; Dutz, Hayri, and Ibarra 2000; Teravaninthorn and Raballand 2009; Winston and others 1990; World Bank and IRU 2016; Ying 1990; Ying and Keeler 1991).

Consolidation and increased cooperation in the container shipping industry can bring benefits in terms of economies of scale and scope and lower search costs, but it has also raised concerns about higher prices among shippers and governments because of increased market power. There is evidence that larger trade flows prompt carriers to use larger vessels, to take advantage of economies of scale, which yields lower shipping rates on thick routes (Asturias 2020). There is also evidence of market power in container shipping, although it is weaker on thicker routes (Hummels and others 2009). Evidence also shows that on routes with several carriers, the cost of requesting and analyzing quotes allows container carriers to price discriminate, charging lower rates for the same service to larger shippers (Ardelean and Lugovskyy 2023). Hence, it is important to assess the extent of concentration at the route and country level as well as its costs and benefits to determine whether shipping rates are above an efficient level.

Competition between and within ports is conducive to lower maritime shipping costs. Ports operating in more competitive environments need to perform more efficiently to attract and retain traffic, which leads to lower maritime shipping costs. The competition environment in the container port sector varies significantly across ports. It is strongly associated with the operational efficiency captured in the World Bank's Container Port Performance Index and with efficiency in the use of port facilities (technical efficiency) (Herrera Dappe, Serebrisky, and others 2024).

Trucks and cargo vessels that run empty are a common feature across the world; they are associated with higher transport prices. The lower the chances the return trip will be empty, the lower the price for the front leg. Regulations that forbid or limit the ability of trucks and vessels to pick up cargo at the destination and information frictions that limit the ability of shippers and carriers to find each other increase the probability of empty trips and hence transport prices for loaded trips. Measures to tackle these market failures and government-created frictions will increase asset utilization and reduce transport prices.

The distribution of economic activity—particularly differences in economic density—is an important determinant of transport demand and the incidence of empty trips. For a given origin, the lower the economic density of the destination, the higher the price of the trip to the destination. Data on contract prices for trucking services to deliver food in low- and middle-income countries facing food security issues show that the price to deliver cargo to a destination with economic density in the 75th percentile is about 14 percent lower than the price to a destination whose economic density is in the 25th percentile (Herrera Dappe, Lebrand, and others 2024). The difference tends to be larger for spot than contract prices, because shipping contracts allow transporters to plan the utilization of their trucks and vessels and to optimize their route by signing up with shippers in the destination area to reduce the empty backhaul. Measures to promote cargo aggregation from neighboring areas can increase demand and reduce the problem of empty backhauls on long-distance trips.

Trucking prices are higher in fragile and conflict-afflicted locations. In Somalia, for example, trucking prices are $0.14–$0.56 per ton-km—above international benchmarks for low- and middle-income countries (World Bank 2021). The price per ton-km for transporting food in areas experiencing conflict is 3–7 percent higher than the average price in low- and middle-income countries (Herrera Dappe, Lebrand, and others 2024). Prices are higher because of the cost of checkpoints, roadblocks, and other security measures; the need to pay higher salaries; and the risk premium charged by carriers.

SHRINKING ECONOMIC DISTANCE REQUIRES EFFICIENT MARKETS FOLLOWED BY EFFICIENT PLACES

All countries are different; the content and pace of implementation of the reform agenda to achieve efficient, high-quality transport and reduce economic distance needs to be tailored to the frictions and institutional and socio-political characteristics of each country as well as to government capacity. In all settings, however, **the reform agenda must include efforts to reduce frictions that make markets and places inefficient** (refer to figure O.5). Making markets efficient requires tackling the market failures and market frictions caused by governments along the transport supply chain; making places efficient requires tackling the frictions of physical and economic geography and those related to infrastructure availability, quality, and operation. **Without efficient markets, the full benefits of measures to ensure efficient places will not be realized, so places should follow markets.**

Making markets efficient is critical

Achieving efficient market outcomes in the freight transport sector requires an enabling business environment. Such an environment is created through laws, rules, and regulations that set conditions on transport operators, workers, and equipment and reduce frictions in input, intermediate service, and transport service markets. Well-functioning institutions with the capacity to enforce laws, rules, and regulations are paramount to creating and sustaining an enabling business environment.

Achieving efficient market outcomes will require different measures in different countries and markets. These measures can be grouped

FIGURE O.5 Building blocks for shrinking economic distance

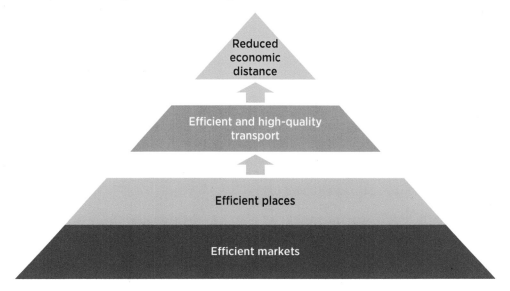

Reduced
economic
distance

Efficient and high-quality
transport

Efficient places

Efficient markets

Source: Original figure for this publication.

into three high-level actions: strengthening competition for and in the market, promoting the development of efficient transport service providers, and promoting demand aggregation and matching.

- **Strengthening competition for and in the market** requires enacting a competition law, creating and empowering an independent competition authority capable of enforcing the law, and aligning government interventions in markets with competition principles. The latter includes avoiding regulating prices unless there is a natural monopoly; avoiding restricting market access, particularly through quotas and quantitative restrictions; and separating the regulatory function from the service provision function. In the port sector, competition for and in the market can be strengthened by encouraging private sector participation through the landlord model and ensuring transparent and competitive concession bidding. Implementation of transparent, market-based slot-allocation mechanisms for access to cargo at ports and multimodal terminals can help prevent anticompetitive practices.

- **Promoting the development of efficient transport service providers** requires regulating access to the profession by setting clear standards and requirements for transport service providers, transport workers, and equipment. These standards and requirements need to be designed in a way that does not promote informality or restrict competition. Regulations should be standardized and homogenized across subnational governments, and they should be consistent with international best practices. Measures that promote the skill development of transport operators and workers, tackle frictions distorting input markets and ancillary sectors hindering operators and workers access to the profession, and support the formalization of operators will go a long way toward developing efficient transport service providers. Enforcement of the laws and regulations applicable to transport is essential for achieving an efficient, high-quality transport sector; developing strong enforcement capacity is therefore critical.

- **Promoting demand aggregation and matching** will support efficient market outcomes. It can be done by supporting the development of competitive intermediaries, including online platforms and marketplaces, and consolidation centers and logistics clusters, to increase the density of demand and reduce information frictions.

Once markets are efficient, policy makers need to help make places efficient

Efficient places mean that all places in the transport network—from road, rail, and water links to the nodes such as ports and border posts—are properly planned and function well. Ports and border posts must be efficiently operated, and traffic, particularly in urban areas, must be effectively managed.

Making places efficient requires different measures in different countries. They can be grouped under three high-level actions: developing adequate transport infrastructure, improving the efficiency of ports and border crossings, and managing urban congestion.

- **Developing adequate transport infrastructure** starts with identifying, appraising, and selecting all transport infrastructure investment projects together, as part of an integrated transport master plan based on robust appraisal methodologies. It also requires a strong project implementation process, from procurement to monitoring of the physical and financial execution of projects, and the consistent application of all-weather and climate-resilient construction standards and axle-load limits.

  Two requisites for high-quality transport infrastructure are (a) implementation of asset management systems to monitor the state of existing infrastructure and ensure that their maintenance needs are met on a timely basis, based on prespecified standards, and (b) the availability of adequate funding. Funding can be provided through dedicated maintenance funds, such as road funds. Such funds must be held to strict governance and transparency standards, and their accounts must be fully reflected in the government's accounts.

  Another important measure to ensure adequate funding for maintenance is the preparation of sufficiently disaggregated rolling medium-term expenditure frameworks to guide the annual budget process. These frameworks should incorporate the projected maintenance costs of ongoing and approved new investment projects. Mobilizing the private sector through public-private partnerships (PPPs) can also help develop adequate infrastructure. Doing so requires a robust PPP preparation, procurement, and contract and fiscal management framework.

- **Developing efficient ports and border crossings** requires aligning the investments in infrastructure and superstructure with the integrated transport master plan and implementing policies and regulations, such as customs and land use policies, that promote efficient operation of the nodes and prevent unnecessary trips. Investing in the digitalization of ports and border crossings can also promote efficiency and encourage private sector participation in the port sector.

- **Managing urban congestion** can be done through several measures. They include supply-side measures, such as targeted infrastructure investments, on-street parking management, vehicle-related access restrictions and lane management, and demand-management measures, such as freight demand and land use management, congestion pricing, intelligent transport systems, last-mile delivery practices, and mode shifts measures for passenger travel.

Several considerations need to be taken into account in appraising policies to reduce economic distance

Policy makers are likely to face tradeoffs when designing policies to achieve efficient, high-quality transport, partly because of the heterogenous impacts of policies on transport prices and time across space and groups of firms (refer to figure O.6). For example, policies that reduce the cost of providing trucking services on some routes can benefit shippers on

FIGURE O.6 Theory of change of transport interventions to reduce economic distance

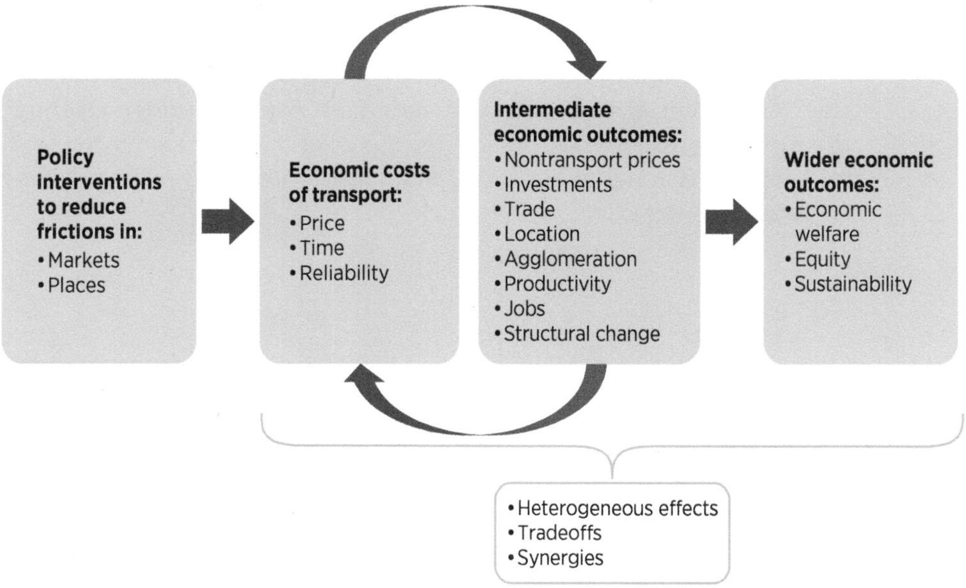

Source: Original figure for this publication.

those routes but might hurt shippers on other routes if there is a relocation of truckers to the less costly routes. Policies to build new transport infrastructure might reduce the funding for maintenance of the existing network, jeopardizing the service level. Policies that increase competition might hurt small shippers if they face significant search costs.

Policy makers may also face tradeoffs and synergies from outside the transport sector. Some places and groups may gain more than others, and some may actually lose out, mostly because of the relocation of economic activity. There is a potential tradeoff between efficiency and equity. Policies that yield the highest economic return by promoting various efficiency gains may, for example, increase inequalities; policies generating lower returns may be more beneficial to the poor and people in disadvantaged locations (Lall, Schroeder, and Schmidt 2014; Roberts and others 2019). Another important tradeoff may arise between economic welfare and environmental quality. Policies that expand market access increase trade and income, but they may lead to deforestation. There are potential synergies between economic welfare and equity, with reductions in transport costs yielding productivity gains and investments, increasing wages, and creating new jobs in areas with unemployment.

Appraisal of policies to reduce economic distance needs to start with a clear understanding of the main problem the policy aims to address and the key market failures and policy-driven frictions that warrant government intervention. It is important to properly estimate the quantity effects—that is, the changes in employment, output, and other outcomes of interest caused by the policy relative to a scenario without it—differentiating between creation and relocation of economic activity. It is also important to properly value the quantity changes, ensuring that they are of net social value (Duranton and Venables 2018; Laird and Venables 2017).

Properly establishing the quantity effects, valuing them, and considering potential tradeoffs and synergies requires understanding the mechanisms at work—that is, the theory of change from intervention to changes in transport prices, costs, and reliability, and to changes in intermediate and wider economic outcomes.

NOTE

1. Shipper-borne economic costs of transport are often referred to as generalized transport costs or the transport-related component of logistics costs.

REFERENCES

Akbar, P.A., V. Couture, G. Duranton, L. Fan, and A. Storeygard. 2024. "Around the World in 24 Days? The Speed of Intercity Road Travel." World Bank, Washington, DC. Background paper prepared for this report.

Allen, T., D. Atkin, S. Cantillo Cleves, and C.E. Hernández. 2024. "Trucks." Background paper prepared for this report.

Antras, P., and D. Chor. 2022. *Handbook of International Economics*. Amsterdam: Elsevier.

Ardelean, A., and V. Lugovskyy 2023. "It Pays to Be Big: Price Discrimination in Maritime Shipping." *European Economic Review* 153.

Ardelean, A., V. Lugovskyy, A. Skiba, and D. Terner. 2022. "Fathoming Shipping Costs: An Exploration of Recent Literature, Data, and Patterns." Policy Research Working Paper 9992, World Bank, Washington, DC. Background paper prepared for this report.

Asturias, J. 2020. "Endogenous Transportation Costs." *European Economic Review* 123.

Atkin, D., and D. Donaldson. 2015. "Who's Getting Globalized? The Size and Implications of Intra-National Trade Costs." NBER Working Paper 21439, National Bureau of Economic Research, Cambridge, MA.

Blankespoor, B., T. Bougna, R. Garduno-Rivera, and H. Selod. 2017. "Roads and the Geography of Economic Activities in Mexico." Policy Research Working Paper 8226, World Bank, Washington, DC.

Blimpo, M. P., R. Harding, and L. Wantchekon. 2013. "Public Investment in Rural Infrastructure: Some Political Economy Considerations." *Journal of African Economies* 22 (Suppl. 2): II57–II83.

Burgess, R., and D. Donaldson. 2010. "Can Openness Mitigate the Effects of Weather Shocks? Evidence from India's Famine Era." *American Economic Review* 100 (2): 449–53.

Collier, S., C. Ruehl, S. Yoon, K. Boriboonsomsin, T.D. Durbin, G. Scora, K. Johnson, and J. Herner. 2019. "Impact of Heavy-Duty Diesel Truck Activity on Fuel Consumption and Its Implication for the Reduction of Greenhouse Gas Emissions." *Transportation Research Record* 2673 (3): 125–35.

Combes, P.P., and M. Lafourcade. 2005. "Transport Costs: Measures, Determinants, and Regional Policy Implications for France." *Journal of Economic Geography* 5: 319–49.

Coşar, A.K. 2022. "Overland Transport Costs." Policy Research Working Paper 10156, World Bank, Washington, DC. Background paper prepared for this report.

Díaz de Astarloa, B., and N. Pkhikidze. 2024. "Internal Trade Costs in Developing Countries." Policy Research Working Paper 10789, World Bank, Washington, DC. Background paper prepared for this report.

Díaz-Ramirez, J., N. Giraldo-Peralta, D. Flórez-Ceron, V. Rangel, C. Mejía-Argueta, J.I. Huertas, and M. Bernal. 2017. "Eco-Driving Key Factors That Influence Fuel Consumption in Heavy-Truck Fleets: A Colombian Case." *Transportation Research Part D: Transport and Environment* 56: 258–70.

Donaldson, D. 2018. "Railroads of the Raj: Estimating the Impact of Transportation Infrastructure." *American Economic Review* 108 (4–5): 899–934.

Donaldson, D., A. Jinhage, and E. Verhoogen. 2017. "Beyond Borders: Making Transport Work for African Trade." IGC Growth Brief Series 009, International Growth Centre, London.

Duranton, G., and A. J. Venables. 2018. "Place-Based Policies for Development." Policy Research Working Paper 8410, World Bank, Washington, DC.

Dutz, M., A. Hayri, and P. Ibarra. 2000. "Regulatory Reform, Competition, and Innovation: A Case Study of the Mexican Road Freight Industry." Policy Research Working Paper 2318, World Bank, Washington, DC.

Faber, B. 2014. "Trade Integration, Market Size, and Industrialization: Evidence from China's National Trunk Highway System." *Review of Economic Studies* 81(3): 1046–70.

Freund, C., and N. Rocha. 2011. "What Constrains Africa's Exports?" *World Bank Economic Review* 25 (3): 361–86.

FSIN (Food Security Information Network), and Global Network Against Food Crises. 2023. *Global Report on Food Crises 2023*. Rome.

Ganapati, S., and W.F. Wong. 2023. "How Far Goods Travel: Global Transport and Supply Chains from 1965–2020." *Journal of Economic Perspectives* 37 (3): 3–30.

Hernández, C.E., and S. Cantillo-Cleves. 2024. "A Toolkit for Setting and Evaluating Price Floors." *Journal of Public Economics* 232.

Herrera Dappe, M., and M. Lebrand. 2024. "Infrastructure and Structural Change in Africa." *World Bank Economic Review*.

Herrera Dappe, M., M. Lebrand, B. Rowberry, and A. Stokenberga. 2024. "Moving Goods: Road Transport Costs in Developing Countries." World Bank, Washington, DC. Background paper prepared for this report.

Herrera Dappe, M., T. Serebrisky, A. Suárez-Alemán, and B. Turkgulu. 2024. "Being Efficient Pays Off: The Case of Ports and Maritime Transport Costs Worldwide." World Bank, Washington, DC. Background paper prepared for this report.

Hummels, D., V. Lugovskyy, and A. Skiba. 2009. "The Trade Reducing Effects of Market Power in International Shipping." *Journal of Development Economics* 89: 84–97.

Iimi, A. 2023. "Estimating Road Freight Transport Costs in Eastern Europe and Central Asia Using Large Shipping Data." Policy Research Working Paper 10533, World Bank, Washington, DC. Background paper prepared for this report.

Ksoll, C., and C. Kunaka. 2016. "Malawi Country Economic Memorandum Trade and Logistics Background Paper." World Bank, Washington, DC.

Laird, J., and A. J. Venables. 2017. "Transport Investment and Economic Performance: A Framework for Project Appraisal." *Transport Policy* 56: 1–11.

Lall, S. V., E. Schroeder, and E. Schmidt. 2014. "Identifying Spatial Efficiency–Equity Trade-Offs in Territorial Development Policies: Evidence from Uganda." *Journal of Development Studies* 50 (12): 1717–33.

Lall, S., S. Sinha-Roy, and F. Shilpi. 2022. "Trucking Costs and the Margins of Internal Trade: Evidence from a Trucking Portal in India." Policy Research Working Paper 10059, World Bank, Washington, DC.

Molnar, A., and F. Shilpi. 2024. "Urban and Infrastructure Determinants of Freight Cost in India." World Bank, Washington, DC. Background paper prepared for this report.

Redding, Stephen J. 2022. "Trade and Geography." In *Handbook of International Economics,* ed. Gita Gopinath, Elhanan Helpman, and Kenneth Rogoff, 147–217. Amsterdam: Elsevier-North Holland.

Rizet, C., C. Cruz, and M. Mbacké. 2012. "Reducing Freight Transport CO_2 Emissions by Increasing the Load Factor." *Procedia—Social and Behavioral Sciences* 48: 184–95.

Roberts, M., U. Deichmann, B. Fingleton, and T. Shi. 2012. "Evaluating China's Road to Prosperity: A New Economic Geography Approach." *Regional Science and Urban Economics* 42 (4): 580–94.

Roberts, M., M. Melecky, T. Bougna, and Y. Xu. 2019. "Transport Corridors and Their Wider Economic Benefits: A Quantitative Review of the Literature." *Journal of Regional Science* 60: 207–48.

Stifel, D., and B. Minten. 2017. "Market Access, Welfare, and Nutrition: Evidence from Ethiopia." *World Development* 90: 229–41.

Storeygard, A. 2016. "Farther on Down the Road: Transport Costs, Trade and Urban Growth in Sub-Saharan Africa." *Review of Economic Studies* 83 (3): 1263–95.

Teravaninthorn, S., and G. Raballand. 2009. *Transport Prices and Costs in Africa: A Review of the International Corridors.* Washington, DC: World Bank.

Walnum, H.J., and M. Simonsen. 2015. "Does Driving Behavior Matter? An Analysis of Fuel Consumption Data from Heavy-Duty Trucks." *Transportation Research Part D: Transport and Environment* 36: 107–20.

Winston, C., T.M. Corsi, C.M. Grimm, and C.A. Evans. 1990. *The Economic Effects of Surface Freight Deregulation.* Washington, DC: Brookings Institution.

World Bank, and IRU (International Road Transport Union). 2016. *Road Freight Transport Services Reform: Guiding Principles for Practitioners and Policy Makers.* Washington, DC: World Bank.

World Bank. 2021. *Somalia Country Economic Memorandum: Towards an Inclusive Jobs Agenda*. Washington, DC: World Bank.

Yang, R. 2024. "Geographic Imbalance, Search Frictions, and Regulation: Causes of Empty Miles in Freight Trucking." Policy Research Working Paper 10775, World Bank. Washington, DC. Background paper prepared for this report.

Ying, J.S. 1990. "The Inefficiency of Regulating a Competitive Industry: Productivity Gains in Trucking Following Reform." *Review of Economics and Statistics* 72 (2): 191–201.

Ying, J.S., and T.E. Keeler. 1991. "Pricing in a Deregulated Environment: The Motor Carrier Experience." *Rand Journal of Economics* 2 (2): 264–73.

1

The Cost of Moving Goods across the World

MAIN MESSAGES

1. Transport costs fell over the past decades, but the world is still far from a single integrated economy, and poorer countries face higher freight transport costs than wealthier countries. On average, domestic transport costs to export and import in low- and middle-income countries are twice as high as in high-income countries, and differences for within-country transport costs can be even larger.

2. Trucking rates vary significantly across countries. Roughly 75 percent of the variation in the per ton-kilometer cost of shipping food in countries facing food insecurity is within countries, with the remaining 25 percent between countries.

3. It takes significantly longer to move goods within poorer countries. Intercity travel tends to be persistently slower in poorer countries, with transport in a country in the top decile of intercity road speed about twice as fast as in a country in the bottom decile. Domestic times to export goods are higher in developing countries, with a significant share of the time within the exporting country spent at the port.

4. Border frictions are significantly greater in low- and middle-income countries than in high-income countries. The average time to comply with border regulations to export ranges from 24 hours in high-income countries to 97 hours in low-income countries, with the time in middle-income countries falling in between.

INTRODUCTION

Declining international trade costs over the past several decades has helped spur the growth of trade, a main driver of economic growth and economic convergence between developing and developed economies. Despite the decline in international trade costs, however, the world is still far from being a single integrated economy. Trade does not start or stop at national borders; high domestic transport costs limit the integration of firms and households with the global economy. Distance matters; geography creates barriers to mobility for goods, services, innovations, and people. Economic distance—the cost of traveling and moving goods—matters both across and within countries, creating obstacles to progress and increasing regional inequalities.

Shippers care not only about the direct costs of transport but also about the time it takes to transport goods and its reliability. Direct costs refer to the price shippers pay to a third party that provides the transport service or the cost of using their own vehicles and vessels. The quality of freight transport services, measured by time and reliability, affect firms' costs through inventory costs, the design of supply chains, the location of warehouses and production facilities, and other decisions firms need to make to cope with long transport lead times and poor reliability.

This chapter presents empirical evidence—based on both new and existing databases—that international and domestic transport costs are higher in developing countries than in developed countries. New data also show that domestic times to export goods are higher relative to the distance traveled within the country. Time at borders and ports represents a large share of the time it takes for goods to be exchanged across borders. Travel speed in interurban roads varies widely across countries, with richer countries able to move goods within their borders more quickly than poorer countries do.

This chapter is organized as follows. The first two sections present evidence of higher international maritime and domestic trucking costs in developing countries, respectively. The third section provides evidence of longer time and lower reliability of international and domestic transport in developing countries, focusing on port and border bottlenecks as well as the time spent moving goods from the port to the hinterland and between cities.

HIGH AND VOLATILE INTERNATIONAL TRANSPORT COSTS IN DEVELOPING COUNTRIES

Declining international trade costs over the past several decades have been an important contributor to the rapid growth of trade, a main driver of economic growth. The period between 1870 and 1914 saw an almost uninterrupted fall in maritime shipping costs relative to the prices of the commodities carried along almost all routes; that decline stopped with World War I (Mohammad and Williamson 2004). Transport costs fell dramatically in the post–World War II period, declining by 33–39 percent by weight and 48–62 percent by value over the past half-century, reflecting large productivity increases and technological advances (refer to figure 1.1).

Technological innovations and investments in infrastructure have led to major reductions in transport costs since the 1850s. Economic historians have documented how technological change led to substantial reductions in shipping costs between 1850 and 1913 (Harley 1980; North 1968; Mohammed and Williamson 2004). The decades since World War II also witnessed significant technological change in shipping, including the development of jet aircraft engines and the use of containerization in ocean shipping, first introduced in 1956. The cost of air transport fell by a factor of more than 10 between 1955 and 2004, and the container price index declined by about 50 percent between 1985 and 2004 (Hummels 2007). By 1983, almost 90 percent of countries had container-handling infrastructure (Rua 2014). By the end of 2015, the largest containership built that year (the *MSC Oscar*) had a capacity 24 times that of the first container ships.

As costs fell, use of global transport soared. Transport usage can be measured by weight or value multiplied by distance traveled (the weight measure puts emphasis on bulk cargo; the value places emphasis on the transport of goods with higher value-per-weight, such as machinery, automobiles, and electronics). After accounting for economic growth, real transport use per unit of final consumption more than doubled between 1965 and 2020, increasing 100 percent by weight and 160 percent by value (Ganapati and Wong 2023). Three factors can explain this increase: (a) increasing participation of

FIGURE 1.1 International transport costs, by weight and value, 1965–2013

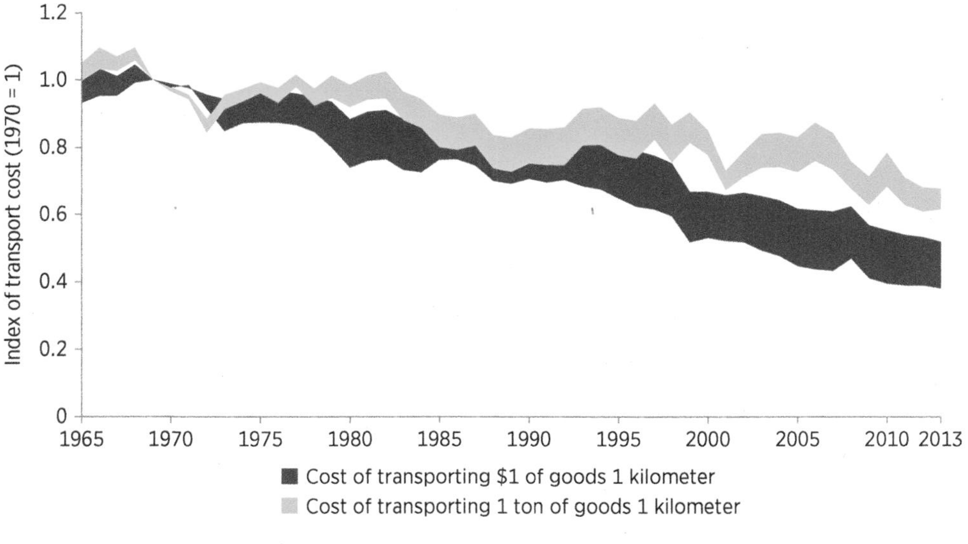

Legend:
- ■ Cost of transporting $1 of goods 1 kilometer
- ▨ Cost of transporting 1 ton of goods 1 kilometer

Source: Ganapati and Wong 2023.
Note: Figure is based on the sum of all global transportation costs in a given year, divided by trade use for that year (either value of or tons of trade) multiplied by distance. The upper-bound estimate is based on the scenario in which all aggregate transport spending is on international trade; the lower-bound estimate reflects spending on both international and domestic trade. Values are normalized to 1 in 1970. Figure is based on a consistent sample of 24 countries representing 90 percent of world gross domestic product.

emerging economies, particularly China, in global trade; (b) increasing trade between countries that are farther apart; and (c) shifts in the composition of traded goods, from natural resources to manufactured goods.

Lower transport costs have permitted the integration of countries and industries into trade networks and global supply chains. Between 1950 and 2004, world trade grew at an average rate of 5.9 percent a year (Hummels 2007). Manufacturing trade grew even faster, at 7.2 percent a year. Manufacturers are no longer located close to their customers; firms have expanded and even fragmented their production supply chains, altering the geographic location of economic activity (Antras and Chor 2022; Redding 2022).

However, it remains more expensive for low- and middle-income countries to export to large markets than it is for high-income countries to do so. For example, it is 57 percent more expensive to export to the United States from a low-income country than from a high-income country and 32 percent more expensive to export to Australia from a lower-middle-income country than from a high-income country for the same distance, weight, and value of exports (refer to figure 1.2).

Despite decades of downward trends, transport prices remain very volatile, and the transport network is vulnerable to unforeseen disruptions. Transport prices have always been volatile following economic and geopolitical shocks as well as during commodity booms and busts. Real dry bulk freight rates are estimated to have followed a downward but undulating path (refer to figure 1.3), with real dry bulk freight rates nearly tripling in some years. Over the long run, shipping demand shocks explain most of the variation in real dry bulk freight rates. In recent years, the COVID-19 pandemic and

FIGURE 1.2 Average transport price per dollar of goods exported to the United States and Australia, by country income group

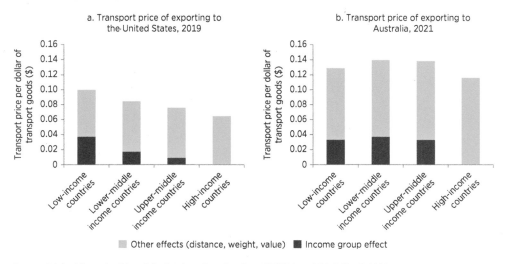

Source: Original figure for this publication based on data from UNCTAD and World Bank 2024.
Note: Figure is based on a simple regression to explain transport costs per value of shipment. Variables include the income group of the exporter, distance, weight, freight on board value, and two-digit commodity codes.

FIGURE 1.3 Dry bulk shipping costs, 1850–2020

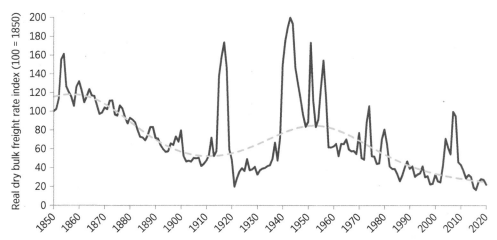

Source: Jacks and Stuermer 2021.
Note: The solid dark blue line represents the real dry bulk freight rate index constructed by Jacks and Stuermer (2021). The dotted orange line is an estimate of the long-run trend derived from the Christiano-Fitzgerald band pass filter, which assumes a cyclical component of 70 years' duration in the real dry bulk freight rate index.

other events, such as the closure of the Suez Canal in 2021 after a container ship ran aground, disrupted the transport network, leading to huge price volatility. The pandemic had the greatest effect on freight rates on trade routes to developing countries. By early 2021, for example, container freight rates from China to South America had jumped 443 percent, compared with 63 percent on the route between Asia and North America's east coast (UNCTAD 2021).

HIGH DOMESTIC TRANSPORT COSTS IN DEVELOPING COUNTRIES

Trade does not start or stop at national borders; high domestic transport costs limit the integration of firms and households with the global economy. International shipping costs have drastically decreased, but domestic transport costs remain a substantial share of overall trade costs. Domestic distribution costs can reach 55 percent of producer prices—more than twice the share of international transport costs (Anderson and Van Wincoop 2004). In India, trade barriers within the country make up 40 percent of total trade barriers (barriers within the country and at the border) on average, although they vary substantially by state (Van Leemput 2021).

Domestic trade costs, which include transport costs, remain high in many low- and middle-income countries. Using the price gap methodology discussed in appendix B, Atkin and Donaldson (2015) find that the cost of distance in Ethiopia and Nigeria is approximately 4–5 times as large as in the United States. The same methodology was applied to a wider sample of countries for this report. This analysis reveals that the cost of distance is 3–14 times as large in the countries studied as in the United States (Díaz de Astarloa and Pkhikidze 2024). These estimates imply that the cost of transporting goods from their origin to relatively remote locations can represent between 7 percent of the final price of goods (in Tanzania) and 17 percent (in Madagascar) (refer to figure 1.4).

Cross-country surveys of traders reveal that domestic transport costs are higher in low- and middle-income countries than in high-income countries. Doing Business surveys provide cross-country estimates of the costs associated with transporting a shipment from a warehouse in a country's largest business city to the most widely used port or border. For a given distance, purchasing power parity–adjusted domestic transport costs to export and import in richer countries are half the level faced by low-income countries (refer to figure 1.5).

Trucking rates in developing countries

Road transportation remains the main mode of shipment in many countries. Except in India, railroads typically account for a small share of the transport system of developing countries, whose infrastructure investments occurred mostly during the second half of the 20th century, after the motorized transportation revolution. In Africa, for example, roads carry 80–90 percent of passenger and freight traffic (Gwilliam 2011). Almost all intra-national trade in mountainous Colombia is done by truck, with trucks accounting for 96 percent of tonnage excluding coal and oil transported within Colombia in 2018 (Ministerio de Transporte 2018).

FIGURE 1.4 **Estimates of transport costs as a percentage of the mean destination price for locally produced goods in selected countries**

Source: Díaz de Astarloa and Pkhikidze 2024.
Note: Estimates are for locally produced goods only and for the following periods: Georgia, January 2012–December 2020; Kenya, October 2018–January 2022; Madagascar, January 2010–April 2021; Nigeria, January 2001–July 2010; Rwanda, January 2013–December 2020; Tanzania, January 2012–April 2021.

FIGURE 1.5 Domestic transport costs to import and export, by country income group

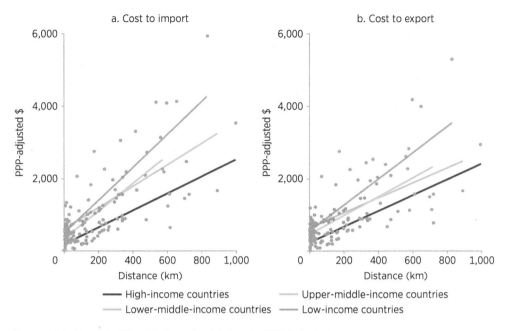

Source: Original figure for this publication using data from the 2020 Doing Business survey.
Note: Dots show observations by country. Lines are the fitted lines per income group. PPP = purchasing power parity.

Trucking rates vary significantly across countries. They are higher in isolated and conflict-ridden locations, such as Somalia, where they range from $0.14 to $0.56 per ton-kilometer (ton-km)—well above international benchmarks for low- and middle-income countries (refer to figure 1.6). Colombia and Bangladesh have among the highest rates in the world—higher than some African countries. Trucking rates in Bangladesh range from $0.06 per ton-km for a 16-ton truck to $0.12 per ton-km for a trailer. These rates are so high that trucking costs represent 31–88 percent of direct logistics costs (Herrera Dappe and others 2020). At the other end, trucking rates in Argentina, Australia, Brazil, the Lao People's Democratic Republic (PDR) and the United States are just below $0.04 per ton-km. In India and South Africa, rates average about $0.06 per ton-km; in Malawi, Tanzania, Uganda, and Zimbabwe, rates are slightly higher, at about $0.08 per ton-km.

The cost of shipping food within countries facing food security issues also varies by country. Using data on contracted trucking services by a large humanitarian organization across 60 low- and middle-income countries, Herrera Dappe and others (2024) find that the cost per ton-km tends to be higher in countries facing conflicts (refer to figure 1.7). Their analysis also finds that 75 percent of the variation in trucking prices per ton-km is within countries, with the remaining 25 percent between countries, and that 60 percent of the variation in unit prices can be explained by differences between destinations for the same origin. Country features, such as geography, infrastructure, and market structure, explain most of the rate differences.

FIGURE 1.6 Trucking prices in selected countries

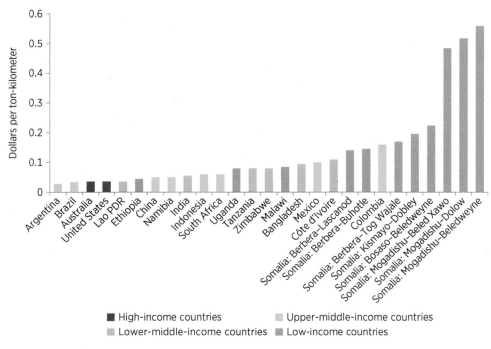

Source: ADB 2016; Herrera Dappe and others 2020; World Bank 2021; Molnar and Shilpi 2024; Nick Porée and Associates 2023.
Note: Figure presents average prices for each country and, for Somalia, the average prices for each corridor. In Bangladesh, the average is for a 7-ton truck, the most used truck in the country.

FIGURE 1.7 Contract trucking prices to ship food in selected countries

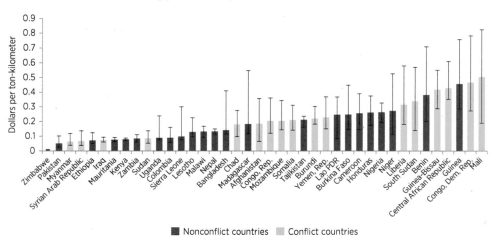

Source: Herrera Dappe and others 2024.
Note: Bars show median price. Whiskers show 25th and 75th percentiles. Sample includes countries with more than 100 observations. Data are from 2019–20.

Within-country variation in trucking rates

Molnar and Shilpi (2024) document the variation in trucking rates within India. They show that poorer regions in the north and east of the country are more expensive to reach. Rates vary with vehicle and cargo attributes but primarily over space. The average unit rate between each pair of states (or union territories) ranges from Rs. 1.50 to Rs. 9.70 per ton-km, with a standard deviation of Rs. 1.89.

The spatial variation can also be seen in terms of the rate premia or discount for delivering cargo in a state and the cost per kilometer of crossing a state. An interstate trip to a state in the northeast of the country incurs a rate premium of Rs. 9,000–Rs. 54,000; trips to Gujarat or Maharashtra enjoy a rate discount of Rs. 6,000–Rs. 18,000.[1] Premia and discounts are independent of the kilometers traveled (refer to map 1.1, panel a).

MAP 1.1 Premia and costs of trucking through states in India

a. Premium for traveling to each state (thousand Rs.)

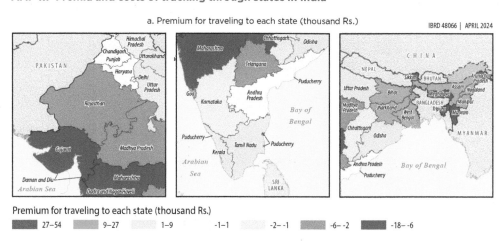

Premium for traveling to each state (thousand Rs.)

| 27–54 | 9–27 | 1–9 | -1–1 | -2–-1 | -6–-2 | -18–-6 |

b. Cost of going through each state (Rs. per kilometer)

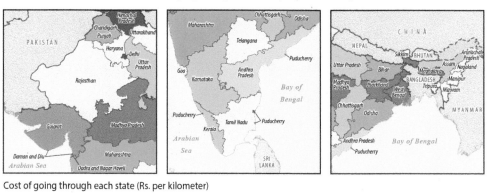

Cost of going through each state (Rs. per kilometer)

| 76–142 | 43–76 | 41–43 | 39–41 | 32–39 | 30–32 | 22–30 | Not available |

Source: Molnar and Shilpi 2024.

Panel b of map 1.1 shows the variation in the per-km rate that can be attributed to traveling through each state. It ranges from 1.6 to 3.1 times the average rate in mountainous states and Delhi. In the four states where it is lowest (Haryana, Rajasthan, Tamil Nadu, and Telangana), the per-km rate is 0.48–0.65 of the average rate. Chapters 3 and 4 examine the determinants of these costs.

The cost of shipping goods within Colombia varies significantly across regions. Average trucking prices in 2021 ranged from $0.08 to $0.67 per ton-km, depending on the destination (refer to map 1.2). Areas in the Chocó (west) faced the highest prices; rates were lower in the north. There is also substantial variation in the prices per ton-km to deliver cargo to a given destination. Figure 1.8 shows the variation in unit trucking prices in 2021 across the same origin-destination pairs and across different origins for routes to Bogotá and Cartagena.

MAP 1.2 Average trucking prices in Colombia, by destination, 2021

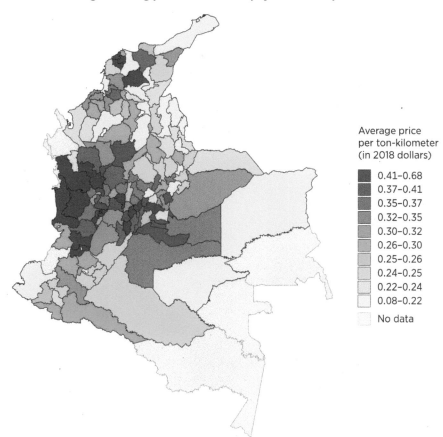

Average price per ton-kilometer (in 2018 dollars)

- 0.41–0.68
- 0.37–0.41
- 0.35–0.37
- 0.32–0.35
- 0.30–0.32
- 0.26–0.30
- 0.25–0.26
- 0.24–0.25
- 0.22–0.24
- 0.08–0.22
- No data

Source: Original map for this publication based on Allen and others 2024.
Note: Map shows weighted-average price (in 2018 dollars) per ton-kilometer per destination.

HIGH TIME COSTS IN DEVELOPING COUNTRIES

Domestic times to export goods are high. Overland distances within exporting countries comprise a very small share of the overall shipment distance, but the share of total time spent within the exporting country is substantial.

Export times from developing countries

Detailed data on distance and time of export shipments from China, India, Indonesia, Malaysia, Thailand, Türkiye, and Viet Nam to Canada, the European Union, and the United States show that overland distance is less than 3 percent of the total export distance for ocean shipments in six of the seven countries analyzed (refer to figure 1.9). The exception to this pattern is India, where a large fraction of shipments originates far from the coast. Time spent moving and waiting within China, India, Türkiye, and Viet Nam accounted for 14–17 percent of the entire export time for exports to Canada and the United States (refer to figure 1.10). The pattern is similar for exports to the European Union, with domestic time shares slightly lower for the more distant exporters in East Asia and higher for Türkiye (27 percent) and India (19 percent).

FIGURE 1.8 Variation in trucking prices per ton-kilometer to Bogotá and Cartagena, by origin, 2021

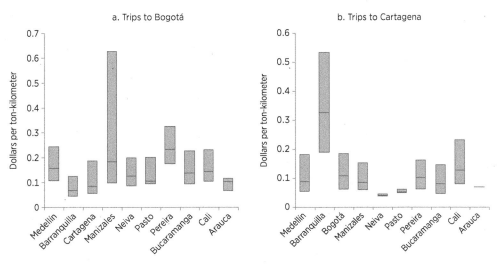

Source: Original figure for this publication based on Allen and others 2024.
Note: Box plots report the 25th, 50th, and 75th percentiles. Prices are in 2018 dollars.

FIGURE 1.9 Decomposition of average shipment distance of exports by sea to Canada and the United States and to the European Union

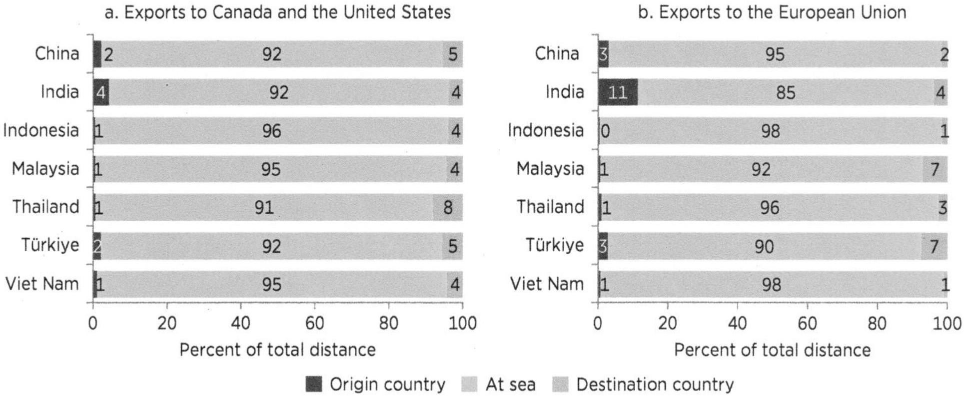

a. Exports to Canada and the United States

	Origin country	At sea	Destination country
China	2	92	5
India	4	92	4
Indonesia	1	96	4
Malaysia	1	95	4
Thailand	1	91	8
Türkiye	2	92	5
Viet Nam	1	95	4

b. Exports to the European Union

	Origin country	At sea	Destination country
China	3	95	2
India	11	85	4
Indonesia	0	98	1
Malaysia	1	92	7
Thailand	1	96	3
Türkiye	3	90	7
Viet Nam	1	98	1

Percent of total distance

■ Origin country   ■ At sea   ■ Destination country

Source: Original figures for this publication based on data from a major logistics company.
Note: Observations are averaged at the country level.

A significant share of the time within the exporting country is spent at the exporting port (refer to figure 1.10). Time spent waiting at port within the seven countries analyzed accounted for 7–15 percent of the entire export time for exports to Canada and the United States. Time spent at the exporting port also varies significantly within countries (refer to figure 1.11). The large variation reflects differences in the products shipped, logistics choices made by the sellers and the logistics firms, and potentially unreliability at ports and customs.

The variability of shipment times also depends on whether shipments use direct services or go through transshipment ports. The median export to Canada and the United States from India, Indonesia, Malaysia and Türkiye goes through international transshipment hubs. For Indonesia, Malaysia, and Türkiye, the median time there is 4–5 days. In contrast, in China and Viet Nam, 75 percent or more of transactions ship directly to the destination country without an international transshipment. The variability in most countries is large, with an interquartile range of 116–217 hours for Türkiye and 66–168 hours for India to export to Canada and the United States (refer to figure 1.12).

Domestic transport times to export are higher in low- and middle-income countries than in high-income countries. Doing Business surveys provide cross-country estimates of the time associated with transporting a shipment from a warehouse in the largest business city of the country to the most widely used port or land border. For a given distance, domestic transport times to export faced by traders in low-income countries are around three times longer than in high-income countries, with middle-income countries closely following low-income countries (refer to figure 1.13).

FIGURE 1.10 Decomposition of average shipment time of exports by sea to Canada and the United States and to the European Union

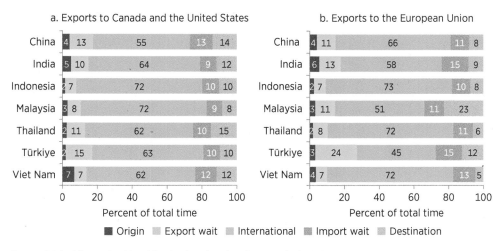

a. Exports to Canada and the United States   b. Exports to the European Union

■ Origin   ■ Export wait   ■ International   ■ Import wait   ■ Destination

Source: Original figures for this publication based on data from a major logistics company.

FIGURE 1.11 Distribution of wait times within and between exporting countries of exports to Canada and the United States and to the European Union

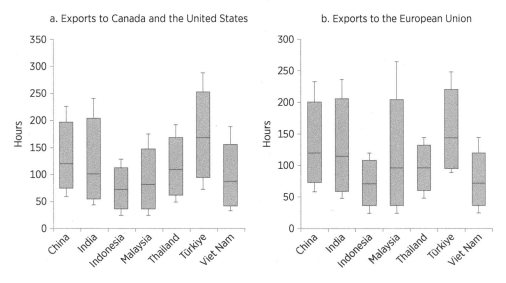

a. Exports to Canada and the United States   b. Exports to the European Union

Source: Original figures for this publication based on data from a major logistics company.
Note: Box plots report the 25th, 50th, and 75th percentiles. Whiskers represent minimum and maximum values.

Delays on the road, at ports, and at borders

Maritime transport represents the largest share of travel time and distance for international shipments. But time at borders and ports represents a large share of the time it takes for goods to be exchanged across borders.

FIGURE 1.12 Distribution of wait times at international transshipment hubs for exports to Canada and the United States

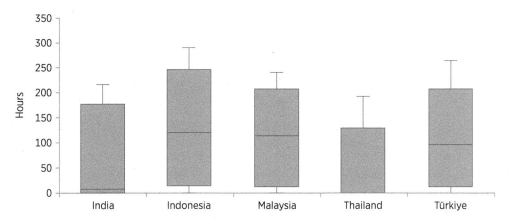

Source: Original figure for this publication based on data from a major logistics company.
Note: Box plots report the 25th, 50th, and 75th percentiles. Whiskers represent minimum and maximum values.

FIGURE 1.13 Domestic transport time to import and export, by country income group

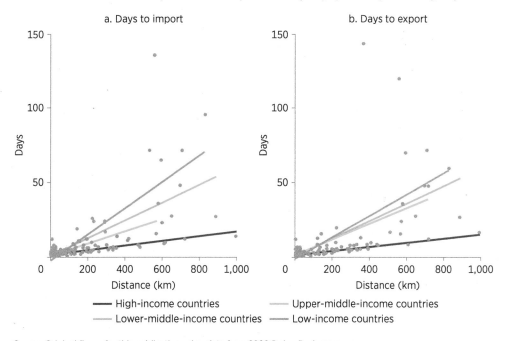

Source: Original figure for this publication using data from 2020 Doing Business survey.
Note: Lines are fitted lines per income group.

Poor-quality road infrastructure and congestion add significant delays and unpredictability for goods to be shipped from the border to the hinterland.

Delays on the road

Both travel to the main port and border crossing and intercity travel takes longer in lower-income countries than in high-income countries. In research conducted for this report, Akbar and others (2024) study how travel speed varies across roads connecting cities of more than 50,000 people in 134 countries. Overall, mean speed for the 134 countries is 70.5 kilometers per hour. The fastest countries in the sample are about 2.5 times faster than the slowest, with the average road speed increasing with a country's level of income (refer to figure 1.14). The standard deviation of average speed is 16 km per hour, and the difference between countries in the top and bottom deciles is 43 km per hour. Travel in a country in the top decile of intercity road speed is about twice as fast as travel in a country in the bottom decile.

Delays at ports

Port performance is generally worse in low- and middle-income countries, hampered by diseconomies of scale and lower levels of digitalization, creating congestion and delays. On average, ports in low- and lower-middle-income

FIGURE 1.14 Correlation between speed of traffic and per capita income

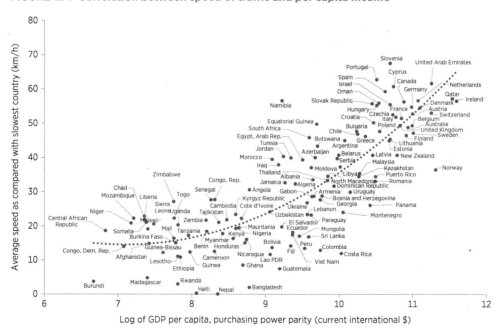

Source: Akbar and others 2024.
Note: Figure reports average speed in a country above the average speed in the slowest country in the sample (Nepal). The average speed is obtained as the country fixed effect in an ordinary least square regression including speed measures for more than 36 million road segments covering all countries.

countries operate much less efficiently than their peers in other countries, as indicated by the World Bank's Container Port Performance Index, which is based on port times (refer to figure 1.15).[2] The median time spent by container ships in ports is more than twice as high in low-income countries as in high-income countries (refer to figure 1.16).

Averages hide variation across counties. Countries with fewer arrivals, only small ships, and a small number of containers loaded and unloaded during each port call have faster turnarounds, as do countries with the latest port technologies and infrastructure that can accommodate the largest container vessels. For most other lower-income countries, poor infrastructure investments and lack of reforms have translated into port inefficiencies and long waiting times (World Bank 2023).

FIGURE 1.15 World Bank's Container Port Performance Index, by country income group, 2022

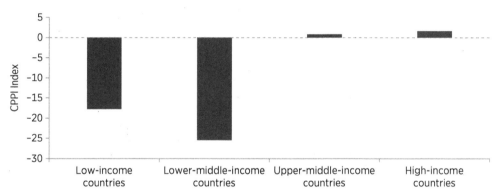

Source: Original figure for this publication based on data from the World Bank's Container Port Performance Index (CPPI).
Note: Port-level CPPI indexes are first averaged at the country level.

FIGURE 1.16 Average median port time, by country income group, 2019

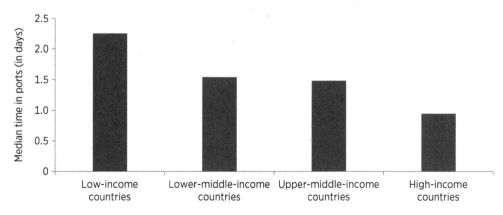

Source: Original figure for this publication based on data from UNCTADstat Database.

Delays at borders

Borders remain major trade bottlenecks for many countries. Trucks are not allowed to cross the border between India and Bangladesh. As a result, cargo must be transloaded, adding to transport and trade costs (Herrera Dappe and Kunaka 2021). On average, crossing the India–Bangladesh border at Petrapole–Benapole, the most important border post between the two countries, takes 138 hours, including 28 hours spent transloading cargo.

Border frictions are significantly greater in low- and middle-income countries than in high-income countries. According to Doing Business, the average time to comply with border export regulations ranges from 24 hours in high-income countries to 97 hours in low-income countries (refer to figure 1.17). Average import times are larger than export times in low- and middle-income countries.

Border-crossing times also vary significantly across corridors in the same country. Figure 1.18 reports the distribution of border-crossing times for the main corridors to each destination country in Southern Africa. The shortest median times are in Malawi, Namibia, and South Africa; the longest are in Zambia and Zimbabwe. Border times also vary significantly across corridors, particularly in Malawi and Namibia. Similar patterns are found in West Africa. In 2022, the average border-crossing time was 48 hours at the Kantchari–Torodi crossing (between Burkina Faso and Niger) and 78 hours at the Cinkanse crossing (between Burkina Faso and Togo) (World Bank 2022). At the Noe–Elubo crossing (between Côte d'Ivoire and Ghana), the average crossing time was 47 hours (World Bank 2019).

FIGURE 1.17 **Average time to comply with border requirements for imports and exports, by country income group**

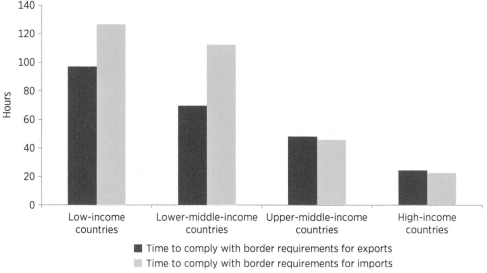

Source: Original figure for this publication based on data from Doing Business Indicators 2020.

FIGURE 1.18 Border-crossing time for imports in selected African countries of destination, 2023

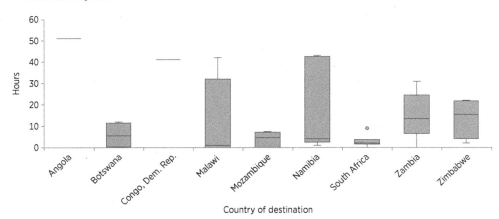

Source: Original figure for this publication based on data from WCO (2023).
Note: Figure shows median time to cross land borders on corridors to enter to Southern African countries. Box plots report the 25th, 50th, and 75th percentiles. Whiskers represent minimum and maximum values.

There is also significant variation along the same corridor, indicating the unreliability of border crossings. For example, the 95th percentile of crossing time from Mozambique to Malawi on the Nyamapanda border post is 10 times the median time, and the 95th percentile of crossing time from Botswana to South Africa (through the Groblersbrug border post) is eight times the median time. In some corridors, queuing time can be almost five times the median border-crossing times, as it is at the Kasumbalesa border post going from Zambia to the Democratic Republic of Congo.

Delays at borders come from a variety of sources, including customs and duty procedures, sanitary regulations, the lack of modern information technology, corruption, and the fact that border posts and customs offices are often physically separated (Barka 2012). Border delays increase firms' costs of production (Marius Adom and Schott 2024), because of the opportunity costs associated with storing and depreciation, especially when production processes rely on speedy delivery.

In African countries, border delays are not only long, they are also highly uncertain (refer to figure 1.19). The countries with the highest average delays also tend to be the countries with the largest variance in delays. Border costs also create misallocations in the economy that hinder the most productive firms (Restuccia and Rogerson 2008), as long and uncertain delivery times disproportionately affect firms that import foreign inputs, which tend to be the most productive.

FIGURE 1.19 Border delays across firms within countries in Africa

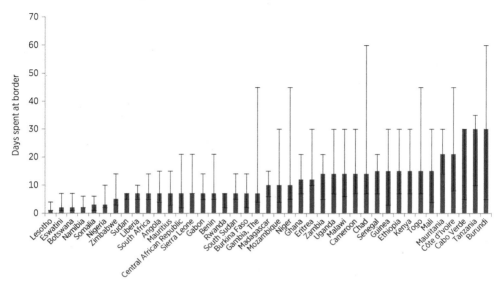

Source: Marius Adom and Schott 2024.
Note: Bars report the median time per country; whiskers show the 25th and 75th percentiles. Data are from World Bank Enterprise Surveys of African countries based on the survey question "In the last complete fiscal year, when this establishment imported material inputs or supplies, how many days did it take on average from the time these goods arrived at their point of entry (for example, port, airport) until the time these goods could be claimed from customs?"

NOTES

1. Rs. 54,000 is about 1.26 times the average rate; Rs. 18,000 is about 40 percent of the average rate.
2. The World Bank's Container Port Performance Index (CPPI) provides a standardized measurement of port performance intended to help policy makers and port operators identify areas for improvement. It is based on how much time ships wait to access port facilities and spend at berths to offload and load containers. A high CPPI score indicates that the port operates efficiently relative to its peers and that ships can expect a quicker turnaround.

REFERENCES

ADB (Asian Development Bank). 2016. "Myanmar Transport Sector Policy Note: How to Reduce Transport Costs." Mandaluyong City, the Philippines.

Akbar, P.A., V. Couture, G. Duranton, L. Fan, and A. Storeygard. 2024. "Around the World in 24 Days? The Speed of Intercity Road Travel." World Bank, Washington, DC. Background paper prepared for this report.

Allen, T., D. Atkin, S. Cantillo Cleves, and C.E. Hernández. 2024. "Trucks." Background paper prepared for this report.

Anderson, J.E., and E. Van Wincoop. 2004. "Trade Costs." *Journal of Economic Literature* 42: 691–751.

Antras, P., and D. Chor. 2022. *Handbook of International Economics*. Amsterdam: Elsevier.

Atkin, D., and D. Donaldson. 2015. "Who's Getting Globalized? The Size and Implications of Intra-National Trade Costs." Working paper 21439, National Bureau of Economic Research, Cambridge, MA.

Barka, H.B. 2012. "Border Posts, Checkpoints, and Intra-African Trade: Challenges and Solutions," Working paper, African Development Bank. Tunis.

Díaz de Astarloa, B., and N. Pkhikidze. 2024. "Internal Trade Costs in Developing Countries." Policy Research Working Paper 10789, World Bank, Washington, DC. Background paper prepared for this report.

Ganapati, S., and W.F. Wong. 2023. "How Far Goods Travel: Global Transport and Supply Chains from 1965–2020." *Journal of Economic Perspectives* 37 (3): 3–30.

Gwilliam, K. 2011. *Africa's Transport Infrastructure: Mainstreaming Maintenance and Management*. Washington, DC: World Bank.

Harley, K. 1980. "Transportation, the World Wheat Trade, and the Kuznets Cycle, 1850–1913." *Explorations in Economic History* 17: 218–50.

Herrera Dappe, M., and C. Kunaka. 2021. *Connecting to Thrive*. Washington, DC: World Bank.

Herrera Dappe, M., C. Kunaka, M. Lebrand, and N. Weisskopf. 2020. *Moving Forward: Connectivity and Logistics to Sustain Bangladesh's Success*. Washington, DC: World Bank.

Herrera Dappe, M., M. Lebrand, B. Rowberry, and A. Stokenberga. 2024. "Moving Goods: Road Transport Costs in Developing Countries." World Bank, Washington, DC. Background paper prepared for this report.

Hummels, D. 2007. "Transportation Costs and International Trade in the Second Era of Globalization." *Journal of Economic Perspectives* 21: 131–54.

Jacks, D., and M. Stuermer. 2021. "Dry Bulk Shipping and the Evolution of Maritime Transport Costs, 1850–2020." *Australian Economic History Review* 61: 204–27.

Marius Adom, I., and M. Schott. 2024. "Inputs Delays, Firm Dynamics, and Misallocation in Sub-Saharan Africa." *Review of Economic Dynamics* 53: 147–72.

Ministerio de Transporte. 2018. *Transporte en cifras: Estadísticas 2018*. Technical Report. Bogotá.

Mohammed, S.I.S., and J.G. Williamson. 2004. "Freight Rates and Productivity Gains in British Tramp Shipping 1869–1950." *Explorations in Economic History* 41: 172–203.

Molnar, A., and F. Shilpi. 2024. "Urban and Infrastructure Determinants of Freight Cost in India." World Bank, Washington, DC. Background paper prepared for this report.

Nick Porée and Associates. 2023. "Road Freight Transport Costs in Sub-Saharan Africa." Background paper prepared for this report.

North, D. 1968. "Sources of Productivity Change in Ocean Shipping, 1600–1850." *Journal of Political Economy* 76 (953).

Redding, Stephen J. 2022. "Trade and Geography." In *Handbook of International Economics,* ed. Gita Gopinath, Elhanan Helpman, and Kenneth Rogoff, 147–217. Amsterdam: Elsevier-North Holland.

Restuccia, D., and R. Rogerson. 2008. "Policy Distortions and Aggregate Productivity with Heterogeneous Establishments." *Review of Economic Dynamics* 11: 707–20.

Rua, G. 2014. "Diffusion of Containerization." Finance and Economics Discussion Series, Divisions of Research & Statistics and Monetary Affairs, Federal Reserve Board, Washington, DC.

UNCTAD (United Nations Conference on Trade and Development). 2021. *Shipping during Covid-19: Why Container Freight Rates Have Surged*. https://unctad.org/news/shipping-during-covid-19-why-container-freight-rates-have-surged.

UNCTAD and World Bank. 2024. Trade and Transport Dataset, UNCTADstat Data Centre, available at https://unctadstat.unctad.org/datacentre/.

Van Leemput, E. 2021. "A Passage to India: Quantifying Internal and External Barriers to Trade." *Journal of International Economics* 131.

World Bank. 2019. *Implementation Completion and Results Report for the Second Phase Project of the Abidjan-Lagos Trade and Transport Facilitation Program.* Washington, DC: World Bank.

World Bank. 2021. *Somalia Country Economic Memorandum: Towards an Inclusive Jobs Agenda.* Washington, DC: World Bank.

World Bank. 2022. *Project Appraisal Document for the Burkina Faso, Niger, and Togo Lome-Ouagadougou-Niamey Economic Corridor Project (P168386).* Washington, DC: World Bank.

World Bank. 2023. *The Container Port Performance Index 2022.* Washington, DC: World Bank.

WCO (World Customs Organization). 2023. "Weekly Cross-Border Report: Week Ending May 7, 2023." Gauteng, South Africa.

2

Drivers of the Economic Costs of Transport

MAIN MESSAGES

1. The economic costs of transport depend on several factors, which interact in complex ways to determine the price, time, and reliability of transport. The physical and economic geography, the infrastructure in place, the inputs required to provide transport services, the structure of the transport market, policies and regulations, and information on business opportunities affect the operation of transport service providers and, hence, the price they will have to receive to be willing to provide the services. The economic geography and information on available services and prices are important determinants of the demand for transport services and the price shippers are willing to pay. All these factors also play a role in determining the quality of the transport service in terms of time and reliability.

2. The composition of carrier costs in the trucking sector varies across countries, with variable costs representing 60–90 percent of trucking costs (per ton-kilometer), depending on the country. The cost of weak security conditions can be high.

3. The costs of maritime shipping operators are typically split among capital, operating, and voyage costs. Fuel costs can represent more than 75 percent of the operating and voyage costs of a large ship; labor costs represent around 40 percent of operating costs on average.

INTRODUCTION

Research on trade and transport costs accumulated over the past several decades points to multiple drivers of the transport costs incurred by shippers and traders. Many policy analyses focus on individual drivers, particularly those that have a direct effect on vehicle operating costs or carrier costs. These costs and their drivers are important, but focusing only on them can lead to incorrect diagnostics and policies that have unintended consequences. To design policies that foster the efficiency of the sector, it is important to understand the broad range of factors that determine the transport costs incurred by shippers and traders and the mechanisms at play.

This chapter is organized as follows. The first section presents a simple framework linking the factors that determine the economic costs of transport with their components and identifying the interactions among them, which helps frame the discussion in the following chapters. The second section dives into the drivers of carrier costs and how they vary across countries.

CONCEPTUAL FRAMEWORK

The economic costs of freight transport incurred by a shipper include the price paid to the transport service provider (or the cost of operating its own transport assets) and the costs of time and uncertainty (or unreliability).[1] Transport time and unreliability have cost implications on shippers through inventory and hedging costs. The economic costs of freight transport depend on the following factors:

- **Physical geography:** distance, topography, climate
- **Economic geography:** spatial distribution of population and industries
- **Infrastructure:** roads, bridges, railways, ports
- **Equipment and labor:** vehicles, vessels, cranes, digital technologies, and workers
- **Policies and regulations:** tariffs and taxes, interest rates, and licensing requirements
- **Information:** search and matching frictions
- **Market structure of transport sector:** competition, scale of formalization, and mark-ups.

These factors interact with each other in complex ways (refer to figure 2.1). The state of technology and exogenous physical geography determine the production possibility frontier of transport services. Within that frontier, the supply of transport services is determined by carrier costs, which are determined by investments in infrastructure, equipment, and supporting structures; the costs of vehicles, vessels, cranes, labor, and fuel and taxes and tariffs on them; and regulations. Economic geography—the

FIGURE 2.1 Economic costs of freight transport and its determinants

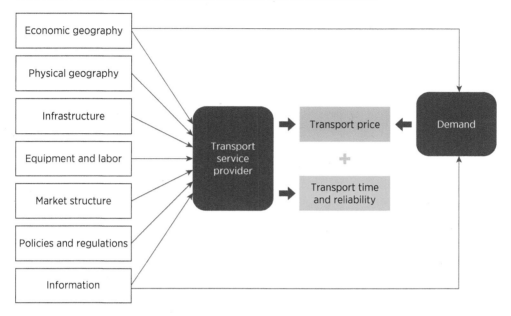

Source: Original figure for this publication.

spatial distribution of populations and industries—is a key determinant of demand for transport services through the level and direction of trade flows. Potential trade imbalances give rise to the backhaul problem (returning empty) and may generate asymmetries in shipping prices between origin and destination locations. Search and matching frictions can make it difficult for carriers willing to transport freight and shippers wanting to ship freight in the same direction to find each other, forcing them to travel empty, which may generate asymmetries in shipping prices. Transport costs and market access affect endogenous location decisions of firms and long-run economic geography. These interactions culminate in an equilibrium market structure in which the level of competition and the scale of formal versus informal service providers determine a markup over carrier costs and thus the ultimate transport prices paid by shippers. The market structure might include intermediaries matching shippers and carriers, which would add a markup by the intermediary.

Inventory costs are the financial cost of goods during their transport. Physical geography; weather; population density; the quality of infrastructure, vehicles, vessels, and cranes; regulations; and the incentives provided by the market interact to determine transport time and reliability. Monetary and financial policies that determine interest rates yield the opportunity cost of cargo during hauling. Hedging costs capture a more complex issue, because hedging strategies can range from deciding to face the risk of disruption of stocks and lost business opportunities when delays surge to reordering early to compensate for potential additional delays in delivery, increasing the inventory and storage costs, to more complex decisions regarding the design of supply chains and the location of warehouses and production facilities.

For private fleets (fleets operated by shippers themselves), what matters is the cost of operating and managing the fleet.[2] All factors except the structure of the transport services market and the information frictions in that market are relevant determinants of the economic costs of transport. The market structure and the quality of the services offered by for-hire transport providers are important determinants of the decision to maintain a private fleet (Herrera Dappe and others 2020; World Bank 2020).

CARRIER COSTS

This section examines the drivers of carrier costs, first for trucking and then for maritime shipping.

Trucking

Conventional wisdom assumes that investing in infrastructure will reduce transport costs. It assumes that reducing variable trucking costs through better transport infrastructure will reduce trucking costs and then transport prices. In fact, variable costs are just one part of the trucking costs, and infrastructure is not the only factor determining them.

Trucking costs include variable and fixed costs. Variable costs for asset-based trucking service providers include the cost of fuel, tires, maintenance, labor, and trip-specific fees, such as tolls and trip-specific formal and informal charges. These costs are directly related to the level of trucking activity, such as kilometers traveled and time on the road.

Fixed costs increase with the size of the operations, typically in a lumpy manner, but are otherwise not directly correlated to the level of activity. Asset-based trucking service providers' fixed costs include expenses related to trucks, systems, facilities, and other capital items. Fixed costs also include asset depreciation and financing costs, insurance, annual vehicle registration, and general overhead (World Bank 2020).

Infrastructure affects trucking costs primarily by reducing distance; increasing commercial speeds, allowing for a higher turnover of trucks; and reducing maintenance and repair costs, with the last two factors largely affected through better-quality infrastructure. Higher turnover of trucks is also affected by the nontravel time needed to complete a job, which includes time spent loading and unloading cargo; waiting to access and be able to unload cargo; and crossing roadblocks, checkpoints, and borders. In some cases, nontravel time is longer than travel time. The poor condition of trucks and overloading can constrain commercial speed even more than the condition of the infrastructure. The age of the fleet also affects costs, as older trucks have higher fuel consumption and maintenance costs.

Reliable access to freight plays a significant role in the balance between fixed and variable costs, by increasing the utilization of trucks. With an increased number of rotations, trucking companies can accommodate higher overheads (for more skilled personnel other than drivers and better facilities), and higher fixed costs (better and larger trucks) without increasing the cost of a trip. Better and larger trucks can allow trucking companies to take advantage of economies of scale and improved fuel efficiency, lowering variable costs. However, gaining reliable access to freight and expediting the completion of a trip sometimes require facilitation payments, which increase variable costs.

The composition of trucking costs varies across countries, but some patterns are evident across countries. Variable costs represent 60–90 percent of trucking costs (per ton-km), depending on the country.[3] In Bangladesh, the costs of drivers and helpers, fuel, maintenance, and tires represent 54 percent of trucking costs (refer to figure 2.2). "Facilitation payments" to drivers unions, traffic police, ferry operators, others, and broker fees, all of which are trip specific, represent 13 percent (Herrera Dappe and others 2020). In Viet Nam, variable costs are at the upper end of the spectrum, at 74 percent of total costs for short-haul and 82 percent for long-haul trips. Tire, repair, and maintenance costs are relatively low, but the costs of tolls and facilitation fees are high, representing 23 percent of total costs for short-haul trips and 28 percent for long-haul trips (Lam, Sriram, and Khera 2019). In India, the cost of fuel represents almost half of trucking costs on average, followed by the cost of tolls, tires, repairs, and maintenance.

FIGURE 2.2 **Composition of trucking costs in selected countries**

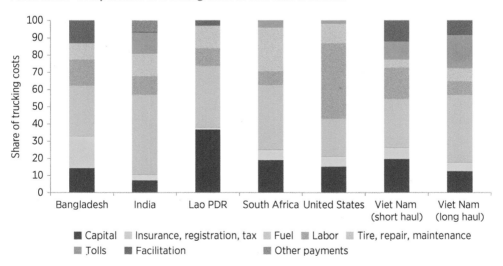

Source: Original figure for this publication based on data from ATKearney 2017; Herrera Dappe and others 2020; Lam, Sriram, and Khera 2019; Nick Porée and Associates 2023; Williams and Murray 2020; and World Bank 2018.
Note: The cost shares for Bangladesh and Viet Nam differ from those in Herrera Dappe and others (2020) and Lam, Sriram, and Khera (2019), who include overhead and fees to brokers (only in Bangladesh); those costs are not included here, in order to standardize the costs shares across countries.

Capital costs represent 7 percent and the cost of insurance, permits, and tax 3 percent (ATKearney 2017).

Total fixed costs are just 25 percent of total costs in South Africa and 38 percent in Lao PDR, but some of their components are high. In South Africa, capital costs represent 19 percent of total trucking costs,[4] the third-largest share after fuel (38 percent) and tire, repair, and maintenance (25 percent). In Lao PDR, depreciation and interest costs represent 37 percent of trucking costs, followed by fuel costs (36 percent). The cost of capital for vehicle financing is relatively high in Lao PDR, with typical interest rates of 10–15 percent a year (usually payable over a period of three years) (World Bank 2018).

In high-income countries, labor wages tend to represent a large share of trucking costs; in low- and middle-income countries, fuel tends to be the main determinant. Another important difference is that facilitation payments are not common in high-income countries. Variable costs represent 79 percent of trucking costs in the United States (Williams and Murray 2020), similar to the figure for long-haul trips in Viet Nam. Employment costs in the United States are 2.4–5.3 times the cost in Bangladesh and Viet Nam, and fuel costs are 28–112 percent higher in low- and middle-income countries than in the United States (refer to figure 2.2).

The cost of poor security conditions can be high. In Somalia, the cost of checkpoints and roadblocks represent as much as 63 percent of trucking costs in some corridors (refer to figure 2.3). Security conditions also lead to higher salary payments over these corridors (World Bank 2021). The most acute

FIGURE 2.3 Composition of trucking costs in Somalia, by corridor

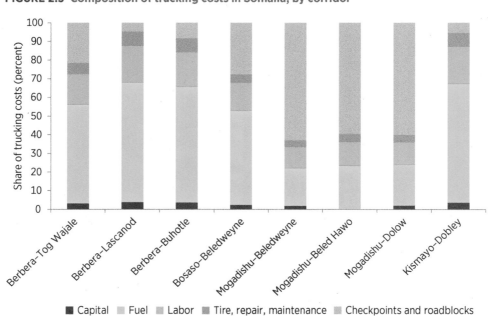

Source: Original figure for this publication based on World Bank 2021.

security-related challenges are observed in the corridors from the ports of Mogadishu, where en-route payments of more than $2,000 per shipment have been observed over the Mogadishu–Beledweyne and Mogadishu–Beled Hawo routes, with higher payments for high-value or sensitive shipments and/or for drivers/traders not backed by strong clans (World Bank 2021). In Central America, the cost of security measures can be as high as 22 percent of freight value (IDB 2013).

Maritime shipping

The costs of maritime shipping operators can be split between fixed and variable costs, but the typical split in the industry is among capital, operating, and voyage costs. Capital costs include depreciation and interest. Operating costs consist of labor-related costs, insurance, repairs, maintenance, dry docking, management and administration, lubricants, spares, and other costs necessary for the running of vessels. Voyage costs consist of fuel costs and port and canal dues (Haralambides 2019).

Port infrastructure, superstructure, and their operation affect carrier costs primarily through shorter port times, which allow for higher turnover of ships. Modern and larger ships allow shipping companies to take advantage of economies of scale and improved fuel efficiency. Voyage speed is an important determinant of fuel costs, with a 10 percent increase in speed leading to a more than 20 percent increase in fuel consumption (Haralambides 2019). Reliable access to freight plays a significant role in the balance between fixed and variable costs, by increasing ship utilization. With increased utilization, shipping companies can accommodate higher overheads and capital costs without increasing the cost of individual trips.

The two most important components of operating and voyage costs are fuel and labor. According to Ronen (2017), fuel costs can represent more than

FIGURE 2.4 Components of operating costs of container and dry bulk vessels

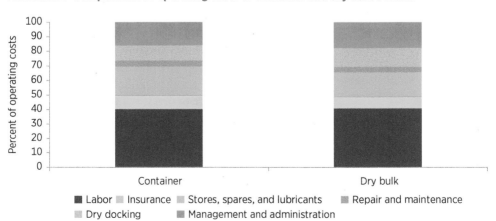

Source: Original figure for this publication based on Drewry 2020.
Note: Shares are averages across vessel sizes.

75 percent of the operating and voyage costs of a large ship. Haralambides (2019) claims that the fuel costs of a large container shipping company represent about half of total costs. Labor costs represent around 40 percent of operating costs, on average, for both container and dry bulk vessels, followed by stores, spares and lubricants, and management and administration (refer to figure 2.4).

NOTES

1. Shipper-borne economic costs of transport are often referred to as *generalized transport costs* or the *transport-related component of logistics costs.*
2. The importance of private truck fleets varies across countries. For the European Union as a whole, less than 30 percent of truck tonnage is moved by private fleets; the figure is 79 percent in Greece (World Bank 2020).
3. These figures assume that all labor and maintenance costs are variable costs, in order to standardize the figures across countries, even though practices vary across countries.
4. Trucking costs in South Africa do not include facilitation payments, which are uncommon in the country, and overhead, the latter because of lack of data.

REFERENCES

ATKearney. 2017. "Estimation of Changes in Trucking Sector Greenhouse Gases Associated with Road Sector Policy and Investment Interventions." Unpublished manuscript.

Drewry. 2020. *Ship Operating Costs Annual Review and Forecast. Annual Report 2020/21.* London.

Haralambides, H.E. 2019. "Gigantism in Container Shipping, Ports and Global Logistics: A Time-Lapse into the Future." *Maritime Economics & Logistics* 21: 1–60.

Herrera Dappe, M., C. Kunaka, M. Lebrand, and N. Weisskopf. 2020. *Moving Forward: Connectivity and Logistics to Sustain Bangladesh's Success.* Washington, DC: World Bank.

IDB (Inter-American Development Bank). 2013. "Trucking Services in Belize, Central America, and the Dominican Republic: Performance Analysis and Policy Recommendations. Department of Infrastructure and Environment." Technical Note IDB–TN–511. Washington, DC.

Lam, Y.Y., K. Sriram, and N. Khera. 2019. *Strengthening Vietnam's Trucking Sector: Towards Lower Logistics Costs and Greenhouse Gas Emissions.* Vietnam Transport Knowledge Series. Washington, DC: World Bank Group.

Nick Porée and Associates. 2023. "Road Freight Transport Costs in Sub-Saharan Africa". Background paper prepared for this report.

Ronen, D. 2017. "The Effect of Oil Price on Containership Speed and Fleet Size." *Journal of the Operational Research Society* 62 (1): 211–16.

Williams, N., and D. Murray. 2020. *An Analysis of the Operational Costs of Trucking: 2020 Update.* American Transport Research Institute, Arlington, Va.

World Bank. 2018. *Transport Costs and Prices in Lao PDR: Unlocking the Potential of an Idle Fleet.* Washington, DC: World Bank.

World Bank. 2020. *Trucking: A Performance Assessment Framework for Policymakers.* Washington, DC: World Bank.

World Bank. 2021. *Somalia Country Economic Memorandum: Towards an Inclusive Jobs Agenda.* Washington, DC: World Bank.

3

Physical Geography and Infrastructure

MAIN MESSAGES

1. Physical geography, particularly distance, is an important determinant of transport times and prices. The prices for trucking services increase with distance, but the increase is less than proportional, with the total transport price of a shipment increasing by about 3.1 percent for every 10 percent increase in trip distance.

2. Transport infrastructure can reduce the frictions of distance and topography. The degree to which it does so depends on the quality and service level of the infrastructure. In a given country, compared with shipments traveling on routes that do not use highways at all, shipments that travel on highways for the entire length of their routes have 20 percent lower transport prices per ton-kilometer, on average.

3. Shipments during the rainy season pay a premium of about 6 percent, on average. The effects are heterogeneous across countries, with the increase higher in countries in which road infrastructure quality is lower.

4. Congestion is less important in intercity than in intracity travel. In intercity travel, the difference between the fastest and the slowest time of day is only about 3 percent; in urban travel, it is 25 percent. Road characteristics—including the number of lanes, surface types, road lighting, and the quality of roads—are among the most important determinants of speed on interurban roads.

5. The availability and quality of port infrastructure and the operation of ports are important determinants of maritime shipping costs. Raising the operational performance of container ports from the 25th to the 75th percentile reduces shipping costs by 37 percent, on average.

INTRODUCTION

Physical geography creates barriers between locations. The longer the distance and the more rugged and mountainous the terrain, the longer a trip takes and the more energy it consumes; inclement weather makes travel even harder. For millennia, civilizations have built road infrastructure to reduce the frictions of physical geography and ports to ease the movement of cargo and people between land and sea.

Answers to several questions can inform governments' policy decisions and allow multilateral development banks and bilateral aid agencies to better support those polices. What are the main determinants behind the variation in travel speed across countries? How much do distance and topography contribute to the variation in transport costs across countries? How much can transport costs be reduced by building more direct routes? Do all types and quality of infrastructure reduce transport costs to the same extent? How much does the operation of container ports contribute to the variation in maritime transport costs across the world?

This chapter presents empirical evidence that answers these important questions. Based on novel datasets and the compilation of existing ones, it assesses the importance of distance, topography, and climate in determining intercity travel speed and reliability, vehicle operating costs (VOCs), and transport prices. The chapter also presents evidence on (a) the ability of transport infrastructure to reduce the frictions of physical geography and how its ability to do so depends on the placement, quality, and service level of the infrastructure and (b) the nature of the relationship between port operations and both maritime and land transport costs.

This chapter is organized as follows. The first section presents novel findings on interurban travel speed, congestion, and reliability across the world. The second section examines the role of distance, topography, and climate as drivers of road transport prices. The third section examines the role of road infrastructure as a driver of carrier costs and road transport prices. The last section presents evidence on the role of ports and their operation as drivers of transport costs.

TRAVEL TIME, RELIABILITY, AND COSTS

Travel time is an important determinant of VOCs, and both travel time and travel time reliability are important determinants of vehicle utilization and shippers' time costs. Travel speed is one of the key determinants of travel time.

Intercity travel is slow in some countries and fast in others, as discussed in chapter 1. Among the 134 countries covered in the study, country characteristics explain 48 percent of the variation in road segment speed, with speeds in countries in the top decile of intercity road speed about twice as fast as those in countries in the bottom deciles, according to research conducted for this report by Akbar and others (2024).

Travel speed tends to be faster on higher-standard roads, such as highways. Primary roads are about 9 percent slower than motorways; secondary roads are about 1 percent slower than primary roads, and tertiary roads are about 5 percent slower than secondary roads. Tortuosity (length divided by the great circle distance between origin and destination[1]) and terrain ruggedness have a negative but small average effect on speed.[2] Road segments close to large cities are slow even when they cross sparsely populated areas (Akbar and others 2024).

Road class explains part of the differences in average travel speed across countries. The share of motorways in the distance traveled on the routed segments ranges from 27 percent in Mozambique to 90 percent or more in France, Germany, and Namibia. Additional road characteristics—including the intersection density per kilometer (km), the number of lanes, the road surface types, streetlighting, and speed limit—and human and physical geography further explain differences in average travel speed across countries.

Part of the differences in average speed is unexplained by such factors, however (refer to figure 3.1). The average speed in Namibia, for example, is 57 km per hour greater than the average speed in Nepal (the slowest country). The difference decreases to 33 km per hour when controlling for road characteristics and human and physical geography. The remaining differences suggest that some countries are intrinsically slower than others.

Analysis of the determinants of speed in intercity travel provides several insights. First, unobserved country characteristics are the most important

FIGURE 3.1 Intercity speed differences with respect to the slowest country (Nepal) with and without controlling for some factors, by world region

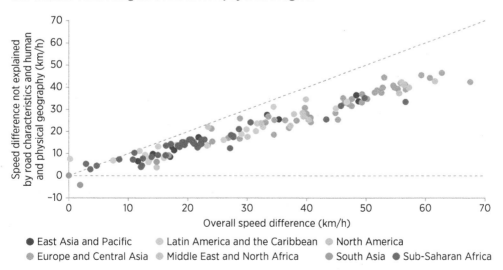

Source: Original figure for this publication based on Akbar and others 2024.
Notes: Road characteristics include road class; the number of intersections per kilometer; the mean speed limit; the mean number of lanes; the share of road surface types (fully paved, partially paved, irregularly paved, and unimproved surfaces); the share of roads with streetlamps; and Google Maps traffic warnings on the route.

determinant of speed, closely followed by road characteristics. Second, population and human geography are secondary determinants of speed. The fact that the unobserved country characteristics explain significant variation in speed across countries suggests that vehicle quality and driving habits are likely to be important in intercity travel. The quality of roads may also be captured by these unobserved country characteristics (a highway in Bangladesh is not of the same quality as a highway in Germany). Unobserved country characteristics are highly correlated with GDP per capita, which supports the hypotheses on the quality of roads and vehicles.

Intercity travel is much less congested than within-city travel. The variation in real-time intercity speed largely reflects variations in uncongested intercity speed (Akbar and others 2024).[3] The difference between the fastest and slowest time of day is only 2 km per hour relative to an average speed of about 70 km per hour (about 3 percent). Congestion matters only close to large cities. Travel speed on segments with population density in the top decile is about 20 percent slower at the worst of the evening peak than at midnight. The difference in the average intercity segment is an order of magnitude smaller than the differences in urban travel found by Akbar and others (2023); differences in denser segments are somewhat similar to those found by Akbar and others (2023). Akbar and others find that on average across 1,119 cities, the slowest time of day in urban travel is 25 percent slower than the fastest. In extreme cases, such as the highly congested city of Bogotá, Colombia, the difference reaches about 50 percent.

Intercity travel shows moderate levels of unreliability across the world, with urban regions presenting higher levels of unreliability than rural regions. The median segment-time-of-day exhibits a measure of unreliability of less than 5 percent (that is, the 90th percentile of travel time is slightly less than 5 percent higher than the median). Unreliability is 42 percent in urban and 16 percent in rural regions (Akbar and others 2024).

EFFECT OF DISTANCE AND TOPOGRAPHY ON TRANSPORT PRICES

Distance, along with quantity shipped, is the largest contributor to the variation in the total transport price of shipments in an analysis of data from shipments of goods within 60 low- and middle-income countries procured by a large humanitarian organization in 2019 and 2020 (Herrera Dappe, Lebrand, and others 2024). Controlling for shipment tonnage and origin- and destination-specific characteristics, the total transport price of a shipment increases by about 3.1 percent for every 10 percent increase in trip distance. Removing 100 km from the trip distance for a shipment that falls at the 25th percentile of the distance distribution (by, for example, building a more direct route between the origin and the destination) is associated with total transport price savings of about 50 percent (after controlling for the shipment quantity, number of trucks used, year-month, and origin city and destination city characteristics).[4] At the 50th and 75th percentiles of distance distribution, the total transport price savings associated with reducing the trip distance by 100 km are about 20 percent and 10 percent, respectively.

The effect of reducing the shipment distance by 100 km at the three percentiles of distance distribution varies widely at the country level (refer to figure 3.2). At the median of the distance distribution, shortening a trip by 100 km is associated with a reduction in the total transport price of 30 percent or more in Lesotho, Iraq, Honduras, and Zimbabwe; the reduction is less than 10 percent in Kenya, Ethiopia, and Colombia. One reason for the difference may be the large differences in the distance distributions across the countries, which means that a 100-km reduction is much more significant for the median trip in Lesotho than in Ethiopia.

A more feasible reduction in shipment distance—by 10 km, for example, through the construction of a bridge or a connecting road segment—is estimated to reduce the total transport price by 1–13 percent at the 25th percentile, by up to 6 percent at the 50th percentile, and by up to 3 percent at the 75th percentile of the trip distribution. However, based on the sample of 60 countries, there is a limit to the extent to which the total transport price of a shipment can be reduced by cutting the travel distance (refer to figure 3.3): For a reduction of 10 km, the potential total cost savings plateau at around 300 km of the original trip distance and disappear once the total original trip distance reaches around 700 km.

A strong positive correlation between transport price per ton and the origin–destination distance has been documented in India, especially for freight of relatively low tonnage transported in containers (refer to figure 3.4). Controlling for the shipment tonnage and local conditions in the origin and destination cities, the marginal cost to the shipper associated

FIGURE 3.2 **Reduction in total transport price associated with reduction in trip distance of 100 kilometers in selected countries, by percentile of initial trip distance**

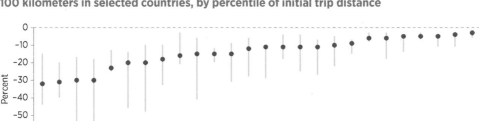

Source: Original figure for this publication based on Herrera Dappe, Lebrand, and others 2024.
Note: Dots show 50th percentile of the distance distribution. Whiskers show 25th and 75th percentiles.

FIGURE 3.3 Decline in total transport price of a shipment from reducing the length of the trip by 10 and 100 kilometers, by original distance

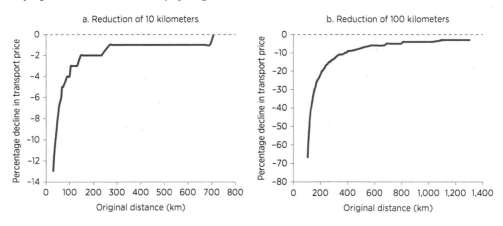

Source: Original figure for this publication based on Herrera Dappe, Lebrand, and others 2024.

FIGURE 3.4 Correlation between distance and transport price per ton in India, by vehicle type and tonnage

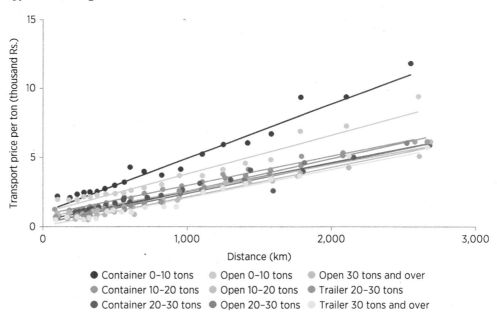

Source: Molnar and Shilpi 2024.
Note: Figure is based on data for 2017–20. Routed distances between origin–destination pairs range from about 300 km for Delhi–Chandigarh to over 2,000 km for Delhi–Chennai, with an average at about 900 km.

with an additional kilometer of distance is around $0.024 (Rs. 1.96) per ton (Molnar and Shilpi 2024).[5]

Shipments that travel over longer distances see a transport price discount per ton-km: The farther the goods travel, the lower the cost per km. This finding suggests some economies of scale in distance, because of the fixed costs associated with each shipment. Herrera Dappe, Lebrand, and others (2024) find that a 10 percent increase in kilometers traveled is associated with a decline of about 7 percent in the transport price per ton-km. Moving from the 25th to the 75th percentile of travel distance for a representative shipment (corresponding to an increase from about 112 km to 420 km) is associated with a 43 percent decline in the unit transport price.

There is significant variation in the effect of distance on unit transport prices across and within countries. In Pakistan, unit transport prices of shipments that travel from Karachi to the farthest destination (Bagh, 1,664 km away) are 78 percent lower than comparable shipments from Karachi to the closest destination (Kotri, 158 km away). In contrast, in the Dominican Republic and Madagascar, the distance-related discount for the longest versus the shortest shipment originating in the main cities is less than 30 percent (refer to figure 3.5). This finding is intuitive, as the difference between the longest and the shortest shipment route is much shorter than in Pakistan. Distance-related transport cost discounts are the most consistent among the group of countries in which the distance differentials exceed 1,400 km.

Data on carrier costs for shipments in Central Asia Regional Economic Cooperation (CAREC) member countries provide evidence of economies of scale. Trucking costs per ton-km decline by 0.4–1.6 percent for every 10 percent increase in distance traveled (Iimi 2023).

Distance is often compounded by, and correlated with, topography, with mountainous and difficult terrain being associated with higher transport prices per kilometer traveled. Globally, road travel is slower where the terrain is more rugged, with speeds in areas of maximum ruggedness 15 km per hour less than speeds on flat terrain, all else equal (Akbar and others 2024).[6] In India, trucking prices are 10 times higher than average on roads on which each 100 meters of distance imply an additional incline of at least 2 meters (Molnar and Shilpi 2024). For example, the price per ton-km for a shipment from Ludhiana (Punjab) to Srinagar (Jammu and Kashmir) is about $0.034 (Rs. 2.83) more expensive than the trip from Ludhiana and Jaipur (Rajasthan), which is about the same length. On the first route, nearly 10 percent of the distance takes place at a grade 1 percent and above; all of the second route takes place at a grade below 1 percent. Moreover, because routes in mountainous areas are more circuitous, the total distance that has to be traveled is longer per equivalent straight-line distance.

The supply of road infrastructure can manifest in the availability of direct rather than circuitous routes, affecting the distance traveled and therefore time and VOC. Across a sample of 134 countries, although the tortuosity of the network matters less than ruggedness, the effect on travel speed is nevertheless significant, with a standard deviation increase in tortuosity associated

FIGURE 3.5 Discount in transport price per ton-km for longest trip compared with shortest trip from main origin city, by difference in distance

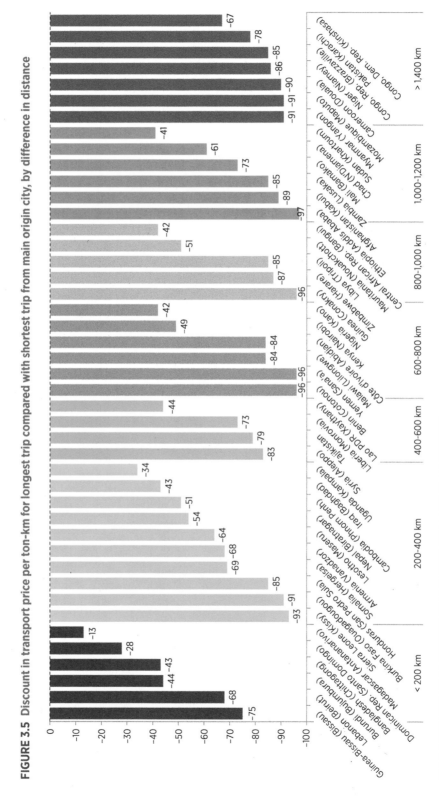

Source: Original figure for this publication based on Herrera Dappe, Lebrand, and others 2024.

with a decline in speed of 1.3 km per hour (Akbar and others 2024). Molnar and Shilpi (2024) quantify the contribution of road supply to routed distance across each state. As expected, the incremental transport cost faced by shippers from path routing is highest in mountainous states and territories (Jammu and Kashmir, Meghalaya, Himachal Pradesh, Assam and Kerala) and lowest in Delhi, where road density is highest (refer to figure 3.6 and map 3.1).

FIGURE 3.6 Total versus routing-related transport costs in India, by state and union territory

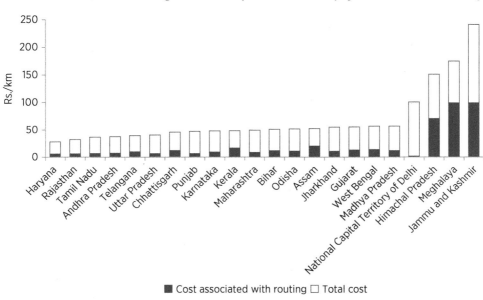

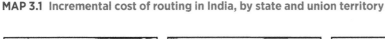

Source: Molnar and Shilpi 2024.

MAP 3.1 Incremental cost of routing in India, by state and union territory

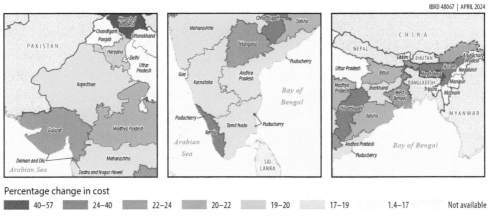

Source: Molnar and Shilpi 2024.

Higher trucking prices in mountainous areas reflect higher trucking costs. Across the CAREC region, the average vertical difference in elevation between origin and destination is 144 meters; it reaches nearly 1,160 meters on some routes. Everything else equal, trucking costs are higher on routes that have significant elevation gain, increasing by about 0.5 percent for every 10 percent increase in the difference in elevation between origin and destination (Iimi 2023). The increase in costs is probably related to the lower speed and fuel efficiency in hilly areas.

EFFECT OF ROAD INFRASTRUCTURE ON TRANSPORT PRICES

Better-quality and higher-capacity road infrastructure can affect the cost of using it: The quality of onshore infrastructure accounts for 40 percent of predicted transport costs for coastal countries and up to 60 percent for land-locked ones (Limao and Venables 2001). Infrastructure affects service delivery through both variable costs of transport and timeliness and supply chain reliability (Arvis, Raballand, and Marteau 2010).

The availability and quality of road infrastructure directly affect VOCs. Roads in poor condition increase fuel consumption and the maintenance costs of trucks. According to the Highway Development and Management Model typically used in the appraisal of World Bank–financed road projects, freight transport VOCs can be reduced by about 15 percent if the road condition, as measured by the International Roughness Index, is improved from 8 (very poor) to 2 (good), holding everything else constant (Iimi 2023).

Regional integration and transport connectivity are of particular importance for the Caucasus and Central Asian region, which is landlocked and located on the crossroads between Europe and East Asia, between the Russian Federation and South Asia (Incaltarau and others 2022). Carrier costs decrease with increasing speed, a proxy for road quality, but the decrease depends on the type of commodity. Once the carrier-specific characteristics are controlled for, costs decrease by 0.3 percent with a 10 percent increase in speed in the case of food products and by 1.1 percent for consumer goods; for other goods categories the effect of speed is not significant (Iimi 2023).

Transport unit prices tend to be lower on routes that use higher-standard and better-quality roads. In the analysis conducted for this report on the drivers of transport prices within and across 60 countries across several regions, Herrera Dappe, Lebrand, and others (2024) calculate for each origin–destination pair the fraction of the total distance traveled on highways[7] rather than more minor roads, an indirect measure of infrastructure availability and quality.[8] The median shipment in the data uses a highway for about 60 percent of the total distance traveled; highway-intensive routes tend to be longer than routes that do not use highways, possibly because traveling farther increases the probability of using a highway (refer to figure 3.7).

FIGURE 3.7 Distribution of trip distance, by fraction of shipment route on highways

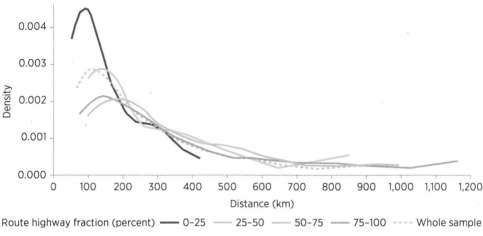

Route highway fraction (percent) ▬▬ 0–25   ▬▬ 25–50   ▬▬ 50–75   ▬▬ 75–100   ···· Whole sample

Source: Herrera Dappe, Lebrand, and others 2024.

In a given country, shipments that travel on highways for the entire length of their routes have 19 percent lower transport prices per ton-km on average than shipments traveling on routes that do not use highways at all (Herrera Dappe, Lebrand, and others 2024). The median transport price per ton-km declines monotonically with the fraction of the route distance traveled on highways, from $0.24 for shipments that use highways for less than a quarter of the route to $0.13 for shipments using highways for over three-quarters of the distance (refer to figure 3.8). If a shipment at the 50th percentile of the distance distribution increases the fraction of kilometers it travels on a highway by 10 percentage points, the unit cost associated with the shipment should fall by about 2.2 percent.

In Afghanistan, for example, shipments from Kabul, the largest origin city, that use highways for a large portion of the route have a 12.4 percent lower unit transport price than otherwise similar shipments from the same city that use highways only for a small fraction of the route.[9] The predicted savings are larger when highways are used more intensively and shipments travel farther (refer to figure 3.9).

Freight rates in India tend to be lower when freight moves along major road corridors such as access-controlled expressways, the Golden Quadrilateral, and the North–South/East–West corridor (Molnar and Shilpi 2024). Access-controlled expressways represent a larger share of the overall freight kilometers in northwestern India. Traveling along these major highways reduces rates by $0.07–$0.08 (Rs. 5.8–Rs. 6.5) per km (about 17.4–19.2 percent) compared with using other district roads or national highways. Analysis of the relationship between freight rates and the speed of movement, another proxy for road quality, suggests that the freight rate per kilometer declines as speed increases but levels out after a speed of 50 km per hour. Eastern India,

FIGURE 3.8 Median transport price based on fraction of route distance traveled on highways

Source: Original figure for this publication based on Herrera Dappe, Lebrand, and others 2024.

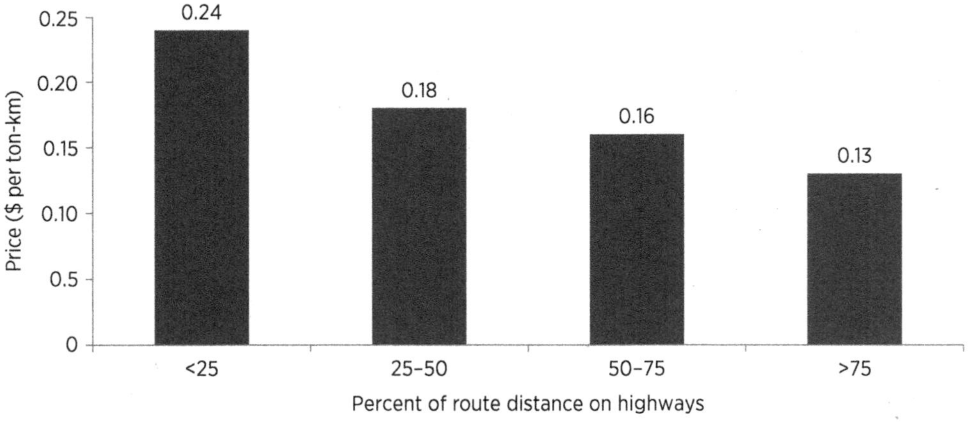

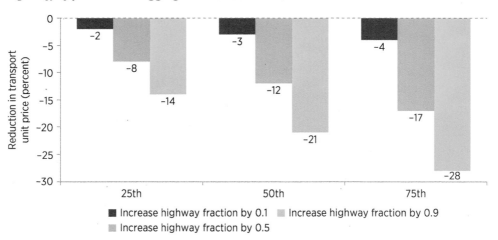

FIGURE 3.9 Predicted reduction in transport unit price from increasing share of trip on a highway, by percentile of aggregate distance distribution

Source: Original figure for this publication based on Herrera Dappe, Lebrand, and others 2024.

which has the lowest road availability (and lowest speeds), has the highest freight rate penalties associated with speed (refer to map 3.2).

The quality of road infrastructure is one of the key determinants of transport prices. In Bangladesh, an estimated 11–36 percent of direct logistic costs are from inadequate road infrastructure (Herrera Dappe and others 2020).[10] In Malawi, infrastructure quality is an important contributor to regional differences in transport prices faced by farmers (Lall, Wang, and Munthali 2009). The quality of the trunk road network is not a major constraint, but

MAP 3.2 Freight rate penalty in India associated with speed, by state

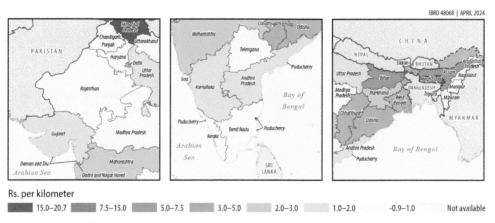

IBRD 48068 | APRIL 2024

Rs. per kilometer

15.0–20.7	7.5–15.0	5.0–7.5	3.0–5.0	2.0–3.0	1.0–2.0	-0.9–1.0	Not available

Source: Molnar and Shilpi 2024.

differences in the quality of feeder roads connecting villages to the main road network significantly affect transport costs, with rates for bad roads 9–15 percent higher than rates on all-weather roads (Ksoll and Kunaka 2016). Similarly, trucking companies in West Africa charge higher rates for trips on roads in poor conditions. The type of roads (that is, number of lanes, urban and interurban) is also an important determinant of trucking costs and rates (Terevaninthorn and Raballand 2009).

Insufficient urban road infrastructure raises the cost of transport on routes that cross urbanized areas. Controlling for tonnage, the cost per kilometer in cities in the lowest quintile of mobility (according to the urban speed indices developed by Akbar and others 2023b) is 2.77 times that of the average urban premium (Molnar and Shilpi 2024). Urban mobility, in turn, depends on the availability and quality of well-planned road networks, among other factors. In India, cities in the lowest quintile of mobility are concentrated in the northeast; they include Arrah, Bihar Sharif and Patna in Bihar and Kolkata, English Bazar, and Santipur in West Bengal (refer to map 3.3). Average speeds in these cities are 13–20 km per hour. The top quintile includes cities in Karnataka, Kerala, and Tamil Nadu, where speeds average 25–33 km per hour (Molnar and Shilpi 2024). The most congested (lowest-mobility) cities thus tend to be in states in which speed is associated with the largest freight rate penalties, as illustrated in map 3.2. All of the largest cities in India except Ahmedabad are in the lowest mobility quintile.

Road conditions interact with many other factors. Climate conditions are increasingly important in many developing countries. Good-quality infrastructure can help mitigate the effect of inclement weather on the transport sector. To understand how road quality and climate conditions jointly affect transport costs, Herrera Dappe, Lebrand, and others (2024) look at whether the cargo shipment occurs during the rainy season. They find that shipments during the rainy season pay a premium of about 6 percent, or about $0.01 per

MAP 3.3 Quintile ranking of cities in India based on speed indices

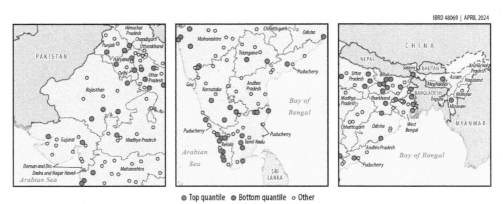

● Top quantile ● Bottom quantile ○ Other

Source: Original maps for this publication based on Akbar and others 2023b.

MAP 3.4 Increase in transport price during the rainy season

Source: Herrera Dappe, Lebrand, and others 2024.

ton-km of the median transport price. The effects are heterogeneous across countries (refer to map 3.4), partly because of differences in road quality.

In Zambia—where road infrastructure conditions tend to be poor to fair and only about half of the distance traveled by the cargo shipments is on highways—the rainy season is associated with a 20 percent increase in the transport cost, or about $0.0168 per ton-km for the country's median shipment relative to the effect of the rainy season in Türkiye, which has some of the best road infrastructure in the sample and uses highways for 93 percent of the overall travel distance. In Zimbabwe, the effect of the rainy season increases transport costs by as much as 36 percent more than it does in Türkiye.[11] The median increase in transport price associated with the rainy season is larger in countries in which road infrastructure quality is assessed to be lower, according to the World Economic Forum (2019). In countries with road infrastructure quality below 2.0 (on a scale from 1 to 7, where 7 is best), such as Chad, the median rainy season premium is $1.61 per ton-km relative to Türkiye. In contrast, the median premium averages just $0.11 per ton-km in countries in which the quality of road infrastructure is 4.0 or above (Namibia, South Africa) (refer to figure 3.10).

Travel on roads managed through various public-private partnership (PPP) schemes can be associated with lower trucking prices, likely because of the positive correlation with road conditions. In India, routes in the top three quintiles in terms of the share of the route covered by PPP roads have the lowest prices, according to analysis based on data from the World Bank's Private Participation in Infrastructure database and a database of PPP projects from the government of India (Molnar and Shilpi 2024). Controlling for shipment-level characteristics and the route kilometers that take place on any PPP road and road type (for example, access-controlled expressway, the Golden Quadrilateral), a kilometer traveled on a PPP road is $0.021 (Rs. 1.7) more expensive on average than a kilometer on non–PPP roads. This premium for PPPs may reflect maintenance and tolls on these roads, but it needs to be interpreted jointly with the fact that major highway corridors were delivered through PPPs; the net estimated effect of such roads is still a discount (for example, a Rs. 4.1 discount for a PPP segment of the Golden Quadrilateral corridor). After netting out the toll fee from the total freight rate, the Rs. 1.7 premium on PPP roads becomes a Rs. 2.7 discount,

FIGURE 3.10 Median increase in transport price during the rainy season for median shipment, by quality of a country's road infrastructure

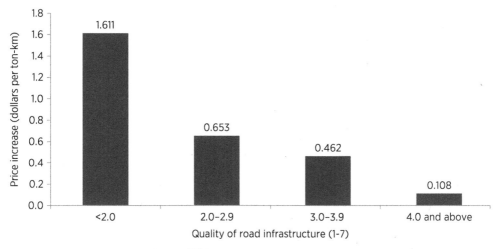

Source: Herrera Dappe, Lebrand, and others 2024.
Note: The increase in transport price is relative to Türkiye, the benchmark country.

suggesting that although the attributes of these roads provide net benefits to freight, the toll fees more than offset them.

EFFECT OF PORT INFRASTRUCTURE AND OPERATION ON TRANSPORT PRICES

Previous empirical work and analysis conducted for this report by Ardelean and others (2022) document a weak correlation between distance and maritime transport costs: A 10-percent increase in maritime distance is associated with an increase in maritime transport costs of just 0.3–2.6 percent. Moreover, the elasticity seems to have decreased between 1989 and 2018, indicating a weaker role of distance as a determinant of transport costs. It is possible that the decreasing trend reflects the larger share of low-income and remote countries in global trade, which specialize in lighter goods, and increased containerization. The effect of fuel costs on shipping costs is smaller for containerized cargo than for bulk cargo, a finding that is consistent with the idea that a larger share of the cost of shipping containers is not related to distance.

The availability and quality of port infrastructure is associated with maritime shipping costs. Improved port infrastructure has a significant impact on freight rates in the Caribbean, especially for the importing country: An increase of one standard deviation reduces the freight rate by $225 (Wilmsmeier and Hoffmann 2008). Wilmsmeier and Sanchez (2009) find similar results for South American ports. In India, a decrease in port quality by one standard deviation is equivalent to an ad valorem trade cost of around 15 percent (Bonadio 2022).

Efficiency in the use of port infrastructure and superstructure at container ports also affects maritime shipping costs. Estimates of the technical efficiency of 286 container ports across 87 countries and its impact on maritime transport costs show that raising port efficiency from the 25th to the 75th percentile of the sample reduces shipping costs by 3.2 percent (Herrera Dappe, Serebrisky, and others 2024). The country with the port sector with the lowest average technical efficiency in the sample could reduce maritime transport costs by 60 percent if it became as efficient as the most efficient country. These findings are similar to those from Herrera Dappe, Serebrisky, and Suárez-Alemán (2021) for a sample of 115 ports in 39 developing countries for the period 2000–07 and Herrera Dappe and Suárez-Alemán (2016) for a sample of 55 ports in 22 countries in the Indian and Western Pacific oceans for the period 2000–10.

Measures of operational performance of container ports are also associated with maritime shipping costs. Analysis using the World Bank's Container Port Performance Index for 259 container ports across 66 countries shows that improving port performance from the 25th to the 75th percentile of the sample reduces shipping costs by 37 percent (Herrera Dappe, Serebrisky, and others 2024). The country with the port sector with the lowest average performance in the sample could reduce maritime transport costs by over 92 percent if it matched the performance of the best-performing country in the sample. Analyses using other measures of port performance reach similar conclusions (Clark, Dollar, and Micco 2004; Wilmsmeier, Hoffmann and Sanchez 2006).

Publicly operated ports tend to be less efficient than ports operated by the private sector; maritime shipping costs at the former also tend to be higher. Analysis of port performance at 203 container ports in 70 developing countries shows that productivity growth rates between 2000 and 2010 varied significantly and that the heterogeneity was explained by changes in pure efficiency, which were higher in ports with private participation (Suárez-Alemán and others 2016). Similar analysis finds that on average, container ports with publicly operated terminals would become 7 percent more efficient in the use of their facilities if they were privately operated; this improvement is associated with maritime shipping costs for shipments that are about 4 percent lower than from a port with average technical efficiency (Herrera Dappe, Serebrisky, and others 2024).

Intermodal connectivity—including landside connectivity—is important for maximizing the efficiency of ports. Port efficiency in 70 developing countries increased from 51 in 2000 to 61 in 2010, on a scale from 0–100, with improvements in multimodal links among the key factors driving the increase (Suárez-Alemán and others 2016). In Spain, intermodal connectivity of a port has a positive influence on its market share in a hinterland region, an indicator of lower transport costs (Caballé Valls and others 2020). At the Port of Mombasa, in Kenya, despite improvements in port performance, upstream inefficiencies on the Northern Corridor that connects to the port consistently undermine the port's quest for greater effectiveness as the region's main trade gateway (Oyaro Gekara and Chhetri 2013).

Inefficient port operations can lead to long wait times for trucks and other inefficiencies on the landside that raise overland transport costs. High levels of congestion at the gate of the ports and in road access raise the inland costs of trade, lowering the productivity of trucks and rail (Ramírez-Nafarrate and others 2017). Port drayage (short hauls from ports to intermodal terminals or warehouses) is an important part of maritime supply chains; it often accounts for a large share of transport costs and a large proportion of truck arrivals at container terminals (Harrison and others 2007; Shiri and Huynh 2016). Drayage truck drivers, most of whom are owner-operators and get paid per successful trip, need to make a certain number of trips per day to pay their expenses. Long wait times reduce the number of potential trips and drivers' earnings (Lange, Schwientek, and Jahn 2017). In the United States, only about 20 percent of drivers at ports operate as hourly employees. Most truckers are independent contractors who are paid per load and are responsible for about 90 percent of trucking expenses, including leasing their trucks and paying for fuel. Federal Motor Carrier Safety Administration regulations cap trucker work hours at 60 per week. Every hour spent waiting at ports is a missed opportunity for an additional delivery that could generate income.

NOTES

1. Great circle distance is the shortest distance between two points on the surface of a sphere, measured along the surface of the sphere.
2. A 1 standard deviation increase in tortuosity and ruggedness is associated with a speed that is about 2 km and 1.3 km per hour slower, respectively.
3. Uncongested speed is derived using travel time under a hypothetical state of no traffic for the same trip on the same route provided by Google Maps.
4. The 25th, 50th, and 75th percentile of the distance distribution are 114, 213, and 428 km, respectively.
5. This figure represents 0.074 percent of the average rate per ton (Rs. 2,643.3).
6. Ruggedness is measured using the index developed by Nunn and Puga (2012), which is measured in hundreds of meters of elevation difference for grid points 30 arc-seconds apart. Countries such as Mauritania and the Netherlands have nearly level terrain (ruggedness of close to 0); highly rugged countries include Lesotho (6.202) and Nepal (5.043).
7. Highways are defined as all roads classified as motorways, trunk, or primary roads by Open Street Maps.
8. The authors abstract from cross-country differences in the quality of highways, which could be significant.
9. These figures correspond to the 81st and 25th percentile, respectively, of the highway fraction distribution in Afghanistan.
10. Direct logistic costs include transport and storage and handling costs.
11. Comparison with Kenya—another country with relatively high road quality and a more comparable climate and geography to most of the countries in the sample—produces very similar results.

REFERENCES

Akbar, P.A., V. Couture, G. Duranton, and A. Storeygard. 2023a. "The Fast, the Slow, and the Congestion: Urban Transportation in Rich and Poor Countries." NBER Working Paper 31642, National Bureau of Economic Research, Cambridge, MA.

Akbar, P.A., V. Couture, G. Duranton, and A. Storeygard. 2023b. "Mobility and Congestion in Urban India." *American Economic Review* 113 (4): 1083–111.

Akbar, P.A., V. Couture, G. Duranton, L. Fan, and A. Storeygard. 2024. "Around the World in 24 Days? The Speed of Intercity Road Travel." World Bank, Washington, DC. Background paper prepared for this report.

Ardelean, A., V. Lugovskyy, A. Skiba, and D. Terner. 2022. "Fathoming Shipping Costs: An Exploration of Recent Literature, Data, and Patterns." Policy Research Working Paper 9992, World Bank, Washington, DC. Background paper prepared for this report.

Arvis, J.-F., G. Raballand, and J.-F. Marteau. 2010. *The Cost of Being Landlocked: Logistics Costs and Supply Chain Reliability*. Directions in Development. Washington, DC: World Bank.

Bonadio, B. 2022. "Ports vs. Roads: Infrastructure, Market Access and Regional Outcomes." Working paper. https://bbonadio.github.io/Bonadio_Ports.pdf.

Caballé Valls, J., P.W. De Langen, L. Garcia Alonso, and J.A. Vallejo Pinto. 2020. "Understanding Port Choice Determinants and Port Hinterlands: Findings from an Empirical Analysis of Spain." *Maritime Economics & Logistics* 22: 53–67.

Clark, X., D. Dollar, and A. Micco. 2004. "Port Efficiency, Maritime Transport Costs and Bilateral Trade." *Journal of Development Economics* 75: 417–50.

Harrison, R., N. Hutson, J. West, and J. Wilke. 2007. "Characteristics of Drayage Operations at the Port of Houston, Texas." *Transportation Research Record: Journal of the Transportation Research Board* 2033: 31–37.

Herrera Dappe, M., C. Kunaka, M. Lebrand, and N. Weisskopf. 2020. *Moving Forward: Connectivity and Logistics to Sustain Bangladesh's Success.* Washington, DC: World Bank.

Herrera Dappe, M., M. Lebrand, B. Rowberry, and A. Stokenberga. 2024. "Moving Goods: Road Transport Costs in Developing Countries." World Bank, Washington, DC. Background paper prepared for this report.

Herrera Dappe, M., and A. Suárez-Alemán. 2016. *Competitiveness of South Asia's Container Ports: A Comprehensive Assessment of Performance, Drivers, and Costs.* Directions in Development. Washington, DC: World Bank Group.

Herrera Dappe, M., T. Serebrisky, and A. Suárez-Alemán. 2021. "On the Historical Relationship between Port (In)Efficiency and Transport Costs in Developing Countries." Technical Note 2203, Inter-American Development Bank, Washington, DC.

Herrera Dappe, M., T. Serebrisky, A. Suárez-Alemán, and B. Turkgulu. 2024. "Being Efficient Pays Off: The Case of Ports and Maritime Transport Costs Worldwide." World Bank, Washington, DC. Background paper prepared for this report.

Iimi, A. 2023. "Estimating Road Freight Transport Costs in Eastern Europe and Central Asia Using Large Shipping Data." Policy Research Working Paper 10533, World Bank, Washington, DC. Background paper prepared for this report.

Incaltarau, C., I. Sharipov, G.C. Pascariu, and T.L. Moga. 2022. "Growth and Convergence in Eastern Partnership and Central Asian Countries Since the Dissolution of the USSR: Embarking on Different Development Paths?" *Development Policy Review* 40 (1): E12547.

Ksoll, C., and C. Kunaka. 2016. "Malawi Country Economic Memorandum Trade and Logistics Background Paper." World Bank, Washington, DC.

Lall, S.V., H. Wang, and T. Munthali. 2009. "Explaining High Transport Costs within Malawi—Bad Roads or Lack of Trucking Competition?" Policy Research Working Paper 5133, World Bank, Washington, DC.

Lange, A.-K., A. Schwientek, and C. Jahn. 2017. "Reducing Truck Congestion at Ports: Classification and Trends." In *Digitalization in Maritime and Sustainable Logistics: City Logistics, Port Logistics and Sustainable Supply Chain Management in the Digital Age, Proceedings of the Hamburg International Conference of Logistics (HICL)* No. 24, ed. Carlos Jahn, Wolfgang Kersten, and Christian M. Ringle, 37–58, epubli GmbH, Berlin.

Limao, N., and A.J. Venables. 2001. "Infrastructure, Geographical Disadvantage, Transport Costs, and Trade." Policy Research Working Paper 2257, World Bank, Washington, DC.

Molnar, A., and F. Shilpi. 2024. "Urban and Infrastructure Determinants of Freight Cost in India." World Bank, Washington, DC. Background paper prepared for this report.

Nunn, N., and D. Puga. 2012. "Ruggedness: The Blessing of Bad Geography in Africa." *Review of Economics and Statistics* 94 (1): 20–36.

Oyaro Gekara, V., and P. Chhetri. 2013. "Upstream Transport Cost Inefficiencies and the Implications for Port Performance: A Case Analysis of Mombasa Port and the Northern Corridor." *Maritime Policy & Management* 40 (6): 559–73.

Ramírez-Nafarrate, A., R.G. González-Ramírez, N.R. Smith, R. Guerra-Olivares, and S. Voß. 2017. "Impact on Yard Efficiency of a Truck Appointment System for a Port Terminal." *Annals of Operations Research* 258 (2): 195–216.

Shiri, S., and N. Huynh. 2016. "Optimization of Drayage Operations with Time-Window Constraints." *International Journal of Production Economics* 176: 7–20.

Suárez-Alemán, A., J. Morales Sarriera, T. Serebrisky, L. Trujillo. 2016. "When It Comes to Container Port Efficiency, Are All Developing Regions Equal?" *Transportation Research Part A: Policy and Practice* 86: 56–77.

Terevaninthorn, S., and G. Raballand. 2009. *Transport Prices and Costs in Africa: A Review of the International Corridors.* Washington, DC: World Bank.

Wilmsmeier, G., and J. Hoffmann. 2008. "Liner Shipping Connectivity and Port Infrastructure as Determinants of Freight Rates in the Caribbean." *Maritime Economics & Logistics* 10: 130–51.

Wilmsmeier, G., J. Hoffmann, and R.J. Sanchez. 2006. "The Impact of Port Characteristics on International Maritime Transport Costs." *Research in Transportation Economics* 16: 117–40.

Wilmsmeier, G., and R.J. Sanchez. 2009. "The Relevance of International Transport Costs on Food Prices: Endogenous and Exogenous Effects." *Research in Transportation Economics* 25: 56–66.

World Economic Forum. 2019. *The Global Competitiveness Report 2019.* Geneva.

4

Market Failures and Frictions

MAIN MESSAGES

1. In several countries, markets for trucking services are not competitive, because of price regulation, entry barriers, and collusion. Eighteen of 83 emerging markets and developing economies (EMDEs) regulate trucking prices, and 31 of 94 (non-island) EMDEs do not allow cross-border delivery of cargo.

2. The regulation of trucking markets has social costs. Price floors for trucking services in Colombia led to a loss to society of 8–12 percent of market revenue. On average, shipping across a border is about 70 percent more expensive than doing so within a country, and the border premium is larger when foreign trucking firms cannot compete in the local market.

3. Competition in the trucking sector leads to lower trucking prices. In Colombia, trucking prices are higher on routes with fewer truckers; a 10 percent increase in a trucker's market share on a route yields a 0.57 percent increase in the price on the route.

4. Competition between and within container ports is strongly associated with higher operational and technical efficiency, and both are associated with lower maritime shipping costs.

5. Market failures, regulations, and the variation on the economic density across space are important determinants of empty trips and, therefore, higher prices. The price for trucking services to deliver cargo to a destination with economic density in the 75th percentile is about 14 percent lower than the trucking price to a destination with the economic density in the 25th percentile.

INTRODUCTION

In efficient markets service providers, workers, and suppliers have the incentive and ability to invest, innovate, increase productivity, and supply the best possible goods and services at the lowest possible prices and buyers can find the goods and services they need. Market failures and frictions, including those created by government policies, can distort these incentives, leading to high prices, low quality, and unrealized trades.

Answers to several questions can inform governments' policy decisions and allow multilateral development banks and bilateral aid agencies to better support those polices. What market failures and frictions, including those created by government, are making trucking markets inefficient? How much do they increase trucking prices? How conducive to competition is the market structure of the container ports and maritime shipping sectors? How much do they contribute to the variation in maritime shipping costs across the world?

This chapter presents empirical evidence that answers these important questions. Using novel datasets and compiling existing ones, it shows how competition in the trucking, port, and maritime shipping sectors varies across countries and routes and how the level of competition affects prices and market efficiency. It also examines different sources of noncompetitive markets. The analysis shows how search and information frictions, together with the spatial distribution of economic activity and regulations restricting access to cargo, cause trucks and cargo vessels to travel empty and how prevalent this problem is. It also examines potential interactions of market power with information frictions and economic geography, which can lead to higher prices and even discriminatory pricing practices.

The chapter is organized as follows. The first section presents the evidence on regulation and market structure in the trucking sector. The second section presents the evidence on market structure in the ports sector. The third section examines the evidence on regulation and market structure in the maritime shipping sector. The last section examines the evidence on empty trips, their impact on prices, and the frictions behind this phenomenon.

EFFECT OF REGULATION AND MARKET STRUCTURE ON TRUCKING PRICES

Trucking services are not competitive in many countries, because of price regulation, formal and informal entry barriers that lead to high concentration, and collusion.

Regulation

Regulation can be approached from different angles. One view is that governments regulate to address market failures, ensuring, for example, that economic agents with market power do not reduce social welfare in pursuit of their own benefits. Based on this view, regulation should be used only in markets where unrestricted competition will not yield efficient outcomes (Armstrong, Cowan, and Vickers 1994). Another view of regulation contends that the government uses it to redistribute economic rents for political benefits. Under this view, regulation arises as the result of pressure from interest groups and hence does not necessarily achieve an efficient outcome, leading to a loss in social welfare.

Most regulations in the trucking sector focus on addressing negative externalities, related to accidents, noise pollution, air pollution, traffic congestion, and damage to road infrastructure from overloaded vehicles. These social, environmental, and economic concerns are usually addressed through road safety standards, rules on weights and measures, rules on traffic and driving conditions, rules on vehicle emissions, regulations on the transport of hazardous substances, and some form of direct or indirect user charges for the use of infrastructure. Price and entry regulations in the trucking sector, however, seem to be driven by the goal of redistributing economic rents rather than improving economic efficiency and overall welfare. This was the case in France and the United States when they regulated their trucking sectors in the 1930s (refer to box 4.1).

Eighteen of 83 countries for which data were available still regulate trucking prices, by setting mandatory or reference prices. In Latin America, Argentina, Brazil, Colombia, Honduras, and Uruguay regulate the prices of some trucking services, following slightly different regulatory approaches. In Argentina, shippers and carriers are free to set the prices of their transactions, but the Ministry of Transport has established reference prices for the road transportation of grain since 2012, which have been frequently updated as input costs changed. Trucking rates for the transportation of grains can be up to 30–35 percent lower than the reference prices or exceed them in response to excess demand. The government of Uruguay has also set reference prices for trucking services (Barbero, Fiadone, and Millán Placci 2020).

Brazil and Honduras follow stricter approaches. In 2018, in response to national trucking strikes, Brazil established mandatory minimum prices per kilometer traveled for several types of cargo. The National Transport Regulatory Agency has the authority to impose fines on anyone hiring trucking services at prices below the price floors (Barbero, Fiadone, and Millán Placci 2020). In 2019, Honduras set mandatory minimum rates for tractor units with semi-trailers.

In 1997, Colombia's Ministry of Transport established the regulation of prices for trucking services paid by intermediaries to truckers by setting

BOX 4.1

Price and entry regulation in the trucking sector: The experiences of France and the United States

France

In 1934, the French government started regulating entry into the trucking services market. Over time, it granted authorizations to operate to a limited number of firms. In 1961, it started setting the price that trucking firms charged for shipping goods in order to protect the French national railroad company from competition. The lack of free entry and competition led to an inefficient outcome, with trucking prices higher than in a competitive market and freight flows along roads lower than they otherwise would have been. Beginning in 1979, the government gradually eliminated quotas for transport licenses; in 1986, it liberalized the pricing of trucking services (Combes and Lafourcade 2005).

United States

In the United States, the trucking sector was highly regulated between 1935 and 1980. In 1935, Congress enacted the Motor Carrier Act and gave the Interstate Commerce Commission (ICC) authority over truck rates and entry into some trucking markets (transportation of unprocessed agricultural goods was exempted). The action came in response to strong lobbying by railways, which were fearful of growing competition from trucking. The 1948 Reed-Bulwinkle Act gave the trucking industry antitrust immunity to set rates collectively in regional rate bureaus (Winston and others 1990).

The ICC severely limited entry, and the operating licenses that were granted were very restrictive in terms of the commodities and routes that could be served. As a result, some carriers were unable to completely fill their trucks in the direction in which they had authority to operate and forced to return with empty backhauls. Route restrictions lengthened trips, increasing delivery times and costs. Limited entry and route restrictions gave trucking firms monopoly power over some routes, allowing them to charge higher than competitive prices. Rate bureaus served as cartels, and the pricing structure encouraged by the ICC led to high prices relative to costs for many commodities (Ying and Keeler 1991).

In 1980, Congress passed the Motor Carrier Act, which substantially deregulated the trucking sector. The deregulation was triggered by the significant inefficiencies caused by price and entry and exit regulations (Winston and others 1990).

minimum prices on the most important routes. The regulation (Decree 1150) was adopted in response to demands from trucking associations, which complained of low prices (as a result of oversupply of services). The Ministry of Transport estimated the efficient costs of providing trucking services for different types of trucks and different routes, which it planned to use as a base in the determination of the price floors. The price floors bore no relation to the estimated costs, however, which were the outcome of agreements with unions and associations (Eslava 2000).

The price floors were revoked in 2011 but reenacted in 2013, in response to a national strike. The new price floors were based on the estimated costs of a typical carrier on each route. In principle, intermediaries were not allowed to pay lower prices. However, the regulation has not always been enforced on every route, as Hernández and Cantillo-Cleves (2024) show. The lack of enforcement triggered new strikes in 2015 and 2016. In response, the government enacted new price floors and promised to enforce them. This time, the price floors were below the costs estimated by the ministry, which led to a new strike in 2021 and higher price floors aligned with the estimated costs (Hernández and Cantillo-Cleves 2024).

The market for trucking services in Colombia does not present any monopsony or oligopsony characteristics that would justify the imposition of price floors on efficiency grounds, as Eslava (2000) and Hernández and Cantillo-Cleves (2024) show. Moreover, on the routes and products for which the price floors were binding in 2016 and 2017, the price floors led to about 50 percent higher prices on average and a 40 percent average reduction in the shipped tonnage, reducing the efficiency of the market. As a result, the price floors led to a loss to society of 8–12 percent of the market value of transportation services in a competitive market, with a significant welfare transfer from shippers to carriers (Hernández and Cantillo-Cleves 2024).

Cross-border entry barriers

Several countries still limit the entry of foreign companies to trucking markets, to protect their industry. The most restrictive barrier is the prohibition on delivering freight. When trucks are allowed to deliver freight, they may not be allowed to provide cabotage services (pickup and delivery of cargo inside the same country), triangular services (pickup of cargo to be delivered in a third country), or backhaul services (pickup of cargo to deliver in country of origin). Entry may also be limited by quotas. Another typical constraint is a limit on foreign ownership of domestic trucking companies.

In 31 of 94 (non-island) emerging markets and developing economies, cross-border delivery of cargo is not permitted; in 10 of 87 EMDEs, foreign majority ownership of trucking companies is prohibited (refer to figure 4.1, panel a.). Detailed data on 43 of the 63 countries that allow cross-border delivery of cargo show that 41 of them allow backhaul services, 32 allow triangular services, and 7 allow cabotage services (refer to figure 4.1, panel b.).

FIGURE 4.1 Restrictions on foreign entry in trucking markets in emerging markets and developing economies

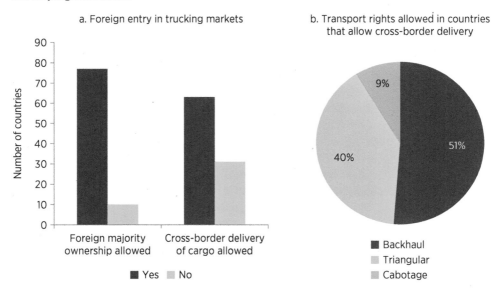

a. Foreign entry in trucking markets

b. Transport rights allowed in countries that allow cross-border delivery

Source: Original figure for this publication based on Services Trade Policy Database and authors' data collection.
Note: The bars in panel a indicating whether foreign majority ownership is allowed and panel b include only non-island EMDEs; the bars indicating whether cross-border delivery of cargo is allowed in panel a include both island and non-island EMDEs. EMDEs = emerging markets and developing economies.

Regulations that limit the entry of trucking companies from neighboring countries into the domestic market can lead to high concentration in trucking markets, undermining the economic efficiency of the national and regional fleets. Although foreign-registered companies can engage in cross-border freight delivery in Costa Rica, El Salvador, Guatemala, Honduras, Nicaragua, and Panama, cabotage services and majority foreign ownership of a trucking company are prohibited. The top three trucking firms by origin perform 34 percent of all trips on national routes—more than twice their 16 percent share on international routes. The number of trucking companies serving national routes is also significantly lower than on international routes relative to market size (Osborne, Pachon, and Araya 2014).

Entry barriers limit competition and cost reductions through innovation and greater technical efficiency. As a result, domestic shippers pay higher trucking prices and become less competitive. Concentration in national trucking markets explains a significant share of average trucking prices in Central America. Osborne, Pachon, and Araya (2014) find that excess mark-ups as a result of imperfect competition account for at least 35 percent of mean prices on national routes throughout the region. They also find that more competition is associated with lower prices on both national and international routes, with the sensitivity of price to additional competition greater on national routes.

Entry barriers for international companies also increase the cost of shipping goods from neighboring countries. On average, shipping food across the border of a low- and middle-income country is about 70 percent more expensive than making a similar shipment within the country (Herrera Dappe, Lebrand, and others 2024). The border effect tends to be smaller when shipments originate in richer countries with more developed, and potentially more competitive, transport markets. The mitigation effect is especially pronounced when the destination market allows foreign truckers to do business, particularly when they are granted cabotage and triangular rights.

Bilateral freight-sharing treaties, which establish quotas for the fleets of neighboring countries, may be economically disadvantageous to countries trying to protect their trucking industry. The quotas usually apply to the cargo movements between coastal and landlocked countries (refer to box 4.2). These quotas limit competition; in some cases, they even create de facto cartels. They can also create opportunities for players in the industry to extract rents from carriers. Forcing shippers to use local trucking firms increases their costs (because of higher prices, lower quality, or bribes), which is detrimental, rather than beneficial, to the interests of the country.

BOX 4.2

Freight-sharing rules in the Economic Community of West African States (ECOWAS)

The ECOWAS Inter-State Road Transport Convention allows pairs of member states to conclude bilateral treaties that give specific percentages of the freight passing through a coastal country's port to a landlocked country to truckers in each of the two countries. Typically, strategic goods are 100 percent allocated to the landlocked country, and nonstrategic goods are allocated two-thirds to the landlocked country and one-third to the coastal country. Several such bilateral treaties exist. Shippers' councils from landlocked countries oversee their application.

Price competitiveness for long distance transport does not appear to exist on some routes, such as the Dakar–Bamako route. The freight allocation scheme creates a quasi-monopoly situation, in which a shipper has no real choice of a carrier and tariffs are de facto fixed by transport unions (World Bank 2017).

The freight-sharing rules grant shippers' councils at ports and transporter associations the power to allocate freight on a quasi-discretionary basis, giving them an opportunity to extract rents. For this reason, the bilateral quota system is also prone to bribery, as those in charge of enforcing quotas may sell freight market shares to truckers or trucking companies ready to pay the highest price. For instance, when the Nigerian fleet cannot service its quota during peaks in demand, the Nigerien Council of Public Transport sells the options to trucks registered in other countries (Zerelli and Cook 2010).

Source: Bove and others 2018.

Intermediaries, entry barriers, and collusion

In theory—and in practice in some countries—intermediaries play an efficiency-enhancing role by matching carriers and shippers, reducing search frictions. In some countries, however, intermediaries that are closely linked to unions and associations distort trucking markets by controlling access to cargo and prices. The involvement of unions, associations, and intermediaries disincentivizes the provision of good-quality services and innovation, encourages on-account service provision, and limits the entry of international service providers. Trucking companies have no incentive to compete by offering higher-quality services, as they are not remunerated based on the quality of their services. As a result, companies have no incentive to innovate and be efficient.

The trucking services market in Bangladesh is highly fragmented, with a large number of single-truck operators and small to medium-size firms. It is dominated, however, by strong owners, associations and drivers unions. Through designated brokers, they act as intermediaries between shippers and truckers, playing a critical role in price-fixing and cargo allocation. In the case of spot contracts, shippers approach brokers in designated truck markets with their shipping needs and are quoted a price by a broker. The brokers operating in a market collude and fix the minimum prices that can be charged to shippers for a particular route. In thick markets, such as Dhaka and Chittagong, brokers allocate the loads to truckers through a bidding process and capture the benefits from competition. In thin markets, brokers allocate loads on a first come/first served basis to truckers at a set price. As a result, trucking companies, particularly small ones, barely break even, but the prices paid by shippers can be high (Herrera Dappe and others 2020).

Drivers unions can also influence the prices of large service providers that do not go through brokers. They do so when service providers outsource the operation of their trucks to third-party drivers who belong to the drivers union. When brokers establish that the prices quoted by a service provider are lower than the rates prevalent in the market, they force the drivers to refuse to operate the trucks of the service provider. Service providers are thus forced to quote prices in line with the prices prevalent in the market as set by the brokers.

A similar situation exists in Central and West Africa, where the sector is characterized by the strong influence of informal intermediaries and trade unions, which intervene in the negotiation of freight rates and through a myriad of formal and informal rules that increase transport prices while keeping the profitability of small firms very low and distorting the incentives to be efficient. In Burkina Faso and Côte d'Ivoire, about 65 percent of transport companies access loads via intermediaries, who tend to engage in uncompetitive practices and charge high fees that are not necessarily related to the costs of intermediation (Bove and others 2018). At ports, trucking unions implement truck queuing (*tour de rôle*), which gives them a central role in cargo allocation. This entry barrier is formal, as the process requires truckers to be affiliated with a transporter association to access cargo (Bove and others 2018).

In Colombia, shippers in most nonagricultural sectors are not allowed to contract directly with truckers; they have to hire an intermediary or broker, who then hires truckers to fulfill the shipper's transportation needs.[1] Brokers are mostly non-asset-based firms—less than 2.6 percent of trucks are owned by brokers—providing ancillary services such as security and tracking of cargo in addition to arranging for the movement of the cargo and ensuring regulatory compliance. Truckers can become brokers, but they need to demonstrate equity of around $250,000 (Hernández and Cantillo-Cleves 2024), a significant entry barrier for the small truckers who dominate the sector (82 percent of truckers are owner-operators who own a single truck) (Allen and others 2024).

In Colombia, intermediaries do not seem to exercise market power, at least not on the most important routes. The number of intermediaries varies by route, with the monthly average ranging from 1 to 383 in 2021. On the 17 routes Hernández and Cantillo-Cleves (2024) study—which are the most important routes, including those between the three largest Colombian cities and the Buenaventura Port (Colombia's main port)—intermediaries behave competitively. On those routes, the number of intermediaries is large, with a median of 67. On the rest of the routes in the country, there are significantly fewer intermediaries, with a median of just 1 and a 75th percentile of just 1.5 (refer to figure 4.2).

Market structure and competition within countries

The cost of providing trucking services tends to vary by route, not just because of the length of the route and inefficiencies along it, such as the quality of the infrastructure, congestion, and waits and delays, but also because of the costs to get to and from a route. In research conducted for this report, Allen and

FIGURE 4.2 Number of intermediaries in Colombia, 2021

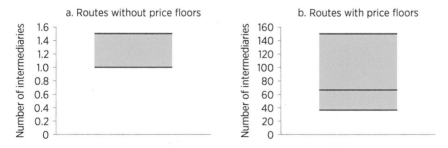

Source: Original figure for this publication based on Allen and others 2024; Hernández and Cantillo-Cleves 2024.
Note: Horizontal lines are 25th, 50th, and 75th percentiles of the origin–destination pair distribution in the average month of 2021. In panel a, the 25th and 50th percentiles are the same. Sample is restricted to origin–destination pairs with at least 100 trips in 2021.

others (2024) define the remoteness of a route as the weighted-average cost of servicing the route (which includes travel to pick up a good, carry it to its destination, and travel back home) for truckers across the country.[2]

Routes that are more costly to serve because they are farther away from economic activity have higher market concentration and are served by smaller truckers. A 10 percent increase in remoteness is associated with a 14 percent increase in market concentration (refer to figure 4.3). A 10 percent increase in the market concentration on a route leads to a 25 percent decrease in the average capacity of truckers (Allen and others 2024). This means that if routes in the 25th percentile of remoteness had the remoteness of those in the 75th percentile, its market concentration would be 63 percent higher, and they would be served by truckers with 71 percent lower average capacity.

Imperfect competition on routes across Colombia means that prices are higher on routes with less intense competition. A 10 percent increase in a trucker's market share on a route yields a 0.57 percent increase in the average price on the route. The effect on prices is greater on small and medium-size routes (where the size of a route is measured by the number of trips). The prices charged by truckers for delivering cargo in the provinces in the east and south tend to be higher than in the center of Colombia (refer to map 4.1).

In India, as in most other countries, the market structure in the trucking industry is fragmented, with both large, national firms and a large number of small and medium-size firms with varying degrees of formalization. On some routes, financially mature trucking firms provide services, in addition to other firms. These firms meet certain requirements set by the Indian Bank Association

FIGURE 4.3 Correlation between number of trucking intermediaries and remoteness in Colombia, 2021

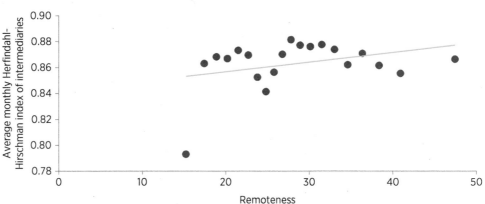

Source: Original figure for this publication based on Allen and others 2024.
Note: The Herfindahl–Hirschman Index is the sum of the square market shares of all truckers. Figure is a scatterplot with 20 bins. Remoteness is defined as follows: $Remoteness_d = (\sum_h (travel\ time_{ho} + travel\ time_{od} + travel\ time_{dh})^{-1} T_h)^{-1}$, where $travel\ time_{ho}$, $travel\ time_{od}$, and $travel\ time_{dh}$ are the travel time between home and origin, origin and destination, and destination and home pairs, respectively, in 2021, measured in hours and T_h is the number of truck owners living in location h in 2021.

MAP 4.1 **Average prices paid to truckers in Colombia, by destination province**

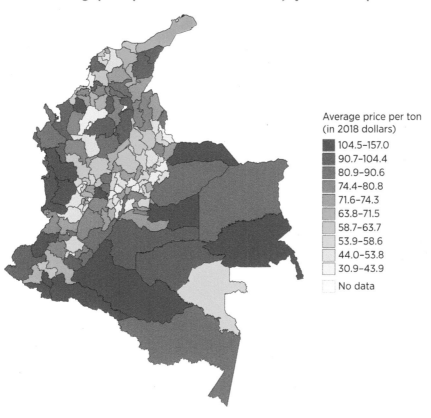

Average price per ton
(in 2018 dollars)

- 104.5–157.0
- 90.7–104.4
- 80.9–90.6
- 74.4–80.8
- 71.6–74.3
- 63.8–71.5
- 58.7–63.7
- 53.9–58.6
- 44.0–53.8
- 30.9–43.9
- No data

Source: Original map for this publication based on Allen and others 2024.

(IBA), which provides discounted lending against trucking receipts.[3] Entry by IBA–qualified firms on a route is associated with lower trucking prices. On average, one additional IBA firm operating on a route is associated with 1 percent lower trucking prices (Molnar and Shilpi 2024). Routes with four IBA firms have about 10 percent lower prices than routes with no IBA firms, and the difference increases monotonically with the number of IBA firms (refer to figure 4.4). This effect may be driven by stronger competition and the thickness of the routes on which IBA firms provide trucking services, allowing all trucking firms to benefit from economies of scale.

Trucking prices in India also vary with the economic density of a route. Lall, Sinha-Roy, and Shilpi (2022) find that, everything else equal, doubling the economic density on a route (measured as the sum of the night lights at the origin and destination) is associated with 17 percent lower spot truck-ing prices. The idea is that locations with higher night light intensity, which is correlated with GDP, are expected to have higher bilateral freight flows. Two potential forces are behind the negative correlation: (a) routes with

FIGURE 4.4 Changes in freight rates by number of Indian Bank Association–qualified transport operators on a route relative to the case of no Indian Bank Association–qualified transport operator

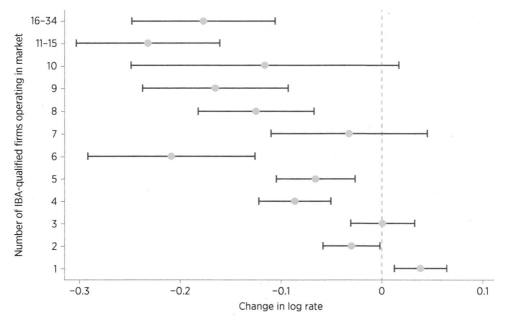

Source: Molnar and Shilpi 2024.
Note: Dots are estimated coefficients for the number of firms listed by the Indian Bank Association (IBA) that operate on a particular route; whiskers are 95 percent confidence intervals.

larger freight flows attract more competition, reducing markups for truckers, and (b) routes with larger freight flows incentivize truckers to invest in bigger trucks with lower marginal costs.

The intensity of competition on a route depends on the alternatives available. When rail or waterways are competitive options for shipping cargo, the ability of trucking operators to charge high prices is weaker than when there is no competitive alternative. The competitiveness of the alternative options depends on the efficiency of rail and water transport and intermodal connectivity (to railway stations and ports) and the cost of transporting the cargo by truck from the shipper's location to the station or port.

Molnar and Shilpi (2024) find that truck freight is cheaper on routes where the alternative provided by rail is more direct. For routes of about 1,100 kilometers or more, trucking prices increase monotonically with the distance by rail for the same origin–destination pair (refer to figure 4.5). On those routes, the estimated rate difference between the smallest and largest rail-to-road distance ratio is Rs. 9,761 (12.3 percent of the average freight rate on routes of about 1,100 kilometers or longer). The estimated difference between rail station access of less than 10 km relative to more than 25 km is Rs. 2,817 (3.6 percent of the average freight rate).

FIGURE 4.5 **Trucking prices, by length of rail option and road distance**

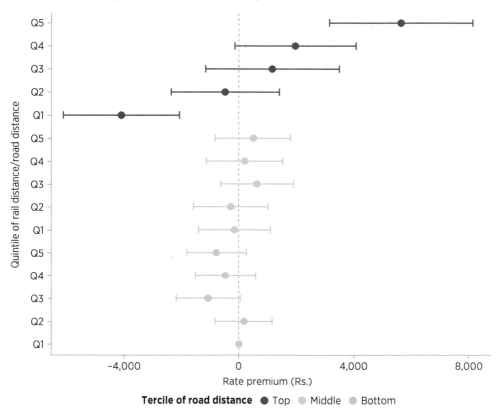

Source: Molnar and Shilpi 2024.
Note: Dots are estimated coefficients for quintiles of the ratio between the shortest distance over railways over the shortest road distance for the same origin–destination pair, interacted with terciles of road distance; whiskers are 95 percent confidence intervals. Terciles of road distance are 1.1–445.1, 445.1–1,081.8, and 1,081.8–3,824.3 km. Quintiles of the distance ratio are 0.02–0.95, 0.95–1.00, 1.00–1.05, 1.05–1.13, and 1.13–31.6.

EFFECT OF MARKET STRUCTURE IN CONTAINER PORTS ON MARITIME TRANSPORT COSTS

Several factors limit competition in the port industry. They include captive port traffic, barriers to establish new ports and enter the terminal market, tariff regulation, high concentration in the port operator market, and the port authority acting as regulator and operator. In some countries, the container port sector has also experienced major changes in its structure, with greenfield ports becoming major players in the market for container traffic. All these changes are likely to affect competition in the sector and hence the performance of the port sector and maritime shipping rates.

Interport competition

Geographic location, proximity to competitors, type of cargo, and specialization in transshipment traffic have significant effects on the level of interport competition.

Market shares

The degree of concentration in container cargo handling in a country is indicative of the intensity of competition in the sector. In countries with small markets, ports can be natural monopolies, requiring their regulation to avoid abusive practices by operators. The market for container handling shows high levels of concentration at the country level, with 94 percent of countries having a Herfindahl–Hirschman Index (HHI) over 1,800.[4]

The more ports operated by different terminal operators serving the same hinterland, the greater the competition for cargo to and from the hinterland. Expansion of the port sector across the world has shifted the port industry from an environment with captive hinterland advantages to one of contestable hinterland (García and Sánchez 2006). For about 40 percent of the container ports in the world, the closest port with a different port operator is within 100 nautical miles; for more than 45 percent of container ports, the closest port with a different port operator is more than 200 nautical miles away. Almost half of all ports lack strong competition for their immediate hinterland.

Inland connectivity between ports and their hinterlands is poor in many countries. The speed of road travel within countries tends to be significantly lower in lower-income countries, as discussed in chapter 1. As a result, although inland markets are contestable in theory, competition in many developing countries is more restricted than in developed countries. In Bangladesh, for example, there is almost no competition between Chittagong and Mongla, the two largest ports. The limited connectivity with the main economic centers in the country, together with the limited handling capacity and shallow waters at Mongla, remove it from consideration by shippers in Bangladesh.

The challenge that crossing borders represents hinders competition between ports in neighboring countries, as discussed in chapter 1. For example, Kolkata and some of the other Indian ports along the eastern coast, which are close to Chittagong and Mongla, could compete for the same hinterland. However, lengthy delays at border crossings and the lack of free transit of trucks between the countries prevents real hinterland competition between Bangladeshi and Indian ports. Similar situations can be found in other regions.

Containerization as a proxy for competition

Containerization has led not only to greater integration of supply chains (Rodrigue 2013) but also to the establishment of a common competition framework among ports specializing in this type of cargo. The technological revolution of containerization has put continuous pressure on transport costs and given increasing power to shipping alliances and large carriers (Limao and Venables 2001; Slack and Frémont 2009; Sys 2009). Logistics and value-added services have become strategic for the survival of ports (Juang and Roe 2010). Ducruet and Notteboom (2012) suggest that the extent of containerization at ports can be used as a proxy for the economic influence of maritime facilities, as ports compete not as individual places that handle ships but as crucial links within global supply chains (Hall and Jacobs 2010; Notteboom and Winkelmans 2001). A port with a higher level of specialization on containerized cargo can therefore be expected to face stronger competition.

Globally, about 45 percent of the berth length at a container port is used to handle containers, on average, with 37 percent of ports using more than half of their berths to handle containers, indicating a high degree of specialization of their infrastructure (refer to figure 4.6). At the ports of JNPT (India), Colombo (Sri Lanka), Port Klang (Malaysia), and Itajai (Brazil), over 80 percent of cargo is containerized.

Transshipment

Transshipment hubs are the facilities along international shipping networks at which cargo is transferred to vessels that serve the final ports of destination and to vessels that serve main routes. They tend to be located along the main maritime routes through Gibraltar, Panama, the Strait of Malacca, and Suez (Notteboom, Pallis, and Rodrigue 2022). The distinction between hinterland

FIGURE 4.6 Global share of berths that handle containers, 2021

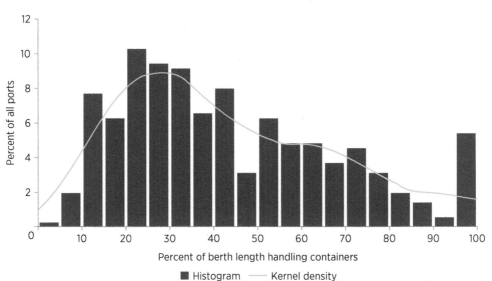

Source: Original figure for this publication based on data from S&P Global.

and transshipment traffic means that two ports that do not serve the same hinterland may still operate in the same geographic market if they compete for the same transshipment traffic (OECD 2011).

Transshipment incidence is the share of total port throughput that is transferred between ships. Following Notteboom, Pallis, and Rodrigue, (2022), ports with a transshipment incidence above 75 percent are considered "pure" transshipment hubs; at ports with an incidence below 25 percent, transshipment is considered an incidental activity. Only about 6 percent of container ports are "pure" transshipment hubs (refer to figure 4.7).

The level of competition among ports handling this kind of traffic is high, forcing ports—particularly terminals—to increase productivity and reduce prices (Rodrigue and Notteboom 2010). Pure transshipment hubs are highly vulnerable, because shipping lines can switch hubs if conditions make it favorable to do so (Wilmsmeier and Notteboom 2011). Ports handling both transshipment and gateway cargo face less risk of shipping lines switching ports (Notteboom, Parola, and Satta 2014).

Intraport competition

Intraport competition refers to competition among terminals within the same port run by different operators. Competition comes through pricing adjustments (such as volume discounts) and service quality improvements (such as preferential berth access).

In all world regions except North America, over 40 percent of ports have a single operator; only in East Asia and Pacific and North America do about 40 percent of ports have three or more operators (refer to figure 4.8). In South Africa, Transnet, a state-owned enterprise, operates all container terminals in Cape Town, Durban, Ngqura, and Port Elizabeth. In the

FIGURE 4.7 Transshipment incidence

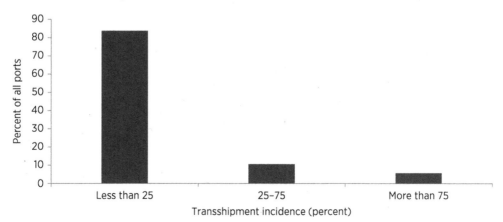

Source: Original figure for this publication based on data from Notteboom, Pallis, and Rodrigue 2022.

FIGURE 4.8 Number of operators at ports, by region

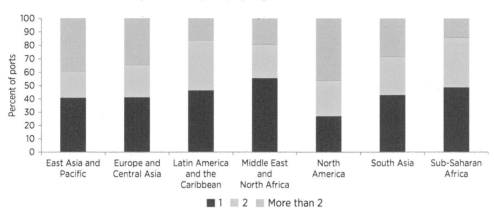

Source: Original figure for this publication based on data from S&P Global.

Luando Port in Angola, each of the three terminals is operated by a different operator. In the Middle East and North Africa, the sector is largely dominated by local state-owned operators. However, as the recent experience of Morocco's Tanger-Med shows, public and private operators can co-exist in the same port.

Focusing on ports with annual throughput above 1 million 20-foot equivalent units (TEUs) shows a slightly more competitive picture in most regions. In Latin America and the Caribbean, most large ports have only two operators. Of the 20 ports with annual throughput above 1 million TEUs, however, 7 (35 percent) have 3 or more operators, 11 (55 percent) have 2 operators, and 2 have 1 terminal operator. In East Asia and Pacific, Europe and Central Asia, and North America, over 60 percent of ports have three or more operators. In the Middle East and North Africa, half of the large ports have a single operator. In Sub-Saharan Africa, most ports have at most two operators.

Competition environment, port performance, and transport costs

A competition index was developed to capture differences in the competitive environment in which container ports operate. The competition environment of a port is ranked as low (1), medium (2), or high (3) on each of the four measures described above, based on the criteria in table 4.1. The score for each port is the simple average of the four criteria. The analysis is based on the potential harm to competition, not the actual behavior of the parties involved. Anticompetitive behavior can arise in ports even if the competition environment is perceived as high, because of other barriers to competition.

TABLE 4.1 Criteria for assessing level of competition at ports

Measure	Low	Medium	High
Country market share (percent)	More than 25	10–25	Less than 10
Containerization (percent of container-handling berth length)	Less than 25	25–50	More than 50
Transshipment (percent of container traffic)	Less than 25	25–75	More than 75
Intraport market structure (number of operators at port)	1	2	More than 2

Note: The European Union was treated as a single country for calculating country market shares.

FIGURE 4.9 Correlations between competition environment and port performance

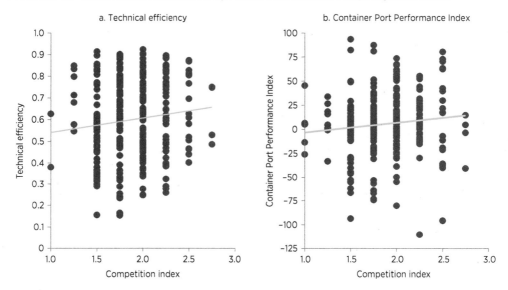

Source: Original figures for this publication based on Herrera Dappe, Serebrisky, and others 2024 and World Bank 2023.
Notes: Yellow lines depict the linear relationship between the variables, which is significant at the 5 percent.
The statistical score of the Container Port Performance Index is used in panel b.

Ports that operate in more competitive environments perform better than other ports, and the maritime shipping costs for their exports are lower. There is a positive correlation between the competition index and technical efficiency, indicating that ports that operate in more competitive environments are more efficient in the use of their facilities than ports in less competitive environments (refer to figure 4.9, panel a). On average, ships loading and offloading at ports that face higher competitive pressures spend less time at port than ships at ports facing less competitive pressures, as indicated by the positive correlation between the World Bank's Container Port Performance Index and the competition index (refer to figure 4.9, panel b). These results are in line with the intuition that ports operating in more competitive environments need to perform more efficiently to attract and retain traffic and that higher performance is associated with lower maritime shipping costs, as Herrera Dappe, Serebrisky, and others (2024) show.

EFFECT OF REGULATION AND MARKET STRUCTURE ON MARITIME TRANSPORT PRICES

The regulation and market structure of the maritime liner shipping industry has changed over time, with important implications on the intensity of competition.

Regulation of maritime shipping

From a legal perspective, the maritime shipping industry is unique, in that collusive agreements were allowed and enforced by the US government from 1984 until 1998 and by the European Union from 1987 until 2006. Until 1998, all carriers within a given liner conference were expected to post a common freight rate for each route serving the United States and for each commodity.[5] Deviations were allowed only in the form of an independent action by a carrier, which had to be publicly announced and offered to all qualified shippers. Any secretive deviation from the common freight rate was subject to a stiff fine by the Federal Maritime Commission. Until 2006, the European Union block exemption on competition law for liner conferences allowed liner shipping companies to set common freight rates, make joint decisions on the limitation of supply, and coordinate timetables.

In 1998, the Ocean Shipping Reform Act abolished the price-fixing requirement, drastically changing the market structure. The vast majority of US and global markets quickly switched to confidential annual contracts between carriers and trading firms (FMC 2001; OECD 2015). Carriers are still allowed to discuss recommended freight rates, but recommended rates are not part of the contracts, so they cannot be legally enforced. Keeping contracts confidential made the detection of these deviations unlikely, weakening the possibility of enforcing the recommended rates.

The European Union repealed the block exemption for liner conferences in 2006, four years after an OECD report that showed that there was no justification for continuing to allow liner shipping companies to coordinate on rates, the level of supply, and timetables (OECD 2002). The repeal resulted in a revision to the EU block exemption on consortia, which has been in force since 1995, to make it more favorable to liner shipping.[6] The block exemption on consortia allows shipping companies to cooperate on the operation of liner shipping services, including the sharing of vessels or other shipping equipment and the allocation of space and slots on vessels.[7] The exemption does not cover agreements related to price-fixing, capacity limitation unrelated to temporary fluctuations in supply and demand, or market or customer allocation.

The container shipping industry has organized itself around global alliances since the mid-1990s. Alliances are cooperation agreements among carriers on sharing vessels and slots on those vessels. Alliances are different from conferences and other forms of cooperation in liner shipping, in that they do not cover joint sales, marketing, pricing, joint ownership of assets, the pooling of revenues, profit or loss sharing, or joint management (ITF 2018).

As a result, several governments have replaced block exemptions for conferences with block exemptions for alliances. Hong Kong SAR, China; Israel; and New Zealand have block exemption regimes for shipping agreements similar to the current EU block exemption regime (Hong Kong Competition Commission 2017; OECD 2015). In Singapore, the block exemption for liner shipping agreements, which was extended until December 2024, allows vessel-sharing agreements for liner shipping services and price discussion agreements for feeder services subject to certain conditions and obligations (CCCS 2023).

Market structure and competition

Concentration in the container shipping industry increased in recent decades. Between 1996 and May 2023, the share of the top 20 carriers in container-carrying capacity rose from 48 percent to 91 percent (UNCTAD 2022; Alphaliner 2023). In May 2023, the shares of the top 4 and top 10 carriers reached 59 percent and 86 percent, respectively (refer to figure 4.10). The HHI increased from around 300 in 1998 to almost 1,400 in 2018 (ITF 2018).[8] According to the US Department of Justice classification of markets, these HHIs classify the market as moderately concentrated (DOJ and FTC 2023).

Market concentration at the route level is even higher. In Chile, the average route HHI was 5,100 in 2009–19, indicating highly concentrated routes (Ardelean and Lugovskyy 2023). Globally, 80 percent of routes in the average country had four or fewer carriers in 2022, suggesting the potential for weak competition, with half of all countries having more than 85 percent of their routes serviced by four or fewer carriers. Many of the countries serviced by four or fewer carriers are least developed countries and Small Island Developing States (UNCTAD 2022). In some trade lanes, such as those between the Mediterranean, North Europe, or North America and the South American east coast, the four largest carriers controlled more than 90 percent of the capacity in 2015, with one carrier (MSC) having 91 percent of

FIGURE 4.10 Concentration in the container shipping industry, May 2023

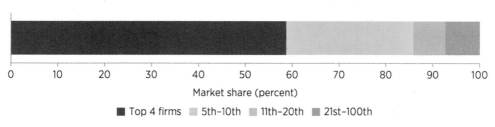

Market share (percent)

■ Top 4 firms ■ 5th–10th ■ 11th–20th ■ 21st–100th

Source: Original figure for this publication based on data from Alphaliner 2023.

the carrying capacity on the Mediterranean–South America east coast routes (ITF 2018).

Between 2015 and 2022, the share of global capacity controlled by alliances increased to more than 80 percent (UNCTAD 2022). The first generation of alliances were agreements among small carriers; in 2022, the top nine container operators organized their activities through three alliances (Ocean, 2M, and THE Alliance). The global alliances operate mainly in the east–west trade lanes, where they control about 95 percent of the market (ITF 2018). In 2022, the global alliances operated in 52 countries, on 40 percent of the routes in those countries on average.

Consolidation and increased cooperation in the container shipping industry can bring benefits in terms of the economies of scale and scope, but they also raise concerns among shippers and governments of higher prices because of increased market power.[9] The increased consolidation, the centrality of the alliances, and the ever-larger size of vessels are seen as a reason for the overcapacity in the container shipping industry, which may be partly a result of entry deterrence strategies. Alliances also provide a vehicle for potential collusion among carriers. Concentration has also increased the monopsony power of a few carriers when it comes to port services (ITF 2018; UNCTAD 2022).

As long as the gains from economies of scale and scope and monopsony power are passed on to shippers, consolidation and cooperation can be beneficial to them. There is evidence that larger trade flows prompt carriers to use larger vessels with lower marginal costs, which reduces shipping rates on thick routes (Asturias 2020). There is also evidence of market power in container shipping, which is weaker on thicker routes. Hummels, Lugovskyy, and Skiba (2009) show that shipping rates for Latin American and US imports decrease with the number of carriers operating on the routes. They find that exporters served by only two carriers face shipping prices that are 21 percent higher than exporters served by eight carriers. They also find that on average, shipping rates for Latin American imports were 30 percent higher than those for US imports, with almost three-quarters of the difference explained by market power.

There is a relatively high degree of vertical integration between container shipping and port terminal operations, which may have implications for competition. Vertically integrated firms that control scarce port capacity could potentially exclude competitors from the market. Vertical integration can increase efficiency; however, the degree of vertical integration could pose a risk of exclusionary practices. For example, a port operator that is vertically integrated with shipping lines, through either property links or exclusivity contracts, could raise port charges for competing carriers or limit their access to the port during peak hours on a discretionary basis, potentially driving these carriers out of the market (World Bank Group 2018).

The switch to confidential contracts after the 1988 Ocean Shipping Reform Act made freight rate dispersion within a route possible. Such dispersion can be across carriers and across shippers. Using data on Chilean and Colombian imports, Ardelean and Lugovskyy (2023) find that carriers implement price discrimination based on the size of the shipper. They find that, on average, Chilean firms in the 90th percentile of annual import size pay 18 percent lower shipping rates than firms in the 10th percentile. The firm size advantage disappears on routes with three or fewer carriers.

The intuition behind these findings is that shippers face a cost in analyzing carriers' quotes for annual contracts; as a result, larger shippers have stronger bargaining power, as they request more quotes, carriers price-discriminate based on size, and thus larger shippers face lower shipping rates. On routes with three or fewer carriers, all shippers obtain the same number of quotes, so there is no room for price discrimination. Information frictions, price discrimination, and market power are thus determinants of shipping rates, explaining the variation on shipping rates across and within routes.

EFFECT OF ECONOMIC GEOGRAPHY, SEARCH FRICTIONS, AND REGULATIONS ON TRANSPORT PRICES

Empty trucks and cargo vessels are a common feature across the world. At any point in time, 42 percent of bulk-carrying vessels are traveling without cargo (Brancaccio, Kalouptsidi, and Papageorgiou 2020). A survey of the literature on empty running trucks conducted for this report finds that estimates of the share of empty trips range from 15 percent to 47 percent, estimates of the share of empty vehicle-kilometers range from 17 percent to 45 percent, and estimates of the probability of an empty backhaul range from 26 percent to 88 percent (Yang 2024). Making some assumptions to standardize all these estimates into estimates of the share of empty vehicle-kilometers,[10] Yang (2024) shows that 95 percent of estimates fall between 15 percent and 45 percent, with a median of 28 percent. If trucks were doing only round-trips between two locations, 45 percent of empty running kilometers would imply that carriers who finish a fronthaul job have only a 10 percent chance of finding a return job.

Trucks run empty more often in low- and middle-income countries than in high-income countries (refer to figure 4.11). High-income countries have lower rates of empty trips, with a median of 20 percent empty kilometers compared with a median of 30 percent in low- and middle-income countries. Several studies of high-income countries use data from the 1970s 1980s, and 1990s; the share of empty trips decreased in those countries. Estimates since 2000 suggest that the gap between high-income countries and low- and middle-income countries has grown. In Bangladesh and Colombia, the share of empty trips is estimated at 35 percent and 28 percent, respectively (Herrera Dappe and others 2020; Holguin-Veras, Thorson, and Zorrilla 2010). In Central American countries, the probability of an empty backhaul is estimated at 30–88 percent, depending on the country (Osborne, Pachon, and Araya 2014). In Viet Nam, it is estimated at

FIGURE 4.11 **Share of trucks that run empty, by country income level**

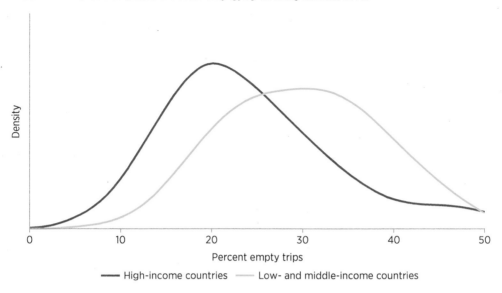

Source: Yang 2024.
Note: Figure plots kernel density estimates of the distribution of estimates of empty vehicle kilometer shares. When estimates of backhaul probabilities are provided, the figure assumes that all fronthaul trips are loaded. The kernel density estimates use a bandwidth of 0.05.

50 percent for logistics service providers and at 70 percent for truck operators (Lam, Sriram, and Khera 2019).

Economic geography, search frictions, regulations, and empty trips

The most important reason why trucks and cargo vessels run empty are freight flow imbalances, search frictions, and regulations. The spatial distribution of economic activity, particularly the uneven economic density across space, leads to imbalances in the flows of freight between geographic areas (countries, regions, and cities), with some geographic areas being net importers and others net exporters. The median country is a net importer, with a ratio of export tonnage to import tonnage of about 0.75 (Yang 2024). However, there is significant variation. The ratio of export tonnage to import tonnage was 0.14 in Burkina Faso, 0.2 in Mali, and 0.3 in Niger (Bove and others 2018). Not all trade between a pair of countries travels along a single route or uses a single mode of transport. Aggregate physical imbalances should therefore be seen as a lower bound on the potential for empty trips.

Trade imbalances and the different compositions of imports and exports, which require different types of trucks, lead to empty trips. In Africa, cargo shipped from ports to landlocked countries and the hinterlands of coastal countries includes industrial supplies, consumer goods, fuel, and other liquid bulks; exports tend to be mineral and agricultural bulk commodities. The trucks required to transport imports and exports are not compatible, so a large proportion of empty trucks ply the corridors. For example, 51 percent of the trucks traveling southbound along the Gauteng–Durban corridor in South Africa are empty, and 41 percent of those traveling northbound are empty. At the Beitbridge border post between South Africa and Zimbabwe, 50 percent of southbound trucks are empty (Nick Porée and Associates 2023). Similar patterns are found in West Africa. Among Cameroonian and Ivorian truckers returning to port, the share of empty trips is about 35 percent; in landlocked West African countries, only about one-fifth of truckers can find a full backhaul load (Bove and others 2018).

The problem of freight flow imbalances also exists within countries. In Bangladesh, in the districts with the two seaports, outward flows to the rest of the country are significantly larger than flows from the rest of the country. In Chittagong, the Interregional Traffic Imbalance Index is −677, which means that flows to the rest of the country are about eight times the flows from the rest of the country (refer to map 4.2). In contrast, in Dhaka and its neighboring districts, Gazipur and Narayanganj, inward flows are three to six times outward flows. In Brazil, outward flows are significantly larger than inward flows in states with significant agriculture or mining activity, such as Pará and Minas Gerais.

Search and matching frictions occur when carriers and shippers are willing to trade but unable to transact immediately. Carriers may either wait and search for a load or travel empty to another market with a greater chance of finding a load. The decentralized nature of the markets for trucking and oceanic bulk shipping and the existence of brokers suggests that information frictions are present.

Search frictions are important in bulk shipping, as Brancaccio and others (2023) show. In Chile, empty vessels arrive to pick up cargo while other vessels depart empty. The biweekly ratio of outgoing empty ships over incoming empty ships—which should be close to zero in the absence of frictions in net exporting countries—is well above zero in a large share of countries. In Bangladesh, the ratio of outgoing to incoming empty trucks is well above zero in most net exporting districts, suggesting important search frictions there (refer to figure 4.12).

Regulations that restrict some carriers from taking jobs from available shippers, which are common, force some carriers to return empty. In international trade, backhaul, cabotage, and triangular restrictions protect domestic carriers by preventing foreign carriers from picking up return and within-country jobs after completing an international delivery. Of 43 countries, 41 allow backhaul services, but only 7 allow cabotage services and 32 allow triangular services (see figure 4.1, panel b). Quotas established in bilateral treaties (in Central and West Africa, for example) lead to empty trips. For example, even if an Ivorian carrier can organize a backhaul load in landlocked Mali, the Malian authorities reportedly will not allow the Ivorian trucker to carry it (Bove and others 2018). In Belize and Central America, regulation prohibits cabotage, even though trucking is a major mode of international trade (IDB 2013).

MAP 4.2 Interregional traffic imbalance index in Bangladesh and Brazil

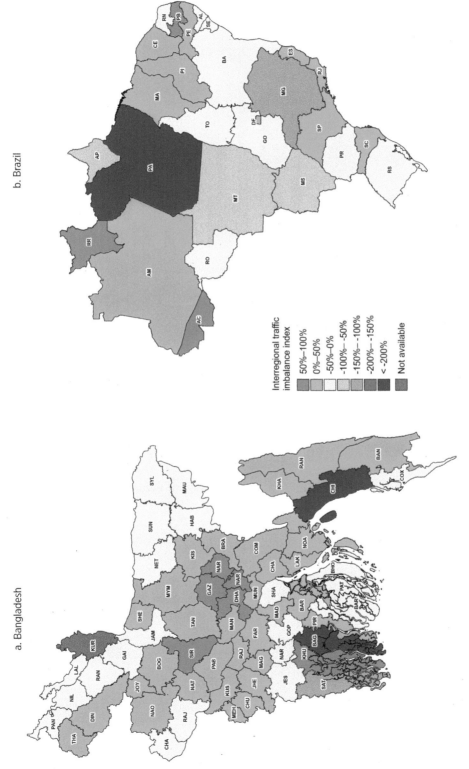

a. Bangladesh

b. Brazil

Interregional traffic
imbalance index

50%–100%
0%–50%
-50%–0%
-100%–-50%
-150%–-100%
-200%–-150%
< -200%
Not available

Source: Original maps for this publication based on Herrera Dappe and others 2020 and Espinet Alegre and Medeiros 2022.
Note: The interregional traffic imbalance index for region n is $(I_n - O_n) / I_n * 100$, where I_n are the freight flows to region n and O_n are the freight flows out of region n.

FIGURE 4.12 **Ratio of outgoing to incoming empty trucks per day in net exporting districts in Bangladesh**

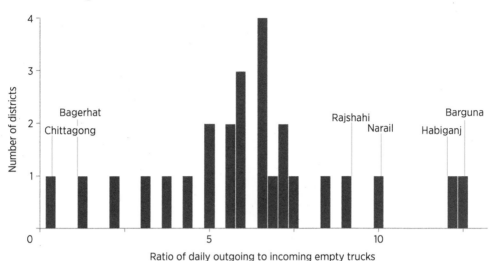

Source: Original figure for this publication based on Herrera Dappe and others 2020.

Even in the European Union, where truckers are allowed to pick up to three cabotage loads after completing an international trip (World Bank 2020), vehicles traveling outside their registration country were empty more than 45 percent of the time and vehicles within their registration country were empty just over 25 percent of the time in 2012 (EC 2014). This difference exists in both specialized and general freight markets, suggesting that cabotage restrictions, rather than search frictions, are the culprit.

The form of business organization can affect the rate of empty trips through several, potentially counteracting, mechanisms. Private carriers, which primarily serve the shipping needs of a parent company, are more likely to have empty backhauls than for-hire carriers (Beilock and Kilmer 1986; Abate 2014). Private carriers often have follow-up commitments after completing a trip, limiting their ability to search for a backhaul load; for-hire carriers have no future commitments, so they are better able to aggregate loads (Abate 2014). In Bangladesh, large shippers place a priority on high service levels; they therefore prefer the control and flexibility of their internal fleet to for-hire carriers, even though it means a high level of empty trips (Herrera Dappe and others 2020).

Formality and sophistication also play a role in carriers' access to trips. In Viet Nam, logistics providers (large for-hire carriers) and private carriers have lower rates of an empty backhaul (around 50 percent) than small informal truck operators (around 70 percent). The reason is that large for-hire and private carriers have more stable demand, through long-term contracts allowing them to better plan the use of their fleet (Lam, Sriram, and Khera 2019). In the United States, empty mile shares are 9–17 percent for large asset-based carriers and more than 30 percent for small independent carriers in the same market (Terrazas 2019). Firms with longer histories or more experience also have lower rates of empty trips (Wilson 1987). The advantage for larger, more experienced, and more sophisticated firms may reflect their better access to shippers and lower search costs.

Carriers that haul specialized cargo, such as refrigerated goods or hazardous materials, tend to experience more empty trips than other shippers. Because specialized carriers cannot pick up general products, they face thinner markets, which may have greater search frictions. In the United States, trucks with the most general trailer types (van, reefer) drove about 34 percent of miles empty; trucks with tank, flatbed, or other specialized trailers drove empty at rates of 38 percent, 44 percent, and 43 percent, respectively (Terrazas 2019).

Holding other frictions fixed, a carrier may spend less time searching for a return load if the cost of the empty trip is smaller, as it is on shorter routes. Trucks on shorter routes have higher rates of empty trips than trucks on longer routes, according to McKinnon and Ge (2006). In Central American countries, trips longer than 150 km are 8.4 percentage points more likely to find a backhaul than trips of less than 150 km (Osborne, Pachon, and Araya 2014).

Empty trips and transport prices

In unregulated markets, transport prices are formed by the optimizing behavior of forward-looking carriers and thus depend on the attractiveness of both the origin and the destination. Competition puts downward pressure on transport prices in the direction in which there is excess supply of transport services; it puts upward pressure on the direction in which there is excess demand. The attractiveness of the destination reflects the intensity of competition and the probability of finding a backhaul load at the destination or in the nearby region. All else equal, the more likely a carrier will have to return empty, the longer it will have to wait to find a load, or the lower the backhaul price will be because of strong competition, the higher the price the carrier will request for the fronthaul trip. The prices for the legs of a round-trip are thus linked and related to the marginal cost of the round-trip. For example, for a round-trip route with a single destination, the higher the rate in one direction, the lower the rate in the opposite direction. For container shipping, Wong (2022) finds that a 1 percent deviation from the average container freight rates from i to j is correlated over time with a negative deviation of 0.84 percent from the average container freight rates from j to i.

The imbalance in freight flows explains the fact that transportation prices are largely asymmetric. In Chile in 2016, the number of containers with imports from the Port of San Antonio to Santiago was 2.5 times the number of containers with exports in the opposite direction. Shipping rates per container were around $380 from San Antonio to Santiago and

$270 in the opposite direction (Farren, Giesen, and Rizzi 2022). China runs a large trade surplus with the United States; the cost to ship a container from China to the United States is more than three times the return cost. Trade between the United Kingdom and the United States is more balanced; the difference in shipping costs in the two directions is therefore small (Wong 2022).

In markets with no frictions, there is a single price for the same service; in markets with search frictions, there are different prices for the same service. In the bulk shipping industry, there is substantial price dispersion, indicating the presence of significant frictions. Brancaccio and others (2023) find that about 30 percent of price variation in bulk shipping contracts cannot be explained by ship size, time of year, or origin and destination characteristics. They also find that the shipping price varied with the value of the product shipped, even though the period studied was one with excess supply of transport services, which in the absence of frictions would have meant prices equal to the ships' opportunity cost.

Contract prices for trucking services to deliver food in low- and middle-income countries facing food security issues suggests that empty backhauls potentially play a role in the pricing of trucking services (Herrera Dappe, Lebrand, and others 2024). Everything else equal, the trucking price to deliver a load to a domestic destination with the market size in the 75th percentile of the sample is about 14 percent lower than the trucking price to a destination with the market size in the 25th percentile. The correlation is weaker for shipments to foreign destinations than to domestic destinations when truckers are allowed to do business in the foreign country, particularly in cabotage and shipments to third countries. The findings support the argument that the higher the probability of finding some business in the destination, the lower the price to transport cargo to the destination, a benefit of free market entry.

Many countries facing food security issues are in conflict. Local conflict is associated with 3–7 percent higher transport prices on average (Herrera Dappe, Lebrand, and others 2024). It is less likely that the potential for empty backhauls is an important determinant of price in conflict countries, as carriers are more interested in returning to the origin as quickly as possible than to avoiding running empty. Among countries facing no conflict, the effect of an empty backhaul is stronger. Everything else equal, the trucking price to deliver a load to a destination whose market size is in the 75th percentile of the sample is about 20 percent lower than the trucking price to a destination whose market size is in the 25th percentile in the sample.

Lall, Sinha-Roy, and Shilpi (2022) find that spot trucking prices per ton-km are negatively correlated with economic density at the destination and positively correlated with economic density at the origin. Doubling the economic density of the destination is associated with 7 percent lower trucking rates; doubling the economic density of the origin is associated with 2.2 percent higher trucking rates. These results confirm the asymmetry in transport prices because of unbalanced demand.

One of the advantages of shipping contracts is that they allow transporters to plan the utilization of their trucks and to economically optimize their route by signing up with other shippers in the destination area to reduce the empty backhaul. This practice could be the reason why the elasticities of spot prices estimated by Lall, Sinha-Roy, and Shilpi (2022) are larger than the elasticities of contract prices estimated by Herrera Dappe, Lebrand, and others (2024).

NOTES

1. Brokers are called *empresas de transporte* in Colombia. The term translates as transport companies, but their role is closest to freight forwarders in the United States (Hernández and Cantillo-Cleves 2024).
2. The weights are the number of truckers in each location.
3. Transport firms need to own at least seven heavy commercial vehicles, meet and maintain the IBA's accounting and solvency standards, and regularly submit documentation to the IBA that includes financial statements.
4. The US Department of Justice classifies markets with HHI above 1,000 as concentrated markets, markets with HHI of 1,000–1,800 as "moderately concentrated," and markets with HHI above 1,800 as "highly concentrated" (DOJ and FTC 2023).
5. Conferences are cooperation agreements in which shipping firms set common freight rates and regulate their capacity.
6. The main changes that favored liner shipping were related to joint capacity adjustments, price discrimination, the obligation to consult transport users, and the possibility of withdrawal of the exemption. See ITF (2018) for a discussion of the changes.
7. Consortia are cost-reducing forms of cooperation that focus on a single maritime service.
8. The HHI is the sum of the squared market shares of all firms.
9. Alliances allow shipping lines to achieve economies of scale by reducing the risk of investing in larger vessels, as they improve fleet utilization and achieve economies of scope by offering customers broader networks.
10. To convert the probability of backhaul estimates into empty miles estimates, Yang (2024) assumes that all trips involve a fronthaul and backhaul leg and that the fronthaul is always loaded. To convert empty trip estimates into empty kilometers estimates, Yang (2024) assumes that loaded and empty trips are of equal length on average, so that estimates of the share of empty trips are comparable to the share of empty kilometers.

REFERENCES

Abate, M. 2014. "Determinants of Capacity Utilisation in Road Freight Transportation Research in Transportation Economics." *Journal of Transport Economics and Policy* 48: 137–52.

Allen, T., D. Atkin, S. Cantillo Cleves, and C.E. Hernández. 2024. "Trucks." Background paper prepared for this report.

Alphaliner. 2023. *Alphaliner Top 100*. https://alphaliner.axsmarine.com/publictop100/. Accessed May 24, 2023.

Ardelean, A., and V. Lugovskyy 2023. "It Pays to Be Big: Price Discrimination in Maritime Shipping." *European Economic Review* 153.

Armstrong, M., S. Cowan, and J. Vickers. 1994. *Regulatory Reform: Economic Analysis and British Experience*. Cambridge, MA: MIT Press.

Asturias, J. 2020. "Endogenous Transportation Costs." *European Economic Review* 123.

Barbero, J.A., R. Fiadone, and M.F. Millán Placci. 2020. "El transporte automotor de cargas en América Latina." División de Transporte, Nota Técnica IDB–TN–1877, Inter-American Bank, Washington, DC.

Beilock, R., and R. L. Kilmer. 1986. "The Determinants of Full-Empty Truck Movements." *American Journal of Agricultural Economics* 68: 67–76.

Bove, A., O. Hartmann, A. Stokenberga, V. Vesin, and Y. Yedan. 2018. *West and Central Africa Trucking Competitiveness.* SSATP Africa Transport Policy Program, World Bank Group, Washington, DC.

Brancaccio, G., M. Kalouptsidi, and T. Papageorgiou. 2020. "Geography, Transportation, and Endogenous Trade Costs." *Econometrica* 88: 657–91.

Brancaccio, G., M. Kalouptsidi, T. Papageorgiou, and N. Rosaia. 2023. "Search Frictions and Efficiency in Decentralized Transport Markets." *Quarterly Journal of Economics* 138 (4): 2451–503. https://doi.org/10.1093/qje/qjad023.

Combes, P.P., and M. Lafourcade. 2005. "Transport Costs: Measures, Determinants, and Regional Policy Implications for France." *Journal of Economic Geography* 5: 319–49.

CCCS (Competition & Consumer Commission Singapore). 2023. "File under Block Exemption Order." https://www.cccs.gov.sg/approach-cccs/file-under-block -exemption-order.

DOJ (Department of Justice), and FTC (Federal Trade Commission). 2023. *Horizontal Merger Guidelines.* Washington, DC.

Ducruet, C., and T. Notteboom. 2012. "The Worldwide Maritime Network of Container Shipping: Spatial Structure and Regional Dynamics." *Global Networks* 12 (3): 395–423.

EC (European Commission). 2014. *Report from the Commission to the European Parliament and the Council on the State of the Union Road Transport Market.* Technical Report, Brussels.

Eslava, M. 2000. "La regulación de precios del transporte de carga por carretera en Colombia. Una visión de economía política." *Desarrollo y Sociedad* 46: 1–41.

Espinet Alegre, X. and T.F. Medeiros. 2022. "Transport Deep Dive." Background paper prepared for the *Brazil Country Climate and Development Report,* World Bank, Washington, DC.

Farren, D., R. Giesen, and L.I. Rizzi. 2022. *The Economics of Empty Trips.* https://ssrn .com/abstract=4493760.

FMC (US Federal Maritime Commission) 2001. *The Impact of the Ocean Shipping Reform Act of 1998.* Technical Report, Washington, DC.

García, L.Y., and R. Sánchez. 2006. "Estadios de la competencia interportuaria: Del marco institucional a la conducta estratégica." Paper presented at the Eighth World Economy Meeting, University of Oviedo, Spain, April 20–22.

Hall, P.V., and W. Jacobs. 2010. "Shifting Proximities: The Maritime Ports Sector in an Era of Global Supply Chains." *Regional Studies* 44 (9): 1103–15.

Hernández, C.E., and S. Cantillo-Cleves. 2024. "A Toolkit for Setting and Evaluating Price Floors." *Journal of Public Economics* 232.

Herrera Dappe, M., C. Kunaka, M. Lebrand, and N. Weisskopf. 2020. *Moving Forward: Connectivity and Logistics to Sustain Bangladesh's Success.* Washington, DC: World Bank.

Herrera Dappe, M., M. Lebrand, B. Rowberry, and A. Stokenberga. 2024. "Moving Goods: Road Transport Costs in Developing Countries." World Bank, Washington, DC. Background paper prepared for this report.

Herrera Dappe, M., T. Serebrisky, A. Suárez-Alemán, and B. Turkgulu. 2024. "Being Efficient Pays Off: The Case of Ports and Maritime Transport Costs Worldwide." World Bank, Washington, DC. Background paper prepared for this report.

Holguin-Veras, J., E. Thorson, and J.C. Zorrilla. 2010. "Commercial Vehicle Empty Trip Models with Variable Zero Order Empty Trip Probabilities." *Networks and Spatial Economics* 10: 241–59.

Hong Kong Competition Commission. 2017. "Block Exemption for Vessel Sharing Agreements." Competition Order 2017.

Hummels, D., V. Lugovskyy, and A. Skiba. 2009. "The Trade Reducing Effects of Market Power in International Shipping." *Journal of Development Economics* 89: 84–97.

IDB (Inter-American Development Bank). 2013. "Trucking Services in Belize, Central America, and the Dominican Republic: Performance Analysis and Policy Recommendations. Department of Infrastructure and Environment." Technical Note IDB-TN-511, Washington, DC.

ITF (International Transport Forum). 2018. *The Impact of Alliances in Container Shipping.* Paris.

Juang, Y.C., and M. Roe. 2010. "A Study on Success Factors of Development Strategies for Intermodal Freight Transport Systems." *Journal of the Eastern Asia Society for Transportation Studies* 8: 722–32.

Lall, S., S. Sinha-Roy, and F. Shilpi. 2022. "Trucking Costs and the Margins of Internal Trade: Evidence from a Trucking Portal in India." Policy Research Working Paper 10059, World Bank, Washington, DC.

Lam, Y.Y., K. Sriram, and N. Khera. 2019. *Strengthening Vietnam's Trucking Sector: Towards Lower Logistics Costs and Greenhouse Gas Emissions.* Vietnam Transport Knowledge Series. Washington, DC: World Bank Group.

Limao, N., and A. J. Venables. 2001. "Infrastructure, Geographical Disadvantage, Transport Costs, and Trade." *World Bank Economic Review* 15 (3): 451–79.

McKinnon, A.C., and Y. Ge. 2006. "The Potential for Reducing Empty Running by Trucks: A Retrospective Analysis." *International Journal of Physical Distribution and Logistics Management* 36: 391–410.

Molnar, A., and F. Shilpi. 2024. "Urban and Infrastructure Determinants of Freight Cost in India." World Bank, Washington, DC. Background paper prepared for this report.

Nick Porée and Associates. 2023. "Road Freight Transport Costs in Sub-Saharan Africa." Background paper prepared for this report.

Notteboom, T., A. Pallis, and J.-P. Rodrigue. 2022. *Port Economics, Management and Policy.* New York: Routledge.

Notteboom T., F. Parola, and G. Satta. 2014. "State of the European Port System: Market Trends and Structure Update." *Partim Transshipment Volumes.*

Notteboom, T., and W. Winkelmans. 2001. "Structural Changes in Logistics: How Will Port Authorities Face the Challenge?" *Maritime Policy and Management* 28 (1): 71–89.

OECD (Organisation for Economic Co-Operation and Development). 2002. *Competition Policy in Liner Shipping.* Final Report. Paris.

OECD (Organisation for Economic Co-Operation and Development). 2011. "Competition in Ports and Port Services." Document Jt03313551, Directorate for Financial and Enterprise Affairs Competition Committee, Paris.

OECD (Organisation for Economic Co-Operation and Development). 2015. "Competition Issues in Liner Shipping." Note for Item IV of the 59th Meeting of Working Party No. 2, OECD Secretariat. Paris.

Osborne, T., M. Pachon, and G. Araya. 2014. "What Drives the High Price of Road Freight Transport in Central America?" Policy Research Working Paper 6844, World Bank, Washington, DC.

Rodrigue, J.P. 2013. *The Geography of Transport Systems,* 3rd ed. New York: Routledge.

Rodrigue, J.P., and T. Notteboom. 2010. "Foreland-Based Regionalization: Integrating Intermediate Hubs with Port Hinterlands." *Research in Transportation Economics* 27 (1): 19–29.

Slack, B., and A. Frémont. 2009. "Fifty Years of Organisational Change in Container Shipping: Regional Shift and the Role of Family Firms." *Geojournal* 74 (1): 23–34.

Sys, C. 2009. "Is the Container Liner Shipping Industry an Oligopoly?" *Transport Policy* 16 (5): 259–70.

Terrazas, A. 2019. *What You Need to Know about Empty Miles in Trucking.* https://convoy.com/blog/empty-miles-in-trucking/#FN5.

UNCTAD (United Nations Conference on Trade and Development). 2022. *Review of Maritime Transport 2022: Navigating Stormy Waters.* New York.

Wilmsmeier, G., and T. Notteboom. 2011. "Determinants of Liner Shipping Network Configuration: A Two-Region Comparison." *Geojournal* 76 (3): 213–28.

Wilson, W. 1987. "Transport Markets and Firm Behavior: The Backhaul Problem." *Journal of the Transportation Research Forum* 28.

Winston, C., T.M. Corsi, C.M. Grimm, and C.A. Evans. 1990. *The Economic Effects of Surface Freight Deregulation.* Washington, DC: Brookings Institution.

Wong, W.F. 2022. "The Round-Trip Effect: Endogenous Transport Costs and International Trade." *American Economic Journal: Applied Economics* 14 (4): 127–66.

World Bank. 2017. *Livre blanc sur le transport et la logistique au Sénégal: Etat des lieux et recommendations.* Internal Report. Washington, DC: World Bank.

World Bank. 2020. *Trucking: A Performance Assessment Framework for Policymakers.* Washington, DC: World Bank.

World Bank. 2023. *The Container Port Performance Index 2022: A Comparable Assessment of Performance Based on Vessel Time in Port.* Washington, DC: World Bank.

World Bank Group. 2018. *Promoting Open and Competitive Markets in Road Freight and Logistics Services.* Washington, DC: World Bank.

Yang, R. 2024. "Geographic Imbalance, Search Frictions, and Regulation: Causes of Empty Miles in Freight Trucking." Policy Research Working Paper 10775, World Bank, Washington, DC. Background paper prepared for this report.

Ying, J.S., and T.E. Keeler. 1991. "Pricing in a Deregulated Environment: The Motor Carrier Experience." *Rand Journal of Economics* 2 (2): 264–73.

Zerelli, S., and A. Cook. 2010. *Trucking to West Africa's Landlocked Countries: Market Structure and Conduct.* West Africa Trade Hub Report 32. Washington, DC: US Agency for International Development (USAID).

Policies to Reduce Economic Distance

5

MAIN MESSAGES

1. To reduce economic distance, governments need to ensure that transport markets and places are efficient. Without efficient markets, the full benefits of measures to ensure efficient places will not be realized. For this reason, measures that make places more efficient should follow measures that increase the efficiency of markets.

2. Achieving efficient market outcomes requires reducing market failures and market frictions caused by governments along the entire transport supply chain, through measures that strengthen competition for and in the market, that promote the development of efficient transport service providers, and that promote demand aggregation and matching.

3. Efficient places means that all places in the transport network are properly planned and function in ways that reduce the frictions associated with distance and topography, which extreme weather events exacerbate, and the costs of agglomeration. Ports and border posts must be efficiently operated and traffic effectively managed, particularly in urban areas.

4. All countries are different; the content and pace of implementation of the reform agenda to achieve efficient, high-quality transport and reduce the economic distance need to be tailored to the frictions and the institutional and socio-political characteristics of each country, as well as government capacity.

INTRODUCTION

Efficient, high-quality transport reduces economic distance, bringing people and firms closer to each other. Achieving efficient, high-quality freight transport requires reducing the frictions keeping transport prices above an efficient level, times high, and reliability low—that is reducing the economic costs of transport. The extent to which these broad objectives can be achieved depends on the targeting of frictions with policy measures and the behavioral responses of carriers and shippers to such measures. A narrow focus on lowering prices at all costs might not reduce the economic costs of transport, because it could lead to longer times and lower reliability. It is important, therefore, to properly identify the frictions and understand the mechanisms at play to design impactful policies that do not have unintended consequences.

Transport prices and times in developing countries are high and reliability is low because of inefficient markets and places. Market failures and market frictions caused by governments along the transport supply chain lead to inefficient market outcomes. The frictions of physical and economic geography and those related to infrastructure availability, quality, and operation lead to broken and inefficient connectivity on segments and nodes along the transport network. Any reform agenda to reduce the economic distance faced by developing countries should, therefore, aim to reduce the frictions making markets and places inefficient (refer to figure 5.1). Without efficient

FIGURE 5.1 Building blocks for shrinking economic distance

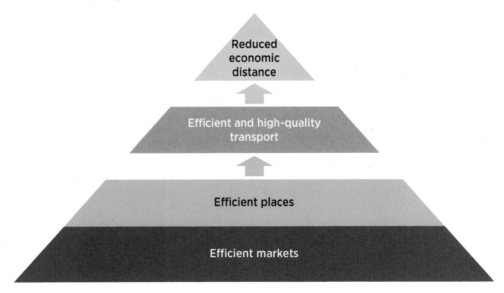

Source: Original figure for this publication.

markets the full benefits of measures to ensure efficient places will not be realized. Measures that make places more efficient should therefore follow measures that increase the efficiency of markets.

All countries are different; the content and pace of implementation of the reform agenda to achieve efficient, high-quality transport needs to be tailored to the frictions and institutional and socio-political characteristics of each country, as well as to government capacity. This chapter aims to help policy makers design reform agendas for their countries by providing a broad range of policy measures and good practices as well as examples in which some of these measures have been implemented and potential tradeoffs policy makers might face.

The chapter is organized as follows. The first section discusses policy measures that seek to make markets efficient, including evidence on their impact. The second section focuses on policy measures to make places efficient, including evidence on their impact.

MAKING MARKETS EFFICIENT

Achieving efficient market outcomes in the freight transport sector requires establishing an enabling business environment. Such an environment is created through laws, rules, and regulations that set conditions for access to the profession and the market and reduce frictions across the transport supply chain. Well-functioning institutions with the capacity to enforce laws, rules, and regulations are paramount to creating and sustaining an enabling business environment. The following sections discuss policy areas and measures to create an enabling business environment that fosters efficient market outcomes.

Strengthening competition for and in the market

Ensuring competition in all segments of the transport supply chain through competition policy is a necessary condition for achieving efficient, high-quality transport. Doing so requires ensuring competition in markets for inputs, including labor, vehicles, and fuel; intermediate services, including pilotage and tug assistance at ports, and equipment repair services; and final freight transport services. Competition policy goes beyond competition law and enforcement to include the alignment of government interventions in markets with competition principles, including regulations and state participation (World Bank Group 2018).

An important policy lever to ensure competition throughout the transport supply chain is competition law and enforcement. An independent competition authority with the power and capacity to enforce competition law in all segments of the transport supply chain can ensure that no market player— including unions, associations, private firms, and state-owned enterprises

(SOEs)—behaves anticompetitively. When sector regulators exist, it is important to clearly delineate the responsibilities of the competition agency and the regulators and ensure adequate coordination between the entities. Where SOEs or authorities participate in any of the segments of the transport supply chain, an independent competition authority can ensure that they do not have a competitive advantage over private firms.

It is important that government interventions not hinder competition. Some policies and regulations may reinforce the dominance of incumbents or limit entry of new market participants, facilitate collusion or restrict firms' choice of strategic variables, and discriminate and protect vested interests. Examples of such interventions include bilateral freight-sharing agreements that give associations the power to allocate freight at ports, the regulation of the trucking sector in France, Mexico, and the United States between the 1930s and 1980s, and rules prohibiting foreign companies from providing trucking services in many countries. Figure 5.2 presents regulations that restrict competition in road transport in Peru, the Philippines and Viet Nam.

Governments should avoid restricting market entry and regulating prices of transport services. Price regulation is justified only in the case of a natural monopoly. A natural monopoly could exist for port services in a small country where the volume of trade can support only a single port and there are no feasible alternatives in neighboring countries. It cannot exist in the trucking sector. Deregulation of the trucking sector in the Czech Republic, France, Hungary, Mexico, Poland, and the United States led to significant entry, higher productivity, lower carrier costs, improvements in the quality of services, and reductions in the trucking prices paid by shippers (refer to box 5.1). The experience in Morocco—where quality decreased after deregulation, mainly because of excess supply—shows that the conditions of the sector at the time of the deregulation are important for the success of the deregulation.

Regulating international trucking services also enhances efficiency. Fears that doing so would leave local carriers worse off while foreign carriers, particularly those whose operating costs are lower, better off were not necessarily justified (refer to box 5.2). Governments should avoid granting exclusivity rights or limiting the number of licenses issued along routes and markets, imposing restrictions on access to cargo, or allowing associations and unions to impose them. It is also advisable that they avoid caps on foreign ownership and more burdensome permit procedures for foreigners—or at least ensure that the benefits of these measures outweigh their costs (World Bank Group 2018).

Experience from across the globe indicates that competition in the port sector is associated with higher port performance and lower maritime shipping costs. Competition can be achieved by encouraging private sector participation through the landlord port model; promoting competition between and within ports, in part through transparent and competitive concession bidding; and ensuring a level playing field in which the port regulator does not operate port terminals or provide port services that the private sector can provide.

FIGURE 5.2 Regulations that restrict competition in road transport in Peru, the Philippines, and Viet Nam

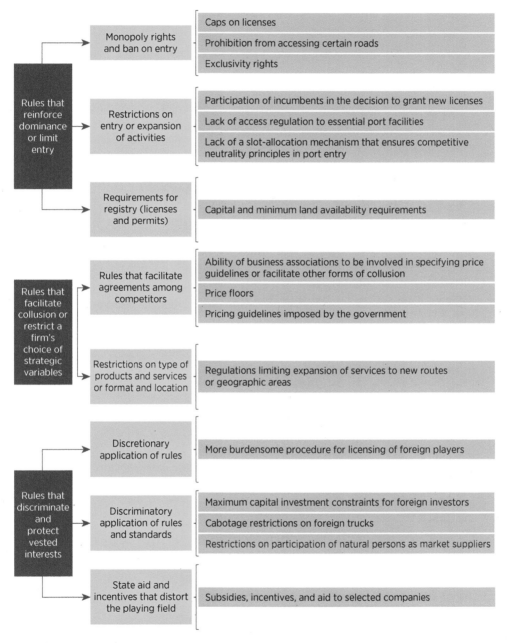

Source: Adapted from World Bank Group 2018.

Strong governance and capacity of port authorities are requisites for the successful implementation of the landlord port model. Under the landlord model, the port authority acts as regulatory body and landlord, and private companies operate the port. Infrastructure is leased to private operating companies. Private operators provide and maintain their own superstructure;

BOX 5.1

Deregulating the domestic trucking sector: Lessons from international experience

France

In 1986, the French government eliminated license quotas, liberalized the pricing of trucking services, and reformed the insurance tax on freight transport allowances and the maintenance contract system. Deregulation led to significant changes in the market structure, with the number of carriers almost doubling the following year. Between 1978 and 1998, carriers' transport costs decreased by 38.3 percent, with 21.8 percentage points attributable to the regulatory changes in the industry (Combes and Lafourcade 2005).

Hungary, Poland, and the Czech Republic

Hungary and Poland liberalized their trucking sectors in 1988; the Czech Republic did so in 1990. These countries were the earliest in Eastern and Central Europe to adopt pro-competition reforms. The privatization of public service providers and the deregulation of the sector, which included the elimination of rate and route controls, led to the entry of many new trucking operators, competitive prices, and better-quality services, including faster delivery times and less breakage and spoilage of cargo (Teravaninthorn and Raballand 2009).

Indonesia

Indonesia liberalized its trucking sector in 1985, removing price regulation, allowing free entry into the market, and banning trucking associations from setting minimum rates (World Bank Group 2018). As a result of the liberalization, the number of truck operators soared, creating a competitive market (Teravaninthorn and Raballand 2009).

Mexico

Mexico deregulated its trucking industry in 1989. It eliminated the obligation to belong to a central cargo station; the structure of regular services by route, specialized by product, and mandatory prices; and the state and regional committees and federal technical committees of road freight transport that had granted permissions for the truck services since 1977. In addition, trucking companies that worked without concessions or permissions were granted permits to operate (World Bank and IRU 2016).

Deregulation had significant impacts on competition, service quality, and prices. By mid-1990, there were about 30,000 new entrants in the trucking industry, and 14,000 illegal operators had been regularized. The frequency of service and the speed of delivery rose (World Bank and IRU 2016). According to the Secretary of Communications and Transport, tariffs for trucking services fell by 23 percent in real terms between 1987 and 1994 (Dutz, Hayri, and Ibarra 2000).

(continued)

BOX 5.1 **Deregulating the domestic trucking sector: Lessons from international experience** *(continued)*

Morocco

In 2003, the government of Morocco abolished the monopoly of freight allocation that the Office National du Transport (ONT) had held. At the time, there was an oversupply of trucks, because many individuals had invested in trucks because of the ONT fleet's low productivity. As a result of the increased competition triggered by the deregulation and the initial large oversupply and low level of professionalism of individual operators, trucking prices decreased below costs, leading to a deterioration in the quality of transport services (Teravaninthorn and Raballand 2009).

United States

In 1980, Congress passed the Motor Carrier Act to substantially deregulate the trucking sector. The act limited collective rate-making, eased entry restrictions, and encouraged pricing freedom. The deregulation had a significant impact on truckers' productivity, reducing costs by 16 percent by 1984, after a 1 percent increase in cost the year after the deregulation (Ying 1990). The impact on trucking prices was even larger. Ying and Keeler (1991) estimate that deregulation yielded price reductions of 15–20 percent by 1983 and 25–35 percent by 1985. Deregulation of trucking is estimated to have generated about $8 billion in annual benefits to shippers, from savings in private trucking operating costs ($3 billion), trucking price reductions ($4 billion), and service improvements ($1 billion) (Winston and others 1990).

---

own and operate the cargo-handling equipment; and, in most cases, employ the dock labor.

Moving from a public sector monopoly to an unregulated private sector monopoly will not bring efficiency gains. Increases in private sector participation should go hand in hand with increased competition for and in the market. Where competition in the market is limited because of large economies of scale relative to the size of the market, regulation should be used to increase efficiency.

Insufficient port capacity leaves room for port terminal operators to give preferential access and conditions to customers that move more cargo or have vertical relationships with the terminal, which could ultimately harm some port users. Increasing port capacity and competition in the port sector weakens the incentives for such practices. In the short term or if the size of the market does not allow for a meaningful increase in competition, putting in place access regulation can prevent exclusionary practices. The use of market-based and transparent slot-allocation mechanisms in ports is another option (World Bank Group 2018).

BOX 5.2

Deregulating the international trucking sector: Lessons from the European Union and Rwanda

European Union

At the beginning of the 1980s, EU member states regulated the number of licenses available for international trucking services, the prices at which shipments could take place, or both. In January 1990, it allowed shippers and carriers to set prices. Starting in 1987, the number of permits was increased by 40 percent a year; all limitations on the number of permits were eliminated in 1993. The need for authorizations to provide cabotage services was eliminated in 1998.

Liberalization of the authorization system had a positive effect on the growth in international trucking in the European Union, according to Lafontaine and Malaguzzi Valeri (2009). It allowed trucking firms to route and use their trucks more efficiently, making it easier for them to arrange backhauls, lowering trucking prices, and increasing the demand for trucking services. Moreover, the distribution of trucking business across countries did not change after liberalization.

Rwanda

In 1994, the Rwandan government deregulated its trucking services sector. Until then, trucking services had been a monopoly of Société des Transports Internationaux du Rwanda (STIR), a parastatal company (Mwase 2003). Deregulation privatized STIR, removed the price protection for local trucking firms, and lowered the fleet size requirements to engage in international transport, among other measures. As a result, the trucking fleet expanded, and trucking prices declined by more than 30 percent (Teravaninthorn and Raballand 2009).

Promoting the development of efficient transport service providers

Deregulation of the freight transport sector, particularly the trucking sector, replaced the system of quotas and quantitative restrictions to enter the profession and the market with free market entry and qualitative requirements to enter the profession.[1] Because of potential market distortions and the negative externalities of transport services (such as accidents), it is important to regulate access to the profession by setting standards and requirements for transport service providers; transport workers (drivers, seafarers, and other workers in the sector); and trucks, vessels, and other equipment. These laws and regulations should define the scope of the criteria to be adopted—whether the rules should apply only to commercial, public, for-hire, and reward transport or also to own-account and private transport. The criteria should cover professional competence and reputation of the people managing the company, the financial standing of the company, and insurance. Additional requirements should be imposed for access to specialized markets, such as the transport of dangerous or hazardous goods or perishable foodstuff. They may cover specialized training for employees and special certification of vehicles, vessels, and other equipment.

Many countries have adopted the European Union's (EU) criteria for access to the profession and the Consolidated Resolution on the Facilitation of International Road Transport (R.E.4) of the United Nations Economic Commission for Europe, which was inspired by the EU criteria (World Bank and IRU 2016). The EU criteria and R.E.4 stipulate that in order to transport goods on the account of others, operators must be licensed. Licensing is granted based on the satisfaction of three criteria: good reputation, adequate financial standing, and professional competence. R.E.4 stipulates that good reputation is met if the manager of the transport operator has not been convicted of a criminal offense (including commercial crimes) or serious breaches of labor or transport law. Adequate financial standing is met when evidence is provided that the undertaking has sufficient resources to ensure that the company is properly set up and managed. Professional competence is met by demonstrating that the manager of the operator has sufficient knowledge to "engage properly and viably in the occupation," in particular in the fields of commercial and business administration; technical standards and operations; road safety; access to market; and elements of company, social and labor, and civil and fiscal law (World Bank and IRU 2016).

Adequate financial and economic understanding is an important requirement for operators; it could be coupled with measures to improve it, such as education. In many developing countries, the lack of a sound financial understanding and education by operators may lead them to offer their services below costs. Once these typically small operators realize that they are losing money, many attempt to round corners, by, for example, evading taxes and overloading their trucks. Strong enforcement of regulations is important to prevent such practices, but without adequate financial skills of operators, achieving an efficient, high-quality transport sector is challenging.

Regulations should also cover the skills and qualifications of drivers, seafarers, and other workers responsible for the operation of equipment. The requirements for professional drivers are not limited to driving; they require competencies in a variety of fields, including environmental laws and regulations; international and national customs regulations; and regulations applicable to the transport of special cargo, such as dangerous goods and perishable foodstuff. Many countries have adopted a Certificate of Professional Competence for professional drivers, certifying the completion of specialized training.

Even high-income countries often suffer from a shortage of skilled drivers and workers to operate transport equipment. Many transport service providers believe that training and hiring skilled workers is a cost and not an investment in human resources, a process to build capacity that will bring better profitability to the company. Introducing new training requirements should therefore be accompanied by incentives and communication to change behavior.

The use of old, inefficient trucks and vessels is common across developing countries. Regulations on access to the profession should include requirements on vehicle and vessel technical characteristics, norms and standards, and technical inspections and control of compliance. Legislation should set the minimum standards that must be complied with for a vehicle or vessel to be operated and require regular technical inspections.

The minimum standards for trucks should be consistent with the quality of fuel available and the availability of maintenance and repair skills in the country. In some countries, trucks that meet the latest emissions standards are imported but the fuels available are not adequate for such standards, damaging the trucks. Developing countries often also lack the skills needed to maintain and repair modern vehicles equipped with advanced systems.

The standards and requirements for operators, drivers and seafarers, and vehicles and vessels should be set in a manner that does not promote informality or hinder competition. Regulations should be easily accessible, simple, and easy to understand. Governments should be as clear and transparent as possible when stating policies and issuing regulations, in order to remove vagueness, ambiguity, and room for individual (especially idiosyncratic) discretion. To minimize opportunities for corruption, little or no room should be left for different interpretations by different government officials. Subnational regulations should be standardized and homogenized across the country. Standardizing regulations across countries can also increase competition: The higher the level of harmonization with international best practices, the fewer reasons there are for exclusion from markets.

It is important that governments assess how markets for inputs work and put in place measures to reduce frictions that may be distorting such markets. When frictions arise from policies and regulations in input markets, governments must ensure that the benefits of those policies and regulations outweigh their costs. For example, trade and nontrade barriers for imports of cargo vehicles, equipment, parts, and fuel can increase the costs of providing transport services and hinder the quality of the services.

In many regions of the world, informal operators populate the freight transport sector, particularly trucking and inland water transport. These providers are not established as commercial entities. They generally maintain no accounting records and operate outdated vehicles. The presence of such operators, whose viability is doubtful, is a disturbing factor in the market, as they operate outside any economic viable model. Freight intermediaries and shippers complain about the situation, but they benefit from the low prices informal operators charge and tend to impose such tariff levels on formal operators, generating a kind of snowball effect. It is important that governments work toward formalizing the sector.

The dominance of small, informal transport operators is undesirable for several reasons. Such operators keep few if any accounting records and do not enter into formal contracts with shippers, hindering their ability to borrow from banks and other financial institutions and forcing them to rely on other sources of financing (including own funds, loans from family members, and supplier financing), which are insufficient to allow them to purchase large trucks in good condition. Old, inefficient fleets are usually a consequence of informality.

Efforts to formalize the sector through the creation of companies, groupings, and cooperatives could be accompanied by incentive measures that reduce some of the constraints operators face. For example, fleet renewal programs are often restricted to companies operating under legal status. Informal operators could be encouraged to formalize their activities by creating a legal entity or joining a grouping or cooperative to become eligible for the program. The program could include fiscal incentives, including direct financial assistance and facilitated access to credit for the purchase of vehicles and vessels. Box 5.3 presents some lessons from fleet renewal schemes.

Enforcement of the laws and regulations applicable to transport is essential for achieving an efficient, high-quality transport sector. If noncompliant transport operators can continue to operate under the same conditions as the operators that make efforts to comply with the rules, the latter will see no sense in complying. Enforcement depends on many factors, including culture, social and economic development, the clarity and applicability of legislation and regulations, the definition of roles and responsibilities, and institutional capacities. Efficient enforcement requires empowered, skilled, and well-trained officers or civil servants, supported at the political and executive levels, and financial resources adequate to the objective.

Promoting demand aggregation and matching

Intermediaries that behave competitively can bring efficiency to the market by reducing search and matching frictions, increasing utilization, and reducing empty trips. Efficiency-enhancing intermediaries include brokers, freight forwarders, and third-party logistics service providers. Brokers are used on demand to find capacity for shippers from a large network of trusted carriers. Freight forwarders typically take responsibility for optimizing and managing the logistics of international and intermodal shipments for shippers. Third-party logistics providers play a strategic role in helping shippers optimize their supply chains and minimize their total logistics costs. Truck brokers and freight forwarders create value, especially for small and medium-size enterprises by giving them access to levels of demand that can yield lower trucking prices through aggregation, providing them with better access to transport capacity at peak periods, and enabling them to work with a larger pool of trucking companies that is collectively less subject to empty trips.

The technology revolution over the last few decades led to the development of online freight markets that reduce search and matching frictions like brokers once did. In the United Kingdom, freight exchanges improved the matching of carriers and shippers, reducing empty trips by 5 percentage points, from a baseline of 28 percent (Mansell 2001). The Uber Freight

BOX 5.3

Lessons from fleet renewal schemes

Several lessons emerge from fleet renewal schemes:

- **Fiscal incentives should be tailored.** They should be sufficient to guarantee enough participation to warrant investment in the program; in the long term, the economic benefits of cleaner or more fuel-efficient vehicles should exceed the provided fiscal incentives. Policy makers should aim to find the tipping point at which owners of the targeted number of older vehicles to be removed participate in the vehicle replacement program, without offering subsidies that are too high.

- **Program design should balance the roles of policy makers at different jurisdictional levels.** Large-scale vehicle replacement programs may initially need to be established and funded by a central authority, but program implementation may be best handled by local policy makers, who have a detailed understanding of local needs and conditions.

- **Fiscal policies should be complemented with other measures and have strong oversight.** Complementary measures, such as mandatory age limits for vehicles and operation restrictions, will incentivize participation in the voluntary vehicle replacement programs and provide additional emissions benefits. Policy makers should ensure that subsidies are not provided for vehicles that have already been abandoned.

Chile

Chile's Swap Your Truck program, which targeted trucks that were more than 25 years old, was implemented entirely by a national body, the Technical Cooperation Service; no complementary policy measures were implemented to further incentivize fleet renewal. Although the subsidy accounted for about a third of the price of the replacement vehicle, access to credit for small fleet operators was challenging. The program removed only 5 percent of the targeted pre-1984 trucks.

China

The Chinese government has initiated multiple programs to encourage voluntary fleet renewal. They include national scrappage subsidies, local scrappage subsidies, and supporting policies, including mandatory vehicle age limits and vehicle activity restrictions. Local programs have tended to be more successful than exclusively national programs. For example, the city of Beijing offered subsidies for the replacement of older vehicles while simultaneously banning older vehicles from traveling in the city center, strongly incentivizing truck owners to take advantage of the subsidies and upgrade their vehicles. The level of the fiscal incentive was increased during program implementation to encourage uptake.

Source: Posada and others 2015.

platform decreased deadhead miles by 22.6 percent among drivers in the United States who used it (Heilmann 2020). Similar digital platforms are in use in developing countries, including Lori Systems and Kobo360 in Africa, BlackBuck in India, and Liftit in Latin America.

When there is an opportunity for making a profit by matching carriers and shippers, established international companies or entrepreneurs will step in and help reduce search and matching frictions, unless there are regulations or market failures that impede them from doing so. Where they do not, policy measures to tackle the impediments may be necessary.

Measures that reduce frictions on the demand side of the market can also improve market outcomes. They include measures to promote freight aggregation, which helps increase vehicle utilization. In agricultural areas, consolidation centers or assembly markets can help farmers aggregate their production and carriers to fully load their trucks, which reduces truck operating costs and prices, if there is competition. Dry ports, inland container depots, container freight stations, and logistics clusters in or near urban areas can help consolidate freight (refer to box 5.4).

BOX 5.4

Lessons from international experience developing logistics clusters

Logistics clusters boost logistics efficiency by facilitating cargo consolidation, increasing capacity utilization, reducing inventory requirements, and promoting multimodality. They have been deployed as anchor nodes in the logistics systems of the world's top-performing countries, as measured by the World Bank's Logistics Performance Index.

There can be multiple approaches to facilitating logistics clusters. In the United States, the development of logistics clusters unfolded organically, based on market and demand-side considerations. Private sector entities, in particular real estate development companies, participated almost always through some form of a public-private partnership arrangement with local, state, or national government participation. The European experience was also market led, but with a more gradual transition from greater incidence of central planning and a strong tradition of collaboration between the public and the private sector and academia. In contrast, the Korean experience involved more participation by the state, through national and subnational planning, goal setting, performance management, supply-demand monitoring, and network design, while still placing emphasis on demand-driven development. All these

(continued)

BOX 5.4 Lessons from international experience developing logistics clusters *(continued)*

countries relied on strong public sector institutions, from the national down to the local level. In all of them, logistics policy and decision-making emphasized agglomeration by seeking to create a small number of high-volume nodes that could naturally develop as clusters.

Lessons from international experience that are relevant for developing countries include the following:

- **A small number of integrated logistics centers** should form the core of a national logistics clusters strategy.
- **Standardization of equipment, information and communication technologies, and cost-effective operations** are necessary to support infrastructure provision to allow logistics clusters to deliver on outcomes such as market uptake, multimodality and modal shift, and logistics cost savings.
- **The availability of a wider set of logistics services** at a given location deepens the economic impact of the cluster and leads to stronger logistics outcomes.
- **The role of government** in the planning and development of logistics clusters will be more critical in regions where land is scarcer and the general public may be more exposed to the negative externalities associated with the transport and handling of freight.
- It is possible to **plan a network of logistics clusters at the national level,** as the Republic of Korea did. The centralized, more predictable nature of this approach allowed the government to pursue complementary policy actions. Some level of overarching planning can help coordinate efforts at more geographically granular levels of decision-making, to support goals such as standardization, national cohesion, international integration, corridor development, and interregional connectivity. This process plays out over time—in the case of Korea over a period of over two decades.

Source: Blancas and others 2022.

Summary of recommendations for making markets efficient

Table 5.1 summarizes the recommendations for making markets along the transport supply chain efficient.

MAKING PLACES EFFICIENT

Efficient places are one of the building blocks to reduce the economic distance between and within countries. Efficient places means that all places in the transport network are planned and function in ways that reduce the frictions associated with distance and topography, which extreme weather

TABLE 5.1 Recommendations for making markets efficient

High-level action	Detailed actions

Strengthen competition for and in the market	• Enact competition law.
	• Create and empower an independent competition authority and clearly delineate responsibility for antitrust issues.
	• Align government interventions in markets with competition principles, including regulations and state participation.
	   • Avoid regulating prices unless there is a natural monopoly.
	   • Avoid restricting market access, particularly through quotas and quantitative restrictions.
	   • Separate the regulatory function from the service provision function.
	• Encourage private sector participation in the port sector through the landlord model.
	• Ensure transparent and competitive concession bidding.
	• Implement transparent, market-based slot-allocation mechanisms.

Promote the development of efficient transport service providers	• Regulate access to the profession by setting clear standards and requirements for transport service provides, transport workers, and equipment.
	   • Ensure that standards and requirements do not promote informality.
	   • Standardize and homogenize subnational regulations.
	   • Harmonize regulation with international best practices.
	• Promote skill development of operators and workers (for example, drivers, seafarers).
	• Tackle frictions distorting input markets and ancillary sectors hindering operators' and workers' access to the profession.
	• Support the formalization of transport operators, by assessing constraints facing operators and considering incentive schemes such as fleet renewal programs.
	• Develop strong enforcement capacity.

Promote demand aggregation and matching	• Support the development of competitive intermediaries, including online platforms and marketplaces. • Support the development of consolidation centers and logistics clusters.

Source: Original table for this publication.

events exacerbate, and the costs of agglomeration. Policy makers can take several steps to ensure that places are efficient.

Developing adequate transport infrastructure

Adequate road infrastructure can reduce the frictions of physical geography and transport costs, as the evidence presented in chapter 3 shows. Developing countries have expanded and improved their road infrastructure, reducing transport times and costs. Ethiopia's Road Sector Development Programme, one of the most impressive large-scale interventions implemented in a developing country, increased travel speeds by 40 percent on asphalt roads and 80 percent on minor gravel roads (Perra, Sanfilippo, and Sundaram 2022). In Colombia, investment in road infrastructure increased seven-fold in real terms between 2002 and 2017 (Ministerio de Transporte 2020). The resulting reduction in travel times led to a decrease in the cost of trucking services and changes in the intensity of competition in some routes, which resulted in a reduction in transport prices of 1.8 percent on average (Allen and others 2024). Box 5.5 presents additional evidence on the impacts of road projects financed by multilateral development banks.

Investments in rail, waterways, and multimodal connectivity can also play a significant role in reducing transport costs (refer to box 5.6). Investments can make rail transport more competitive with trucking, especially over long distances.

Policy makers need to think very carefully about where to invest, what to invest in, and what policies to implement to endow their country with adequate infrastructure. The first step is to develop an integrated transport master plan to identify the mix of investments and infrastructure-related policies that yield the greatest net benefits and provide the blueprint for policy makers (Balboni 2024; Fajgelbaum and Schaal 2020; Kreindler and others 2023). The integrated master plan should be anchored in a transport model that takes into account the impacts on transport time and costs and the wider economic impacts discussed in chapter 6. It should be part of an integrated public investment management system that besides identifying, appraising, and selecting investments selects the best provision modality for each investment based on fiscal affordability and value for money (see Herrera Dappe and others 2023 and Kim, Fallov, and Groom 2020 for in-depth discussions on integrated public investment management systems).

BOX 5.5

Travel time and cost reductions associated with road projects financed by multilateral development banks

Over the past three decades, multilateral development banks invested in interurban road projects that reduced the median travel time on the project roads, with reductions ranging from 30 percent in Latin America and the Caribbean to 59 percent in the Middle East and North Africa. The median travel time savings were greater on roads whose capacity was expanded or that were otherwise upgraded than on roads that were rehabilitated or maintained. The range in travel time savings was widest in large countries, including Ethiopia, China, Pakistan, and India (refer to figure B5.5.1), where the geography and topography was more varied than elsewhere.

The median vehicle operating cost savings resulting from road improvements ranged from 11 percent in Eastern Europe and Central Asia (reflecting initially better conditions) to 33 percent in Sub-Saharan Africa and Latin America and the Caribbean. It reached 55 percent in individual countries (refer to map B5.5.1).

Major regional corridor investments financed by the World Bank in Sub-Saharan Africa resulted in significant reductions in both travel times and travel time variance, a measure of unpredictability. These improvements also benefited landlocked countries (Burkina Faso, the Central African Republic, Chad, Mali, and Rwanda), which have high import and export costs and depend on connectivity to their coastal neighbors for access to international markets.

(continued)

BOX 5.5 **Travel time and cost reductions associated with road projects financed by multilateral development banks** *(continued)*

FIGURE B5.5.1 Median reduction in travel times on roads improved as part of projects financed by multilateral development banks

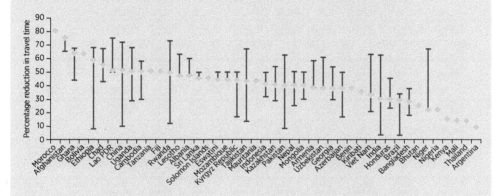

Source: Original figure based on Stokenberga and Ogita 2021.
Note: The unit of observation is a road improved by a project; sample = 223. Diamonds represent the median; whiskers represent the minimum and maximum.

MAP B5.5.1 Median reduction in vehicle operating costs on roads improved as part of projects financed by multilateral development banks

Source: Original map for this publication based on Stokenberga and Ogita 2021.

BOX 5.6

Improving multimodal transport infrastructure to reduce travel times and costs: Lessons from international experience

Kazakhstan

Kazakhstan embarked on a massive road and rail investment program, Nurly Zhol, to connect major cities, logistics centers, and free-trade zones to the regional market—including border crossings, ports on the Caspian Sea, and dry ports—investing about $37 billion between 2013 and 2017. As a result, regional connectivity improved, average transport prices paid by shippers to move cargo on the regional corridors fell from $0.16 in 2013 to $0.09 per ton-km in 2019.

Madagascar

To reduce transport costs and facilitate trade, in 2003–08 the government of Madagascar invested in 145 km of railway replacement, 226 km of railway reinforcement, the rehabilitation of several bridges between Toamasina and Andevoranto, the rehabilitation and renewal of about 35 km of track, and equipment to improve communication capacity, and other projects. As a result, prolonged speed reductions on the Northern Railway affected only 1.2 km of the route, compared with 23 km before the interventions, and transit speed on the Antananarivo–Toamasina railway line doubled. Wagon turnaround time on the Northern Railway decreased by 12 percent, facilitating more than a doubling in freight traffic.

Viet Nam

In the Red River and Northern Delta region, which accounts for 10 percent of Viet Nam's area but produces almost a quarter of the country's agricultural products, inland waterways play a critical role in the movement of cargo. Recognizing the need for and benefits of efficient multimodal transport and logistics services, the government adopted several sectoral policies in the late 2010s, including the upgrading of waterway transport infrastructure. To reduce transport time and costs, it upgraded two key waterway corridors, from Quang Ninh to Viet Tri and from Hanoi to the Lach Giang estuary; built an access channel to connect the sea and inland waterway; and invested in new facilities at Viet Tri and Ninh Phuc cargo ports, among other mea-sures. Completion of the infrastructure reduced the travel and waiting times along the corridor and allowed the operation of more modern vessels with bigger capacity. Travel times of barges fell by 36 percent from Quang Ninh to Viet Tri during the dry season and by 16 percent from Hanoi to the Lach Giang estuary. Waiting times for vessels through the two corridors were reduced by 20–25 percent, and the vessel waiting time to enter or exit the river system at the Lach Giang estuary during the dry season fell from 20 to less than 1 hour. Transport costs declined by more than $1 per ton of cargo, equivalent to several thousand dollars of savings per cargo vessel.

Source: ADB 2020; UNECE 2019; World Bank 2013b, 2023.

The availability of good-quality transport infrastructure depends on a number of policy decisions besides the design of the network and selection of investments. They include the consistent application of all-weather and climate-resilient construction standards and other resilience measures along the lifecycle of the infrastructure assets; axle-load limits to lengthen the useful life of the assets; strong project implementation process, including procurement and monitoring of the physical and financial execution of projects; the proper management and maintenance of the infrastructure assets over time; and sustainable and efficient financing of the infrastructure.

Resilience investments must be based on a rational and evidence-based approach that involves assessing and prioritizing interventions following evaluation of exposure to hazards, system vulnerabilities, risks, direct and indirect impacts, intervention costs, and their benefits in the long run (World Bank Group 2024). Decision-makers should consider the full infrastructure lifecycle, from the systems planning phase to engineering and design, operation and maintenance, contingency planning, and institutional capacity and coordination. Institutional capacity and coordination can leverage innovative private sector solutions to improve resilience and risk allocation among partners. Public-private partnership (PPP) contract provisions that may increase the attractiveness of projects include climate provisions in tender documents, key performance indicators specifying recovery targets, and provisions for flexible tariff models and cost-sharing mechanisms to facilitate climate resilience interventions during the operational phase.

Countries need to move away from the build, neglect, rebuild mindset. It is common across developing countries to build new land transport infrastructure, neglect proper maintenance, and then rebuild it when the infrastructure is dilapidated. Reasons for such behavior include the preference for new infrastructure because of its political benefits, the lack of adequate asset management systems and capacity, and funding. This pattern costs significantly more than building and properly maintaining infrastructure. For example, the South African National Roads Agency estimates that the cost of repairing roads is 6 times the cost of preventative maintenance after three years of neglect and 18 times after five years of neglect (SANRAL 2004).

Several steps can be taken to improve the management of public infrastructure, thereby lengthening its useful life and improving the quality of the services it provides. Analysis and quantification of future maintenance requirements of a new investment should be an integral part of the cost–benefit analysis of the project. Governments should establish guidelines for such analysis. Projected costs of the maintenance of ongoing and approved new investment projects should be incorporated in the country's expenditure framework. Line ministries and other relevant agencies should establish and put into consistent practice systems to monitor the state of infrastructure, such as road asset management systems, to ensure that maintenance needs are met on a timely basis and according to prespecified standards. In most countries, establishing asset management systems is likely to require significant investment in relevant technologies and databases.

Well-prepared medium-term expenditure frameworks (MTEFs) can help safeguard infrastructure assets. MTEFs take into account spending commitments on ongoing projects, make explicit the costs of planned new investments over the entire time horizon of the framework, ensure consistency of both capital and operations and maintenance spending with the projected revenue envelope over the same period, and allocate adequate resources to the operations and maintenance of existing and new infrastructures. An MTEF helps reduce the risk that overambitious infrastructure investment plans end up not being implemented and projects are delayed for lack of adequate budgetary resources.

To help address some of the political economy factors that bias infrastructure spending toward new investments at the expense of the maintenance of existing roads, some countries have created dedicated maintenance funds (road funds). The evidence presented in Herrera Dappe and others (2023) suggests that such funds are effective in increasing the share of maintenance in road spending. It is essential that they be held to strict governance and transparency standards and that their accounts be fully reflected in the government's accounts.

Private participation in road and rail infrastructure financing and operation can help increase the availability of good-quality infrastructure. In Colombia, for example, road network improvement and expansion was supported through a PPP program that mobilized over $10 billion of investment in 32 projects covering more than 3,000 km of roads between 2013 and 2016. Chile mobilized more than $12 billion in investment in 1993–2017 through PPPs, building nearly 3,500 km of interurban and urban roads (Engel, Fischer, and Galetovic 2020).

A successful PPP program requires a robust framework covering PPP preparation, procurement, and contract management, and fiscal management. Given the complexity, magnitude, and long-term nature of PPP contracts, the government should perform rigorous assessments to gauge the viability of infrastructure projects before deciding on PPP procurement and contract design. The framework should establish a procurement process that awards PPPs to the private partner that can deliver the highest value for money. Properly managing implementation of a PPP contract is key to ensuring that the project delivers the expected value for money and does not lead to fiscal surprises. Robust fiscal management of infrastructure requires specific provisions regarding PPPs and especially an integrated management of the fiscal implications of projects delivered through PPPs and public provision. Herrera Dappe and others (2023) and World Bank (2020) provide an in-depth discussion of the requirements of a robust PPP framework.

Improving the efficiency of ports and border crossings

High-quality infrastructure and efficient operation are critical for transport nodes, such as ports and border posts. Physical investments at border-crossing points, such as one-stop border posts, can reduce border-crossing times and their variance. Evidence from countries that have implemented policy measures to improve their maritime connectivity suggests potentially sizable transport cost savings (refer to box 5.7). Such activities include improvement and expansion of port infrastructure; superstructure (quayside container cranes, rubber-tired gantry cranes, forklift trucks, and ancillary equipment); and landside access, including connectivity between gateway ports and inland cities, as well as investment in container-handling capacity and infrastructure that enables transshipment of goods (which may be particularly important for island countries).

In addition to physical investments in ports and border crossings, countries need to ensure that policies and regulations related to transport nodes ensure efficient operation of the nodes and prevent unnecessary trips. Customs policies and regulations that limit the number of commodities that can be cleared at the port can create significant congestion inside the port, lowering its operational performance, as it does in Bangladesh (Herrera Dappe and others 2020). Land use policies that limit the development of container depots by the port or inland can lead to empty containers being transported back and forth from the port and limited use of containers for inland transportation, unnecessarily increasing the number of truck trips and congestion. Reforming such policies to reduce their impact on transport would reduce transport time and costs.

BOX 5.7

Reducing transport costs through port improvements: Lessons from Croatia and Viet Nam

Croatia

To improve the efficiency of the Port of Ploce, in Croatia, new bulk cargo and container and multipurpose terminals were constructed in the late 2000s, in addition to construction and rehabilitation of the supporting port infrastructure within the port area. As a result, gross bulk unloading crane productivity increased sevenfold between 2005 and 2014, and gross general cargo crane productivity increased by over 50 percent, reducing the time related costs at the port.

Viet Nam

The Cai Mep-Thi Vai marine terminal, first opened in 2009, significantly improved Viet Nam's maritime connectivity, allowing ocean carriers to offer direct services from Viet Nam to Europe and North America without the need to use feeder vessels for connections at regional transshipment hubs like Hong Kong SAR, China or Singapore. The elimination of feeder and transshipment costs is estimated to save about $150–$300 per 20-foot equivalent unit for containers shipped to and from Viet Nam.

Source: Blancas and others 2014; World Bank 2016a.

Interventions that improve the performance of border posts can have significant benefits. They include electronic customs processing systems, the strengthening and modernization of national customs departments, the harmonization of weighbridge policies among neighboring countries, electronic cargo tracking, and "green lanes" at border-crossing points (refer to box 5.8).

Noninfrastructure interventions at ports that can reduce costs and wait times include measures to enhance security for cargo, the establishment and operationalization of electronic "single-window" systems to speed up logistics and customs clearance procedures and reduce port dwell time, and the establishment of on-site customs and chamber of commerce offices that issue transit documents. Significant travel time and cost savings for the movement of cargo can also result from proper management of traffic in and around

---

BOX 5.8

Reducing border-crossing times: Lessons from Africa, North America, and Viet Nam

Africa

Countries in the East African Community have been using electronic cargo tracking systems for real-time tracking of shipments for several years. Most of the benefits of the reductions in delays and uncertainty have accrued to the coastal countries, Kenya and Tanzania, but the landlocked countries, Rwanda and Uganda, have also reaped benefits (Kunaka, Raballand, and Fitzmaurice 2016). In 2011, Rwanda implemented a customs-centered electronic single window system that reduced the time needed to clear goods from 11 to less than 2 days and reduced the cost of clearance by 83 percent (TMEA 2017). The Ghana National Single Window program reduced the time and cost of import procedures per consignment by 400 hours and $50, respectively (Arvis, Raballand, and Marteau 2010). In Côte d'Ivoire, automation of customs control based on the database of traders' risk profiles reduced the proportion of cargo subjected to physical inspection from 56 percent to 21 percent (World Bank 2016b), significantly reducing average border-crossing time.

North America

Radio frequency identification enabled lanes implemented on the US–Mexico border in 2009 to reduce congestion, improve toll efficiency, and add potential revenue streams. The program reduced vehicle inspection time from 35 to 10 seconds, saving labor costs (Lam, Sriram, and Khera 2019).

Viet Nam

In 2014, Viet Nam implemented a rules-based e-customs system to replace the paper-based clearance system that was reportedly prone to delays and subject to informal payments. As a result, the average times for import and export clearance were reduced by 18 percent and 58 percent, respectively (Lam, Sriram, and Khera 2019).

the port. For example, dedicated truck lanes have reduced road congestion around US ports (DOT and FHWA 2010), and truck appointment systems have reduced congestion at the port gate in several countries (Davies and Principal 2009).

Port digitization—including ensuring reliable internet access, implementation of port community systems, increased use of scanners, and general electronic systems innovations—can improve efficiency and reduce costs (refer to box 5.9). There is significant variability in the level of digitalization of ports across the regions of the world, reflecting different levels of maturity in adoption of the maritime single-window system and port community systems. For example, 83 percent of ports in East Asia but only about one in three ports in Central and South America, Southeast Asia, and Sub-Saharan Africa have a port community system (IAPH 2022).

Private sector operation of container port terminals can improve efficiency and reduce transport costs. Evidence from across the world points to an increase in total factor productivity associated with private sector operation (Estache, Gonzalez, and Trujillo 2002 for Mexico; Herrera Dappe and others 2024 for a global sample; Trujillo, Gonzalez, and Jimenez 2013 for Africa; Wanke and Barros 2015 for Brazil) and an increase in operational performance (Herrera Dappe and Suárez-Alemán 2016; refer to box 5.10). Herrera Dappe and others (2024) find that across the world, container ports with publicly operated terminals would become 7 percent more efficient in the use of their facilities on average if they were privately operated. This increase is associated with about 4 percent lower maritime shipping costs for shipments from a port with average technical efficiency.

BOX 5.9

Port digitalization in Africa

A 2007 protocol of cooperation between the customs authorities in Côte d'Ivoire and Ghana identified implementation of a port single-window system as likely to speed logistics and customs clearance procedures and reduce port dwell times. The computerized port single window (GUCE) was established in the Port of Abidjan using a public-private partnership. It resulted in 100 percent of cargo manifests being shared electronically through the single window and 100 percent of customs declarations being processed through GUCE, reducing transactions costs and cutting customs processing times.

In Tunisia, the World Bank supported policy actions to improve trade and logistics performance at the Port of Radès, including the streamlining of trade procedures for critical supply chains and digitization of international trade-related procedures. As a result, container dwell times at the port decreased from 18 days in 2019 to 16 days in 2021.

Source: World Bank 2019, 2021.

BOX 5.10

Improving port operations in East Asia and Sub-Saharan Africa

Indonesia

In the mid-2010s the government of Indonesia, with the support of the World Bank, granted concessions to operate ports in over 100 locations and integrated information from port operators with electronic systems in several ports. These actions resulted in a significant increase in the availability of container-handling equipment at the container ports and a reduction in the maximum ship waiting times between 2014 and 2018 from 24 to 2 hours at the Tanjung Priok Port and from 6.0 to 1.5 hours at the Makassar Port.

Madagascar

The container terminal at the Port of Toamasina, which handled about 80 percent of total container traffic in Madagascar, was concessioned in the mid-2000s. As of 2012, the concessionaire had invested about $60 million in infrastructure and equipment. Vessel productivity improved from 29 to 38 moves per hour between 2006 and 2011, and waiting time for ferries was reduced from 1 day to 1 hour between 2003 and 2008.

Mozambique

In the early 2000s, Mozambique sought large-scale involvement of the private sector in the operations and management of all the major ports in the country. Between 2001 and 2005, it granted concessions for the general cargo and container terminals at the ports of Beira, Maputo, and Nacala. Operational efficiency improved significantly as a result, with tons/ship/day increasing by 16 percent and 20-foot equivalent units/ship/day increasing by 43 percent between 1999 and 2008.

Source: World Bank 2009, 2013a, 2019.

Managing urban congestion

The transport of freight through urban areas is growing in importance, because most manufacturing goods are produced and consumed in cities. Urban congestion affects both the speed and the reliability of travel. Reliability may be of greatest concern to shippers; it should be monitored when implementing congestion management policies. Targeting travel time variability—unreliable and extremely variable travel times—and pain points in urban areas with the worst congestion can yield significant transport cost savings and reduce inventory costs.

Countries can tackle urban congestion with a range of policy options, ranging from supply-side policies to transport demand-management measures. Supply-side policies include the provision of road infrastructure such as urban bypasses, which route trucks around highly congested urbanized areas (refer to box 5.11); on-street parking management; and vehicle-related access restrictions and lane management. Transport demand management includes freight demand and land use management, pricing incentives (congestion charging), intelligent transportation systems, last-mile delivery practices, and measures that can shift personal travel to public transport.

BOX 5.11

Reducing urban transport times and costs: Lessons from Croatia, the Netherlands, and the United States

Croatia

In the early 2000s, Croatia's Port of Rijeka was an old industrial facility that stretched for several kilometers along the waterfront in the middle of the city, creating a barrier to the Adriatic. Port traffic passed through city streets, contributing to traffic congestion and increasing the cost of urban transport. Urban planning was difficult, because the port property was administered by the central government. Much of the prime potential waterfront area was occupied by dilapidated warehouses that were no longer suitable for modern port operations.

As part of port–city interface redevelopment in the first decade of the 21st century, a connecting road between Draga and Brajdica was constructed, linking the Rijeka bypass to the Port of Rijeka in order to reduce truck traffic through the congested city center. The Orehovic–Draga–Sv. Kuzam section was constructed to complete the western section of the Rijeka bypass, relieving traffic congestion and providing a through link for tourist traffic from Central Europe, Italy, and Slovenia to the Dalmatian coast. These targeted interventions resulted in significant mitigation of urban congestion, reducing total truck transit time through the city of Rijeka from 60 minutes to just 6 minutes between 2002 and 2012 (World Bank 2013b).

The Netherlands

In the Netherlands, the national government provided financial support for operators in 25 pilot cities in the late 2000s to invest in silent delivery equipment for night deliveries at supermarkets. Companies were estimated to save 30 percent in delivery costs and 25 percent in diesel consumption (Dablanc 2009).

United States

To reduce urban congestion and pollution, New York City's government ran a pilot scheme in 2009–10 to move urban freight delivery windows to nighttime hours by providing incentives to the freight-receiving companies. The participating businesses experienced significant savings thanks to the reduction in delays and parking tickets, higher travel speeds, and reduced fuel costs, and carriers found they could use a smaller fleet of vehicles.

Demand-side measures are likely to be necessary over the long term, given that most traditional congestion relief measures that either free up existing capacity or deliver new road capacity are likely to provide only temporary relief, as new road capacity is filled with suppressed demand, at least in economically dynamic cities.

Summary of recommendations for making places efficient

Table 5.2 summarizes ways policy makers can make places efficient.

TABLE 5.2 Recommendations for making places efficient

High-level action	Detailed actions
Develop adequate transport infrastructure	• Identify, appraise, and select all transport infrastructure investment projects together, as part of an integrated transport master plan based on robust appraisal methodologies. • Strengthen project implementation process, from procurement to monitoring of the physical and financial execution of projects. • Consistently apply all-weather and climate-resilient construction standards and axle-load limits. • Implement asset management systems to monitor the state of existing infrastructure, and ensure that maintenance needs are met on a timely basis, based on prespecified standards. • Create dedicated maintenance funds, such as road funds. Ensure that they are held to strict governance and transparency standards and that their accounts are fully reflected in the government's accounts. • Prepare sufficiently disaggregated rolling MTEFs to guide the annual budget process. Incorporate the projected maintenance costs of ongoing and approved new investment projects in the MTEF. • Develop the databases and staff capacities needed to implement investment projects and manage assets. • Implement a robust PPP preparation, procurement, and contract and fiscal management framework.
Improve the efficiency of ports and border crossings	• Invest in border-crossing and port infrastructure and superstructure based on an integrated transport master plan. • Implement policies and regulations, such as custom and land use policies, that promote efficient operation of transport nodes and prevent unnecessary trips. • Invest in port and border-crossing digitalization. • Encourage private sector participation in the port sector through the landlord model.
Manage urban congestion	• Implement supply-side measures, such as targeted infrastructure investments, on-street parking management, and vehicle-related access restrictions and lane management. • Implement demand management measures, such as freight demand and land use management, congestion pricing, intelligent transport systems, last-mile delivery practices, and mode shifts for passenger travel.

Source: Original table for this publication.
Note: MTEF = medium-term expenditure framework; PPP = public-private partnership.

NOTE

1. "Access to the profession" means holding a license of transport operator; "access to the market" means actually providing freight transport services.

REFERENCES

ADB (Asian Development Bank) 2020. *CAREC Corridor Performance Measurement and Monitoring Annual Report 2019*. Manila.

Allen, T., D. Atkin, S. Cantillo Cleves, and C.E. Hernández. 2024. "Trucks." Background paper prepared for this report.

Ardelean, A., and V. Lugovskyy 2023. "It Pays to Be Big: Price Discrimination in Maritime Shipping." *European Economic Review* 153.

Arvis, J.-F., G. Raballand, and J.-F. Marteau. 2010. *The Cost of Being Landlocked: Logistics Costs and Supply Chain Reliability*. Directions in Development. Washington, DC: World Bank.

Balboni, C. 2024. *In Harm's Way? Infrastructure Investments and the Persistence of Coastal Cities*. https://www.dropbox.com/scl/fi/qrx37phtzxu3954fcnu5v/in_harms_way.pdf?rlkey=cpyf1t9n24wnxfahayettdj4c&dl=0.

Blancas, L.C., C. Briceño-Garmendia, H.-S. Roh, and H. Vrenken. 2022. *Competing with Logistics Clusters: Vignettes from the International Experience*. Mobility and Transport Connectivity Series. Washington, DC: World Bank.

Blancas, L.C, J. Isbell, M. Isbell, H.J. Tan, and W. Tao. 2014. *Efficient Logistics: A Key to Vietnam's Competitiveness. Directions in Development*. Washington, DC: World Bank.

Combes, P.P., and M. Lafourcade. 2005. "Transport Costs: Measures, Determinants, and Regional Policy Implications for France." *Journal of Economic Geography* 5: 319–349.

Dablanc, L. 2009. *Freight Transport for Development Toolkit: Urban Freight*. Washington, DC: World Bank.

Davies, P., and D. Principal. 2009. "Container Terminal Reservation Systems." In *Proceedings of the Third Annual METRANS National Urban Freight Conference*, Long Beach, CA.

DOT (Department of Transportation), and FHWA (Federal Highway Administration). 2010. *Dedicated Truck Lanes Feasibility Study. Phase 1 Final Report: The Business Case for Dedicated Truck Lanes*, prepared for the Missouri, Illinois, and Ohio Departments of Transportation and the US Federal Highway Administration.

Dutz, M., A. Hayri, and P. Ibarra. 2000. "Regulatory Reform, Competition, and Innovation: A Case Study of the Mexican Road Freight Industry." Policy Research Working Paper 2318, World Bank, Washington, DC.

Engel, E., R. Fischer, and A. Galetovic. 2020. "When and How to Use Public-Private Partnerships in Infrastructure: Lessons from International Experience." NBER Working Paper 26766. National Bureau of Economic Research, Cambridge, MA.

Estache, A., M. Gonzalez, and L. Trujillo. 2002. "Efficiency Gains from Port Reform and the Potential for Yardstick Competition: Lessons from Mexico." *World Development* 30 (4): 545–60.

Fajgelbaum, P.D., and E. Schaal. 2020. "Optimal Transport Networks in Spatial Equilibrium." *Econometrica* 88 (4): 1141–52.

Heilmann, K. 2020. "Information Frictions, Load Matching, and Route Efficiency in the Trucking Industry." *SSRN Electronic Journal*. https://ssrn.com/abstract=3545019.

Herrera Dappe, M., V. Foster, A. Musacchio, T. Ter-Minassian, and B. Turkgulu. 2023. *Off the Books: Understanding and Mitigating the Fiscal Risks of Infrastructure*. Sustainable Infrastructure Series. Washington, DC: World Bank.

Herrera Dappe, M., C. Kunaka, M. Lebrand, and N. Weisskopf. 2020. *Moving Forward: Connectivity and Logistics to Sustain Bangladesh's Success*. Washington, DC: World Bank.

Herrera Dappe, M., T. Serebrisky, A. Suárez-Alemán, and B. Turkgulu. 2024. "Being Efficient Pays Off: The Case of Ports and Maritime Transport Costs Worldwide." World Bank, Washington, DC. Background paper prepared for this report.

Herrera Dappe, M., and A. Suárez-Alemán. 2016. *Competitiveness of South Asia's Container Ports: A Comprehensive Assessment of Performance, Drivers, and Costs*. Directions in Development. Washington, DC: World Bank.

IAPH (International Association of Ports and Harbors). 2022. *Closing the Gaps: Key Actions in Digitalization, Decarbonization, and Resilience in the Maritime Sector*. Tokyo.

Kim, J., J. A. Fallov, and S. Groom. 2020. *Public Investment Management Reference Guide*. International Development in Practice. Washington, DC: World Bank.

Kreindler, G., A. Gaduh, T. Graff, R. Hanna, and B.A. Olken. 2023. *Optimal Public Transportation Networks: Evidence from the World's Largest Bus Rapid Transit System in Jakarta*. https://drive.google.com/file/d/10wjoy8qpdt4dolyukvbihokp0wk_lnct/view.

Kunaka, C., G. Raballand, and M. Fitzmaurice. 2016. "How Trucking Services Have Improved and May Contribute to Economic Development." In *Industries without Smokestacks: Industrialization in Africa Reconsidered*, ed. R. Newfarmer and others, 133–50. Oxford: Oxford University Press.

Lafontaine, F., and L. Malaguzzi Valeri. 2009. "The Deregulation of International Trucking in the European Union: Form and Effect." *Journal of Regulatory Economics* 35: 19–44.

Lam, Y.Y., K. Sriram, and N. Khera. 2019. *Strengthening Vietnam's Trucking Sector: Towards Lower Logistics Costs and Greenhouse Gas Emissions*. Vietnam Transport Knowledge Series. Washington, DC: World Bank Group.

Mansell, G. 2001. "The Development of Online Freight Markets. *Logistics and Transport Focus* 3: 2–3.

Mwase, N. 2003. "The Liberalisation, De-Regulation and Privatisation of the Transport Sector in Sub-Saharan Africa: Experiences, Challenges and Opportunities." *Journal of African Economies* 12 (Suppl. 2): 153–92.

Ministerio de Transporte. 2020. *Transporte en cifras vigencia 2019*. Bogotá. https://www.mintransporte.gov.co/documentos/15/estadisticas/.

Perra, E., M. Sanfilippo, and A. Sundaram. 2022. "Roads, Competition, and the Informal Sector." Working Paper, Department of Economics and Statistics, Cognetti De Martiis Campus, Luigi Einaudi, Turin, Italy.

Posada, F., D.V. Wagner, G. Bansal, and R. Fernandez. 2015. *Survey of Best Practices in Reducing Emissions through Vehicle Replacement Programs*. International Council on Clean Transportation. Washington, DC.

SANRAL (South African National Roads Agency Limited) 2004. *Annual Report 2004: Sustainability Report*. Pretoria.

Stokenberga, A., and S. Ogita. 2021. "Anticipating Vehicle Traffic Increase on Improved Inter-Urban Roads: Evidence from Three Decades of Transport Projects in Developing Regions." *Transport Reviews* 41 (3): 285–303.

Teravaninthorn, S., and G. Raballand. 2009. *Transport Prices and Costs in Africa: A Review of the International Corridors*. Washington, DC: World Bank.

TMEA (Trademark East Africa). 2017. *TradeMark East Africa Annual Report 2016-2017*. Nairobi.

Trujillo, L., M.M. Gonzalez, and J.L. Jimenez. 2013. "An Overview on the Reform Process of African Ports." *Utilities Policy* 25: 12–22.

UNECE (United Nations Economic Commission for Europe). 2019. *Logistics and Transport Competitiveness in Kazakhstan*. Geneva.

Wanke, P.F., and C.P. Barros. 2015. "Public-Private Partnerships and Scale Efficiency in Brazilian Ports: Evidence from Two-Stage DEA Analysis." *Socio-Economic Planning Sciences* 51: 13–22.

Winston, C., T.M. Corsi, C.M. Grimm, and C.A. Evans. 1990. *The Economic Effects of Surface Freight Deregulation*. Washington, DC: Brookings Institution.

World Bank. 2009. *Railways and Ports Restructuring Project*. Implementation Completion and Results Report. Washington, DC: World Bank.

World Bank. 2013a. *Rijeka Gateway Project.* Implementation Completion and Results Report. Washington, DC: World Bank.

World Bank. 2013b. *Transport Infrastructure Investment Project.* Implementation Completion and Results Report. Washington, DC: World Bank.

World Bank. 2016a. *Trade and Transport Integration Project.* Implementation Completion and Results Report. Washington, DC: World Bank.

World Bank. 2016b. *Second Regional Trade Facilitation and Competitiveness Development Policy Loan to Burkina Faso and Côte d'Ivoire.* Washington, DC: World Bank.

World Bank. 2019. *Logistics Reform Development Policy Loan.* Implementation Completion and Results Report. Washington, DC: World Bank.

World Bank. 2020. *Trucking: A Performance Assessment Framework for Policymakers.* Washington, DC: Washington, DC: World Bank.

World Bank. 2021. *Tunisia First Resilience and Recovery Emergency Development Policy Financing.* Implementation Status and Results Report. Washington, DC: World Bank.

World Bank. 2023. *Northern Delta Transport Development Project.* Implementation Completion and Results Report. Washington, DC: World Bank.

World Bank, and IRU (International Road Transport Union). 2016. *Road Freight Transport Services Reform: Guiding Principles for Practitioners and Policy Makers.* Washington, DC: World Bank.

World Bank Group. 2018. *Promoting Open and Competitive Markets in Road Freight and Logistics Services.* Washington, DC: World Bank Group.

World Bank Group. 2024. *Disaster and Climate Resilient Transport Guidance Note.* Draft Version, February. Washington, DC: World Bank Group.

Ying, J.S. 1990. "The Inefficiency of Regulating a Competitive Industry: Productivity Gains in Trucking Following Reform." *Review of Economics and Statistics* 72 (2) 191–201.

Ying, J.S., and T.E. Keeler. 1991. "Pricing in a Deregulated Environment: The Motor Carrier Experience." *Rand Journal of Economics* 2 (2): 264–73.

Economic Implications of Policies to Reduce Economic Distance

MAIN MESSAGES

1. Reducing economic distance affects the levels and locations of investments by firms, the levels and patterns of trade and productivity, job creation, the structural composition of economic activity, workers' location decisions, and agglomeration, all of which help determine economic welfare, equity, and sustainability. These impacts can vary across space, firms, and households. There are potential tradeoffs and synergies across policy interventions and across economic outcomes.

2. The appraisal of policies to reduce the economic distance needs to start with a clear understanding of the main problem the policy aims to address and the key market failures and policy-driven frictions that warrant a government intervention. It is key to properly identify and quantify the effects, differentiating between creation and relocation of economic activity. Doing so and considering potential tradeoffs and synergies requires understanding the mechanisms at work—that is, the theory of change from intervention to changes in transport prices, costs, and reliability and changes in intermediate and wider economic outcomes.

INTRODUCTION

Policies that foster efficient, high-quality transport bring people and firms closer to each other and affect economic outcomes that need to be considered when appraising interventions to maximize their net benefits. Transport costs affect the levels and locations of investments by firms, the levels and patterns of trade and productivity, job creation, and the structural composition of economic activity. These outcomes—together with the impact of transport costs on the prices of land, assets, goods, and nontransport services—affect workers' location decisions and agglomeration (refer to figure 6.1). Through these intermediate outcomes, changes in transport costs lead to changes in the levels and distribution of income, affecting economic welfare and equity. Transport costs also affect sustainability, particularly environmental quality (through emissions and deforestation, for example).

Policies to make markets and places efficient can have heterogeneous effects on transport costs across space, households, and firms (as discussed in chapter 5); they can also affect intermediate and wider economic outcomes. There are also potential tradeoffs and synergies across policy interventions in terms of their effects on economic outcomes. These heterogenous effects, tradeoffs, and synergies need to be considered when appraising interventions to maximize their net benefits.

This chapter aims to help policy makers design and appraise policies to reduce economic distance by making markets and places more efficient by examining the economic impacts of policy interventions, the mechanisms behind the impacts, and the evidence on them. The chapter is organized as follows. The first section examines intermediate outcomes. The second section examines wider economic outcomes. The third section examines heterogeneous effects, tradeoffs, and synergies of policies. The fourth section provides guidelines for appraising policies to achieve efficient, high-quality transport.

FIGURE 6.1 Theory of change of transport interventions to reduce economic distance

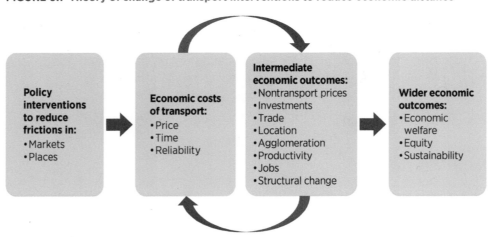

Source: Original figure for this publication.

INTERMEDIATE OUTCOMES

Transport interventions affect trade, location decisions by firms and households, investments, clustering, productivity, jobs and their sectoral distribution, and nontransport prices.

Trade

A reduction in transport costs may stimulate trade volumes and affect the patterns of trade. The decrease in international transport costs was a major driver of the increase in international trade since 1950 (Hummels 2007). The construction of the Panama and Suez canals led to significant increases in trade. Their closure would lead to an estimated reduction in global trade of 3.0–3.5 percent (and close to 30 percent in some regions) (Brancaccio, Kalouptsidi, and Papageorgiou 2020). A reduction in maritime transport costs because of improvement in port efficiency boosts competitiveness and expands trade. Improving port efficiency from the 25th to 75th percentiles would reduce shipping costs and increase exports to the United States by around 22 percent, according to Clark, Dollar, and Micco (2004).

The reduction in international transport costs played an important role in inducing manufacturers to extend production processes beyond national borders, allowing countries to participate in global value chains (GVCs) (World Bank 2020). GVCs use transport more intensively than other types of trade, as parts and components are shipped to a country only to be shipped out after assembly, making GVCs more sensitive to transport frictions than other types of trade.

Interventions that reduce land transport time, unreliability, and costs promote trade. Lower uncertainty in border clearance times for imports translates into higher survival rates for manufacturing exporters (Vijil, Wagner, and Woldemichael 2019). A one-day decrease in overland travel time leads to a 7 percent increase in Africa's exports (Freund and Rocha 2011). Simulations suggest that upgrading the primary road network connecting major cities would increase trade within Sub-Saharan Africa by $250 billion over 5 years (Buys, Deichmann, and Wheeler 2010). In Peru, a road improvement program led to a 3.8 percent increase in firms' average annual growth rate of exports (Volpe Martincus, Carballo, and Cusolito 2017). For Indonesian manufacturing firms, higher road density in a firm's province and in neighboring provinces increases the probability of exporting their goods (Rodríguez-Pose and others 2013). In Türkiye, transportation-intensive industries displayed higher trade growth in regions with above-average improvements in connectivity between 2003 and 2012 (Coşar and Demir 2016).

Interventions that reduce domestic transport costs not only affect international trade, they also affect domestic trade. Expansion of the railways in colonial India (which corresponds to contemporary Bangladesh, India, and Pakistan) decreased trade costs, increasing interregional and international trade (Donaldson 2018). Reductions in the road distance between cities increase trade between them. In Colombia, the elasticity of trade with respect to distance is around –0.60 (Duranton 2015); in the United States it is between –1.63 and –1.91 for weight and between –1.17 and –1.41 for value (Duranton, Morrow and Turner 2014). In Colombia, a 10 percent increase in major roads within a city is associated with about a 2–4 percent increase in exports to other cities. Roads shift economic activity in Colombian cities at the extensive margin toward goods that are tradable and goods that are lighter. In the United States, a 10 percent increase in highways within a city causes about a 5 percent increase in the weight of its exports. Highways in the United States are found to affect trade at the intensive margin and foster the weight of exports but not their value (Duranton, Morrow, and Turner 2014). Reductions in transport costs increase trade. In India a 1 percent reduction in trucking unit costs is associated with a 2.8–3.9 increase in domestic trade flows (Lall, Sinha-Roy, and Shilpi 2022).

Firms' and households' location decisions, clustering, and productivity effects

A transport improvement can make a place either more or less attractive for firms. Firms' location decisions depend on market access, access to firms that are sources of intermediate inputs, competition in markets for their output, and production costs. A reduction in transport costs both improves access to export markets and opens the local market to import competition. When transport costs are high, a reduction makes a location more attractive even if production costs are high; when transport costs are low, a reduction in transport costs increases the importance of production costs on firms' location decisions, potentially making a place less attractive for firms.

A reduction in transport costs increases productivity by promoting the clustering of activity. Lower transport costs make places closer together, increasing the productivity benefits of proximity and agglomeration. Lower transport costs may also trigger investments in the form of firms moving into a cluster of activity, further increasing agglomeration and raising productivity. A major intercity road investment in India (the Golden Quadrilateral) caused higher entry rates of manufacturing firms near improved highways, productivity growth for incumbent firms, adjustments in the spatial sorting of industries, and improved allocative efficiency in the manufacturing industries initially located along the improved highways (Ghani, Goswami, and Kerr 2016). Firms located near the improved highways reduced their inventory holding time after the improvements, an indication that they were being run more efficiently (Datta 2012). In Indonesia, improvements to the highway system during the 1990s led to the clustering of perishable goods production and dispersion of durable manufacturing activities (Rothenberg 2013).

Transport improvements support the specialization of cities and regions. The construction of the Chinese National Trunk Highway System promoted the specialization of centrally located prefectures on manufacturing and the specialization of the hinterland on agriculture (Baum-Snow and others 2020).

Railways can facilitate the movement of industrial production out of city centers, freeing up space for activities such as tradable services, which benefit more from agglomeration spillovers, yielding productivity gains.

Improvements in land transportation also drive migration, particularly within countries, as there are fewer constraints than between countries, potentially favoring larger cities over smaller cities. Access to jobs; wages; the prices of land, goods, and service; and amenities that affect the quality of life determine people's locations decisions. A 10 percent increase in market access induces a 0.8–1.3 percent increase in the population of African cities on average over the following 30 years (Jedwab and Storeygard 2022). In China, a 10 percent increase in roads within 450 km of a prefecture city is associated with a 1.1 percent increase in the population of the largest city and a 1.7 percent reduction in the population in secondary cities (Baum-Snow and others 2020).

Different types of infrastructure can have different effects, however. In China, each radial highway displaced 4 percent of the city center population to surrounding regions, and ring roads displaced an additional 20 percent, with stronger effects on the richer coastal and central regions (Baum-Snow and others 2017). In the United States, a single interstate highway causes about 9 percent of the population of a city to decentralize (Baum-Snow 2007). A reduction in transport costs can also decrease the likelihood of migration. In Tanzania, a road quality improvement decreased the probability of migrating from a rural location by 7.2 percent on average (Gachassin 2013), likely because of the associated increase in per capita consumption.

Transport improvements, particularly through infrastructure investments, can have long-term effects that need to be considered when designing policies. In Africa, railways had large effects on the distribution of economic activity during the colonial period, through creation of economic activity rather than just a spatial reorganization of prior economic activity; these effects persist to this day, even though the original railways collapsed (Jedwab and Moradi 2016). Once a cluster is established it creates a productivity advantage, which might not be possible to overcome over time. Firms and people might fear forgoing the benefits of their location and be uncertain about the benefits of other locations.

Not only trunk but also tertiary infrastructure supports productivity growth. In Sub-Saharan Africa, a 10 percent decrease in travel time from a local crop production location to a nearby city of more than 25,000 people increases local crop production by 23 percent in the long run (Dorosh and others 2012). Rural road infrastructure improvements in southwestern Kenya increase agricultural productivity and market participation by rural smallholder farmers (Kiprona and Matsumoto 2018).

Jobs and structural transformation

The increase in trade and investments and the productivity effects of a reduction in transport costs can create jobs. Increased market access because of road improvements in Mexico during 1986–2014 led to increases in local employment. A 10 percent increase in market access resulted in a 2.9–6.5 percent increase in employment (Blankespoor and others 2017). In Peru, road improvements caused an increase in exports, which accounted for 4 percent of the net new jobs that exports created in 2003–10 (Volpe Martincus, Carballo, and Cusolito 2017). In China, in prefectures that are 443 kilometers away from the coast (the median distance from the coast across prefectures), industry employment is 17 percent lower than in coastal prefectures for an industry with an average export-revenue ratio and 13 percent for an industry with average labor intensity. This negative distance gradient is stronger for export-oriented industries (Coşar and Fajgelbaum 2016).

Reduced transport costs may also lead to a shift of production and labor away from the agricultural sector. In Ethiopia, all-weather road access alone increased services employment, at the expense of manufacturing, and bundled road access with electrification increased manufacturing employment at the expense of agriculture (Moneke 2020). In Cameroon, Chad, Djibouti, Ethiopia, Kenya, Nigeria, and Somalia, investments in paved roads and electricity increased manufacturing and services employment at the expense of agricultural employment (Herrera Dappe and Lebrand 2024). In Indonesia, improved road quality increased employment in the manufacturing sector and triggered a shift from agriculture to manufacturing (Gertler and others 2014). In Georgia and Viet Nam, rural road construction fostered the emergence of rural enterprises and new nonfarm activities (Lokshin and Yemtsov 2005; Mu and van de Walle 2011). In India, new all-weather rural roads triggered a shift from farm to nonfarm employment, particularly nonfarm employment outside the village (Asher and Novosad 2020; Herrera Dappe, Alam, and Andres 2021), and the share of people with primary employment outside their village increased by 35 percent (Herrera Dappe, Alam, and Andres 2021).

Nontransport prices

A reduction in transport costs can reduce the price of goods and their variation across space. In the Democratic Republic of Congo, food price dispersion between products and across regions is significantly related to transport cost differentials (Minten and Kyle 1999). A road rehabilitation program in Sierra Leone led to reductions in transport costs and prices of the two main domestically produced staples (rice and cassava) along the affected corridors (Casaburi, Glennerster, and Suri 2013). Expansion of the railways in colonial India decreased trade costs and interregional price dispersion (Donaldson 2018).

A reduction in transport costs can also increase land values, reflecting the better connectivity and profitability of land. Expansion of the railways in colonial India to the average district caused a 16 percent increase in land rents in that district (Donaldson 2018). In the United States, expansion of the railway network between 1870 and 1890 led to an increase in the value of agricultural land. A 1 percent increase in market access increased land values by approximately 0.51 percent, suggesting that removing all railways in 1890 would have decreased the total value of agricultural land by 60 percent (Donaldson and

Hornbeck 2016). In 17th and 18th century England, parishes served by toll roads experienced an 11–30 percent increase in land rents (Bogart 2009).

WIDER ECONOMIC OUTCOMES

Transport interventions affect economic welfare, equity, and sustainability.

Economic welfare and equity

Reductions in transport costs raise production and incomes and lower prices. In colonial India, the increased trade and lower interregional price dispersion caused by expansion of the railways led to an increase in real agricultural income in connected districts (Donaldson 2018). During the two decades after China opened to trade and market reforms, regions closer to historical transportation networks had higher levels of GDP per capita than regions farther from the network (Banerjee, Duflo, and Qian 2020). The Chinese National Trunk Highway System, built mostly between the 1990s and 2000s, enhanced intra-national trade, leading to an increase in aggregate real income (Roberts and others 2012). In Sub-Saharan African countries where the largest city is a port, a 10 percent reduction in transport costs can lead to a 2.8 percent increase in income for cities that are 500 kilometers from the port (Storeygard 2016).

Firms' and people's location decisions in response to a reduction in transport costs can lead to changes in local GDP. The relocation of industrial production caused by the reduction in transport costs because of railways' investments in China led to a reduction in industrial GDP in city centers, cheaper housing, and higher real wages (Baum-Snow and others 2017). Construction of highways led to a reduction in local GDP growth in peripheral areas between connected metropolitan centers along the way relative to peripheral areas not connected by the highways (Faber 2014). The effect seems to have been driven by a reduction in industrial output growth, which might be a result of the relocation of economic activity.

Reduced transport costs as a result of road investments can have pro-competitive effects on both input and output markets. The clustering of manufacturing activity as a result of lower transport costs helped reduce the monopsony power of Indian firms in labor markets among firms near newly constructed highways relative to firms far from highways. The resulting effect was an increase in labor's share of income of around 2 percentage points (Brooks and others 2021). On average, expansion and improvement of the Colombian road network reduced travel times by 17–18 percent between 2015 and 2020, reducing markups in the trucking sector by 3 percent and increasing welfare by 3 percent (Allen and others 2024).

A reduction of transport costs can have significant welfare and equity implications in rural areas. Investments in last-mile connectivity in rural areas have been found to increase household income (Jacoby and Minten 2009;

Kebede 2021) and consumption (Emran and Hou 2013; Khandker, Bakht, and Koolwal 2009; Nakamura, Bundervoet, and Nuru 2020). Better access to both domestic and international markets has positive effects on per capita income, with the domestic market effect larger (Emran and Hou 2013). Reductions in transport costs in rural areas can reduce poverty (Dercon and others 2009; Khandker, Bakht, and Koolwal 2009). The impacts on inequality are nuanced. In Nepal, for example, rural roads improved the welfare of poor rural households, but they did not reduce inequality (Jacoby 2000). Rural roads can improve resilience to severe droughts, reducing the probability of falling into poverty (Nakamura, Bundervoet, and Nuru 2020).

Reductions in transport costs through improved road connectivity can affect households' opportunity costs of human capital investments, which affects the economic welfare and equity of younger generations. Better transport infrastructure may reduce students' travel costs to school, improving attendance (Adukia, Asher, and Novosad 2020; Aggarwal 2018; Herrera Dappe, Alam, and Andres 2021; Jacoby and Minten 2009; Khandker, Bakht, and Koolwal 2009) and educational performance (Adukia, Asher, and Novosad 2020). Reduced transport costs also expose students to more immediate job opportunities, however, potentially incentivizing students, particularly high school students, to drop out to join the labor market (Aggarwal 2018; Li, Zhao, and Teng 2019).

Interventions that reduce transport cost for cargo and people can affect health outcomes. Improved road access can have a positive impact on the use of preventative health care services (antenatal care, delivery assisted by trained health personnel, modern contraception, health insurance, and water treatment) by women and households in rural areas (Banerjee and Sachdeva 2015; Herrera Dappe, Alam, and Andres 2021). In Africa, improved transport access has been found to reduce food security problems, improving rural household nutrition (Blimpo, Harding, and Wantchekon 2013; Stifel and Minten 2017). By enabling internal trade, the railways in India improved food security, dramatically limiting the ability of rainfall shocks to cause famines in the colonial era (Burgess and Donaldson 2010).

Sustainability

Policies aimed at alleviating the frictions keeping transport time and cost high can either reduce or increase the social costs of transport. Social costs include the negative externalities from congestion, air pollution, the easier spread of epidemics, and accidents and direct costs from environmental impacts such as deforestation, biodiversity loss, and more generally degradation of ecosystems.

Congestion contributes to air pollution through vehicle emissions. Policies aimed at reducing congestion can reduce both the private and social costs of transport. Investments in urban transport, such as subway systems, have been shown to reduce congestion (Gu and others 2021; Yang and others 2018) and improve air quality (Chen and Whalley 2012; Gendron-Carrier and others 2022) in urban areas, which are important sources of frictions keeping transport times and costs high.

In contrast, highway expansion, which is usually put forward as a potential intervention to reduce congestion, has been shown not to decrease and even to increase congestion and pollution in developed countries (Duranton and Turner 2011; Hsu and Zhang 2014), as the increase in road capacity increases traffic by stimulating commercial traffic and inducing people to drive more. Whether these findings apply to developing countries, where the stock of transport infrastructure is underdeveloped, needs to be researched but should be considered when designing policies.

Policies aimed at promoting the development of efficient transport service providers and demand aggregation and matching and reducing waiting times at ports and border crossings reduce emissions. The use of bigger trucks and reductions in empty and less than full truckload trips reduce the number of trips needed to transport a given amount of cargo and hence emissions from road transport (Rizet, Cruz, and Mbacké 2012). Use of more fuel-efficient trucks and more efficient driving practices also reduces emissions from road transport (Collier and others 2019; Díaz-Ramirez and others 2017; Walnum and Simonsen 2015). Trucks lining up at sea and land ports spend significant time idling; improving the efficiency of ports therefore reduces emissions.

Transport can help spread infectious diseases through the movement of people, including transport service workers, labor influx for the construction and operation of infrastructure, and passengers. Short-term migration of workers away from homes and families increases opportunities for sexual relationships with multiple partners, transforming transport routes into critical links in the propagation of HIV/AIDS, with long-haul truck drivers the highest-risk group in the road sector (Regondi, George, and Pillay 2013; World Bank 2004). The spread of COVID-19 was linked to the movements of people, particularly to the frequencies of high-speed train services and flights (Lau and others 2020; Zhang, Zhang, and Wang 2020).

Interventions to reduce transport costs and times through an increase in travel speed can increase road fatalities and injuries. Globally, two-thirds of road traffic deaths occur among people of working age (18–59). Ninety-two percent of traffic deaths occur in low- and middle-income countries, with the risk of death three times higher in low-income than in high-income countries (WHO 2023).

Transport infrastructure may disturb the ecosystem; measures therefore need to reduce its social costs. Land proprietors' decisions to clear forests are highly sensitive to market access, land opportunity values, official protection status, soil quality, and topography. Road building facilitates access to markets and thus raises the probability that forests will be cleared for agriculture, especially near the forest fringe (Chomitz and Gray 1996; Cropper, Puri, and Griffiths 2001; Damania and Wheeler 2015). Some species suffer heavy mortality near roads from vehicle roadkill, increased predation, and hunting. A large proportion of species in tropical forests avoid clearings or forest edges; roads and railways therefore create barriers to faunal movements (Laurance, Goosem, and Laurance 2009).

HETEROGENEOUS EFFECTS, TRADEOFFS, AND SYNERGIES OF POLICIES

Policies that make markets and places efficient are very likely to yield highly heterogenous outcomes across space. Reducing entry costs to remote areas through connectivity improvements may lead to relocation of truckers, reducing transport prices in those areas but increasing prices in other areas, where the supply of truckers declines. For example, average trucking prices in Colombia decreased by over 6 percent for shipments to some provinces as a result of the improvement of the road network, but prices on more central routes rose (refer to map 6.1), as truckers reallocated to more remote routes, reducing competition on more central routes and raising prices there (Allen and others 2024).

MAP 6.1 Changes in prices paid to truckers in Colombia for nonagricultural shipments as a result of road improvements

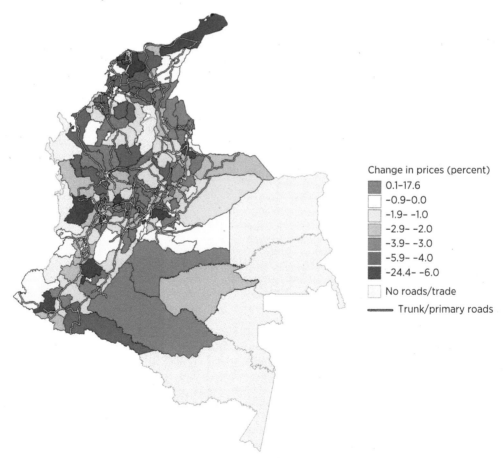

Change in prices (percent)
- 0.1–17.6
- −0.9–0.0
- −1.9– −1.0
- −2.9– −2.0
- −3.9– −3.0
- −5.9– −4.0
- −24.4– −6.0
- No roads/trade
- Trunk/primary roads

Source: Original map for this publication based on Allen and others 2024.
Note: Data are for 2015–21.

Changes in economic geography brought about by transport improvements that result in relocation of economic activity lead to some places winning and others losing, even if aggregate welfare increases. For example, the construction of the Chinese National Trunk Highway System increased real income across prefectures by about 4 percent on average, but it reduced real wages in many prefectures (Roberts and others 2012). Economic output and population increased in the largest city at the expense of other cities in a region (Baum-Snow and others 2020). Road improvements in Mexico had heterogeneous effects across sectors, with employment in commerce and services benefiting more than manufacturing (Blankespoor and others 2017).

The impact depends on the characteristics of the locations being affected. The impact of the rapid expansion of the Brazilian road network from the 1960s to the 2000s on population and economic activity was stronger up to 200 kilometers around cities and for areas with good amenities and a high share of nonagricultural GDP than it was elsewhere (Bird and Straub 2020). The effects of transportation investments on the population of African cities over the longer term varies substantially depending on the context. They are smaller for larger and less isolated cities, more politically favored constituencies, more agriculturally suitable areas, and foreign rather than domestic markets (Jedwab and Storeygard 2022). The Golden Quadrilateral highways in India led to a stronger growth in manufacturing activity in districts within 10 kilometers of the highways than in districts 10–50 kilometers from the network (Ghani, Goswani, and Kerr 2016). The impacts of improvements in rural road infrastructure on crop prices in rural markets in Sierra Leone were largest in the markets farthest away from main urban centers (Casaburi, Glennerster, and Suri 2013).

Several studies assess the potential economic impacts of proposed policies on places and markets, identifying the aggregate and heterogenous effects across locations and sectors. Bird, Lebrand, and Venables (2020) and Lall and Lebrand (2020) examine the impacts of proposed investments under the Belt and Road Initiative, identifying cities and regions that gain and those that lose in Central Asia and China as a result of the infrastructure investments. Other studies look at proposed transport investments in West Africa (Lebrand 2021) and the Horn of Africa and Lake Chad region (Herrera Dappe and Lebrand 2024). Herrera Dappe and Lebrand (2024) identify the regions gaining and losing economic activity and the heterogeneous effects across economic sectors. Herrera Dappe, Lebrand, and Van Patten (2021) assess the impact of liberalizing cross-border trucking services between Bangladesh and India. They show that national real income would increase significantly as result of the liberalization (by up to 16.6 percent in Bangladesh and 7.6 percent in India). However, some states in India might experience reductions in real income, and spatial wage inequality would decrease.

Policies focused on places and markets can have different impacts across space, even if they have the same average effect on transport costs.

In Bangladesh, for example, a reduction in dwell times at Chittagong Port that lead to the same reduction in transport costs as a set of policies to increase competition in trucking services, crack down on facilitation payments, and better match supply and demand of trucking services to reduce empty trips can have significantly different spatial impacts (refer to map 6.2). Market-focused policies increase economic activity in more districts than does a reduction in port dwell times (a place-focused policy). Market-focused policies increase the concentration of employment slightly more in Greater Dhaka than a place-focused policy and decrease it in Chittagong. Western districts increase their share of employment, thanks to market-focused policies (refer to map 6.2, panels a and c). Market policies leverage the comparative advantage of districts more than port-centric policies. Gains in real wages are slightly greater at the district level under market policies than under port-centric policies. The spatial pattern of real wage gains is different in the market-focused policy scenario than in the place-focused scenario, with workers in most districts far from Chittagong Port enjoying larger increases in real wages than workers in Chittagong and districts closer to it in the market-focused scenario (refer to map 6.2, panels b and c).

Policies that make markets efficient can yield heterogenous outcomes across firms. Policies that increase competition may benefit some shippers and hurt others. When the cost of obtaining and analyzing carriers' quotes is nontrivial and higher for smaller shippers who do not have as strong bargaining power as larger shippers, carriers may price-discriminate based on size, causing smaller shippers to face higher shipping rates. Reducing market power in the shipping sector may amplify informational friction distortion and price discrimination in the importing sectors, hurting smaller importers (Ardelean and Lugovskyy 2023).

Policy makers face potential tradeoffs when designing policies to reduce transport costs, partly because of the heterogenous outcomes of some policies. There is a potential tradeoff between efficiency and equity: Policies that yield the highest economic return by promoting various efficiency gains through higher productivity and less factor misallocation may increase inequalities across space and groups of people; policies generating lower returns might be more beneficial to the poor and people in disadvantaged locations (Lall, Schroeder, and Schmidt 2014; Roberts and others 2019). Another important tradeoff may arise between economic welfare and environmental quality. For example, policies that expand market access increase trade and income but may also increase deforestation.

There are also potential synergies of policies. There are synergies between policies to increase competition in trucking and investments in road infrastructure, as better infrastructure may increase competition in remote routes. There are also synergies between economic welfare and equity, with reductions in transport costs yielding productivity gains and investments, increasing wages, and creating new jobs in areas with unemployment.

MAP 6.2 **District-level changes in employment and real wages associated with a one-day reduction in dwell times at Chittagong Port and market policies in Bangladesh**

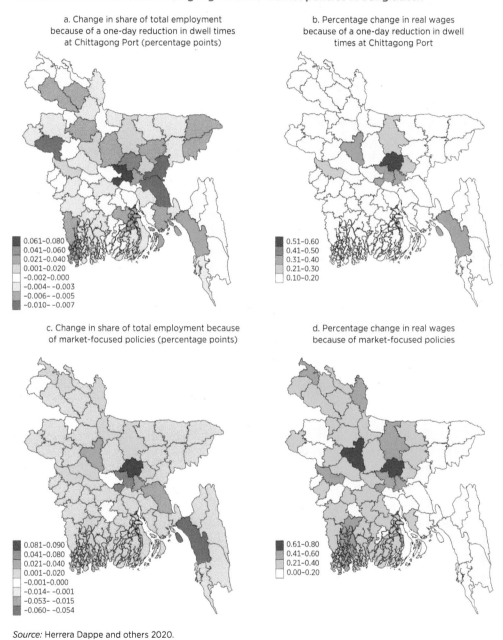

a. Change in share of total employment because of a one-day reduction in dwell times at Chittagong Port (percentage points)

0.061–0.080
0.041–0.060
0.021–0.040
0.001–0.020
−0.002–0.000
−0.004– −0.003
−0.006– −0.005
−0.010– −0.007

b. Percentage change in real wages because of a one-day reduction in dwell times at Chittagong Port

0.51–0.60
0.41–0.50
0.31–0.40
0.21–0.30
0.10–0.20

c. Change in share of total employment because of market-focused policies (percentage points)

0.081–0.090
0.041–0.080
0.021–0.040
0.001–0.020
−0.001–0.000
−0.014– −0.001
−0.053– −0.015
−0.060– −0.054

d. Percentage change in real wages because of market-focused policies

0.61–0.80
0.41–0.60
0.21–0.40
0.00–0.20

Source: Herrera Dappe and others 2020.

GUIDELINES FOR APPRAISING POLICIES

The discussion of the economic implications of policies to make markets and places efficient reveals the complexity of assessing them. Appraisal of a policy needs to start with a clear understanding of the main problem the policy aims to address and the identification of key market failures and policy-driven frictions that warrant a government intervention (refer to figure 6.2). Policy makers then need to quantify the effects, estimating and valuing the changes in employment, output, or other outcomes of interest (Duranton and Venables 2018; Laird and Venables 2017).

When establishing the quantity changes, the analyst should separate direct and indirect effects. Direct effects are the savings in travel time and vehicle operating costs that lead to reductions in the economic costs of transport and resulting changes in travel patterns. The social value of these changes is usually referred to as user benefits. Indirect effects are the changes in investments, employment, output, and other outcomes from the induced changes in private sector behavior. The analyst should differentiate between aggregate quantity changes and relocation of economic activity between places (Duranton and Venables 2018).

When valuing quantity changes, the analyst should clearly identify why the changes caused by the policy are of net social value, distinguishing

FIGURE 6.2 Key steps and considerations in appraising transport interventions

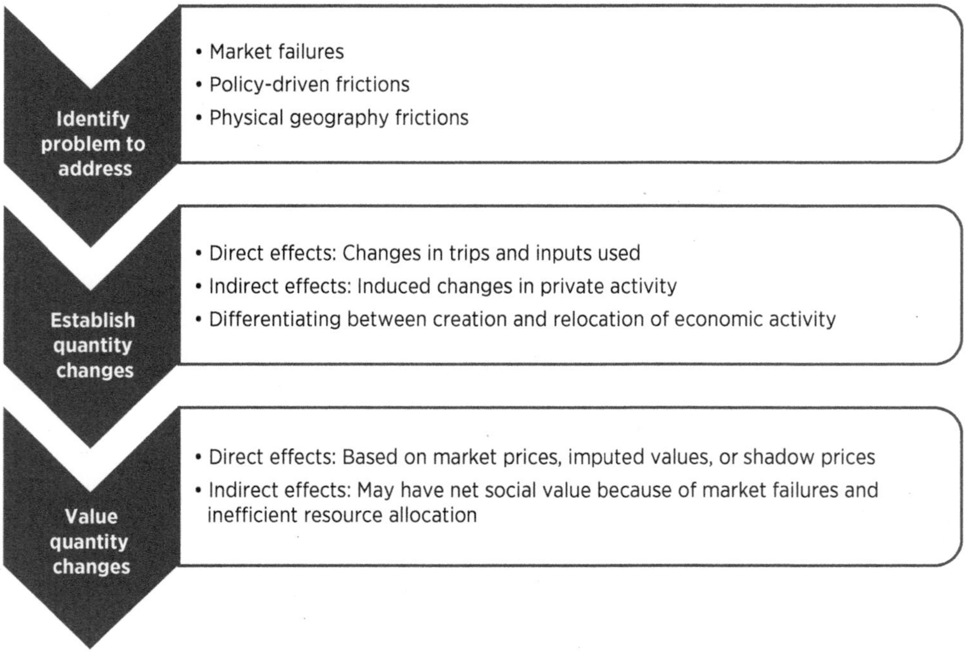

Identify problem to address
- Market failures
- Policy-driven frictions
- Physical geography frictions

Establish quantity changes
- Direct effects: Changes in trips and inputs used
- Indirect effects: Induced changes in private activity
- Differentiating between creation and relocation of economic activity

Value quantity changes
- Direct effects: Based on market prices, imputed values, or shadow prices
- Indirect effects: May have net social value because of market failures and inefficient resource allocation

Source: Original figure for this publication based on Duranton and Venables 2018.

between direct and indirect effects. Direct effects are valued using market and shadow prices and imputed values, as part of standard cost–benefit analysis. Indirect effects may be of net social value because of market failures and inefficient resource allocation. The induced private investments may create some positive externalities (for example, productivity gains from agglomeration) and negative externalities (for example, increased air pollution). The private sector may hire unemployed or underemployed workers, or the induced investments may be made by firms with some degree of market power in input markets, resulting in a difference between the private and social value of the investments (Duranton and Venables 2018).

A comprehensive appraisal of transport policies should assess equity, safety, and environmental implications. Spatial general equilibrium models are useful for assessing the implications of spatial equity. They can be complemented with studies of the potential distributional impacts of policies on different groups of households and firms. Studies of the safety and environmental implications of policies can complement a spatial general equilibrium model.

A challenge analysts and policy makers will face with a collection of studies assessing different effects is how to weigh their findings. One way to deal with the problem is to develop complex computable general equilibrium models covering all relevant aspects. Their complexity goes against a key principle of appraisals—transparency—however. When the mechanisms underpinning the findings of the appraisal are hard to understand, it becomes challenging to get stakeholders to support the proposed policy and creates fertile ground for vested interests to challenge the appraisal and proposed policy. The approach followed should therefore balance comprehensiveness with clarity.

REFERENCES

Adukia, A., S. Asher, and P. Novosad. 2020. "Educational Investment Responses to Economic Opportunity: Evidence from Indian Road Construction." *American Economic Journal: Applied Economics* 12 (1): 348–76.

Aggarwal, S. 2018. "Do Rural Roads Create Pathways out of Poverty? Evidence from India." *Journal of Economic Development* 133: 375–95.

Allen, T., D. Atkin, S. Cantillo Cleves, and C.E. Hernández. 2024. "Trucks." Background paper prepared for this report.

Ardelean, A., and V. Lugovskyy 2023. "It Pays to Be Big: Price Discrimination in Maritime Shipping." *European Economic Review* 153.

Asher, S., and P. Novosad. 2020. "Rural Roads and Local Economic Development." *American Economic Review* 110 (3): 797–823.

Banerjee, A., E. Duflo, and N. Qian. 2020. "On the Road: Access to Transportation Infrastructure and Economic Growth in China." *Journal of Development Economics* 145: 102442.

Banerjee, R., and A. Sachdeva. 2015. "Pathways to Preventive Health: Evidence from India's Rural Road Program." Research Paper 15–19, Dornsife Institute for New Economic Thinking, University of Southern California, Los Angeles.

Baum-Snow, N. 2007. "Did Highways Cause Suburbanization?" *Quarterly Journal of Economics* 122 (2): 775–805.

Baum-Snow, N., L. Brandt, J. V. Henderson, M. A. Turner, and Q. Zhang. 2017. "Roads, Railroads, and Decentralization of Chinese Cities." *Review of Economics and Statistics* 99 (3): 435–48.

Baum-Snow, N., J. V. Henderson, M. A. Turner, Q. Zhang, and L. Brandt. 2020. "Does Investment in National Highways Help or Hurt Hinterland City Growth?" *Journal of Urban Economics* 115: 103124.

Bird, J., M. Lebrand, and A. J. Venables. 2020. "The Belt and Road Initiative: Reshaping Economic Geography in Central Asia?" *Journal of Development Economics* 144: 102441.

Bird, J., and S. Straub. 2020. "The Brasília Experiment: The Heterogeneous Impact of Road Access on Spatial Development in Brazil." *World Development* 127: 104739.

Blankespoor, B., T. Bougna, R. Garduno-Rivera, and H. Selod. 2017. "Roads and the Geography of Economic Activities in Mexico." Policy Research Working Paper 8226, World Bank, Washington, DC.

Blimpo, M. P., R. Harding, and L. Wantchekon. 2013. "Public Investment in Rural Infrastructure: Some Political Economy Considerations." *Journal of African Economies* 22 (Suppl. 2): ii57–ii83.

Bogart, D. 2009. "Turnpike Trusts and Property Income: New Evidence on the Effects of Transport Improvements and Legislation in Eighteenth-Century England." *Economic History Review* 62 (1): 128–52.

Brancaccio, G., M. Kalouptsidi, and T. Papageorgiou. 2020. "Geography, Transportation, and Endogenous Trade Costs." *Econometrica* 88 (2): 657–91.

Brooks, W., J. P. Kaboski, I. O. Kondo, Y. A. Li, and W. Qian. 2021. "Infrastructure Investment and Labor Monopsony Power." NBER Working Paper 28977, National Bureau of Economic Research, Cambridge, MA.

Burgess, R., and D. Donaldson. 2010. "Can Openness Mitigate the Effects of Weather Shocks? Evidence from India's Famine Era." *American Economic Review* 100 (2): 449–53.

Buys, P., U. Deichmann, and D. Wheeler. 2010. "Road Network Upgrading and Overland Trade Expansion in Sub-Saharan Africa." *Journal of African Economies* 19 (3): 399–432.

Casaburi, L., R. Glennerster, and T. Suri. 2013. "Rural Roads and Intermediated Trade: Regression Discontinuity Evidence from Sierra Leone." *SSRN Electronic Journal*.

Chen, Y., and A. Whalley. 2012. "Green Infrastructure: The Effects of Urban Rail Transit on Air Quality." *American Economic Journal: Economic Policy* 4 (1): 58–97.

Chomitz, K.M., and D.A. Gray. 1996. "Roads, Land Use, and Deforestation." *World Bank Economic Review* 10 (3): 487–512.

Clark, X., D. Dollar, and A. Micco. 2004. "Port Efficiency, Maritime Transport Costs, and Bilateral Trade." *Journal of Development Economics* 75 (2): 417–50.

Collier, S., C. Ruehl, S. Yoon, K. Boriboonsomsin, T.D. Durbin, G. Scora, K. Johnson, and J. Herner. 2019. "Impact of Heavy-Duty Diesel Truck Activity on Fuel Consumption and Its Implication for the Reduction of Greenhouse Gas Emissions." *Transportation Research Record* 2673 (3): 125–35.

Coşar, A.K., and B. Demir. 2016. "Domestic Road Infrastructure and International Trade: Evidence from Turkey." *Journal of Development Economics* 118: 232–44.

Coşar A. K., and P. D. Fajgelbaum. 2016. "Internal Geography, International Trade, and Regional Specialization." *American Economic Journal: Microeconomics* 8 (1): 24–56.

Cropper, M., J. Puri, and C. Griffiths. 2001. "Predicting the Location of Deforestation: The Role of Roads and Protected Areas in North Thailand." *Land Economics* 77 (2): 172–86.

Damania, R., and D. Wheeler. 2015. "Road Improvement and Deforestation in the Congo Basin Countries." Policy Research Working Paper 7274, World Bank, Washington, DC.

Datta, S. 2012. "The Impact of Improved Highways on Indian Firms." *Journal of Development Economics* 99 (1): 46–57.

Dercon, S., D.O. Gilligan, J. Hoddinott, and T. Woldehanna. 2009. "The Impact of Agricultural Extension and Roads on Poverty and Consumption Growth in Fifteen Ethiopian Villages." CSAE Working Paper 2007–01, Centre for the Study of African Economies, Oxford University, Oxford.

Díaz-Ramirez, J., N. Giraldo-Peralta, D. Flórez-Ceron, V. Rangel, C. Mejía-Argueta, J.I. Huertas, and M. Bernal. 2017. "Eco-Driving Key Factors That Influence Fuel Consumption in Heavy-Truck Fleets: A Colombian Case." *Transportation Research Part D: Transport and Environment* 56: 258–70.

Donaldson, D. 2018. "Railroads of the Raj: Estimating the Impact of Transportation Infrastructure." *American Economic Review* 108 (4–5): 899–934.

Donaldson, D., and R. Hornbeck. 2016. "Railroads and American Economic Growth: A 'Market Access' Approach." *Quarterly Journal of Economics* 131 (2): 799–858.

Dorosh, P., H. G. Wang, L. You, and E. Schmidt. 2012. "Road Connectivity, Population, and Crop Production in Sub-Saharan Africa." *Agricultural Economics* 43 (1): 89–103.

Duranton, G. 2015. "Roads and Trade in Colombia." *Economics of Transportation* 4 (1–2): 16–36.

Duranton, G., P. M. Morrow, and M.A. Turner. 2014. "Roads and Trade: Evidence from the US." *Review of Economic Studies* 81 (2): 681–724.

Duranton, G., and M.A. Turner. 2011. "The Fundamental Law of Road Congestion: Evidence from US Cities." *American Economic Review* 101(6): 2616–52.

Duranton, G., and A. J. Venables. 2018. "Place-Based Policies for Development." Policy Research Working Paper 8410, World Bank, Washington, DC.

Emran, M.S., and Z. Hou. 2013. "Access to Markets and Rural Poverty: Evidence from Household Consumption in China." *Review of Economics and Statistics* 95 (2): 682–97.

Faber, B. 2014. "Trade Integration, Market Size, and Industrialization: Evidence from China's National Trunk Highway System." *Review of Economic Studies* 81 (3): 1046–70.

Freund, C., and N. Rocha. 2011. "What Constrains Africa's Exports?" *World Bank Economic Review* 25 (3): 361–86.

Gachassin, C. M. 2013. "Should I Stay or Should I Go? The Role of Roads in Migration Decisions." *Journal of African Economies* 22 (5): 796–826.

Gendron-Carrier, N., M. Gonzalez-Navarro, S. Polloni, and M.A. Turner. 2022. "Subways and Urban Air Pollution." *American Economic Journal: Applied Economics* 14 (1): 164–96.

Gertler, P. J., M. Gonzalez-Navarro, T. Gracner, and A.D. Rothenberg. 2014. "The Role of Road Quality Investments on Economic Activity and Welfare: Evidence from Indonesia's Highways." Unpublished manuscript. https://sites.bu.edu/neudc/files/2014/10/paper_250.pdf.

Ghani, E., A.G. Goswami, and W.R. Kerr. 2016. "Highway to Success: The Impact of the Golden Quadrilateral Project for the Location and Performance of Indian Manufacturing." *Economic Journal* 126 (591): 317–57.

Gu, Y., C. Jiang, J. Zhang, and B. Zou. 2021. "Subways and Road Congestion." *American Economic Journal: Applied Economics* 13 (2): 83–115.

Herrera Dappe, M., M.M. Alam, and L. Andres. 2021. *The Road to Opportunities in Rural India: The Economic and Social Impacts of PMGSY.* Mobility and Transport Connectivity Series. Washington, DC: World Bank.

Herrera Dappe, M., C. Kunaka, M. Lebrand, and N. Weisskopf. 2020. *Moving Forward: Connectivity and Logistics to Sustain Bangladesh's Success.* Washington, DC: World Bank.

Herrera Dappe, M., and M. Lebrand. 2024. "Infrastructure and Structural Change in Africa." *World Bank Economic Review.*

Herrera Dappe, M., M. Lebrand, and D. Van Patten. 2021. "Bridging Bangladesh and India: Cross–Border Trade and the Motor Vehicles Agreement." Policy Research Working Paper 9592, World Bank, Washington, DC.

Hsu, W.-T., and H. Zhang. 2014. "The Fundamental Law of Highway Congestion Revisited: Evidence from National Expressways in Japan." *Journal of Urban Economics* 81: 65–76.

Hummels, D. 2007. "Transportation Costs and International Trade in the Second Era of Globalization." *Journal of Economic Perspectives* 21: 131154.

Jacoby, H.G. 2000. "Access to Markets and the Benefits of Rural Roads." *Economic Journal* 110: 713–37.

Jacoby, H.G., and B. Minten. 2009. "On Measuring the Benefits of Lower Transport Costs." *Journal of Development Economics* 89 (1): 28–38.

Jedwab, R., and A. Moradi. 2016. "The Permanent Effects of Transportation Revolutions in Poor Countries: Evidence from Africa." *Review of Economics and Statistics* 98 (2): 268–84.

Jedwab, R., and A. Storeygard. 2022. "The Average and Heterogeneous Effects of Transportation Investments: Evidence from Sub-Saharan Africa 1960–2010." *Journal of the European Economic Association* 20 (1): 1–38.

Kebede, H.A. 2021. "The Gains from Market Integration: The Welfare Effects of New Rural Roads in Ethiopia." *SSRN Electronic Journal.*

Khandker, S.R., Z. Bakht, and G.B. Koolwal. 2009. "The Poverty Impact of Rural Roads: Evidence from Bangladesh." *Economic Development and Cultural Change* 57 (4): 685–722.

Kiprono, P., and T. Matsumoto. 2018. "Roads and Farming: The Effect of Infrastructure Improvement on Agricultural Intensification in South-Western Kenya." *Agrekon* 57(3–4): 198–220.

Lall, S., and M. Lebrand. 2020. "Who Wins, Who Loses? Understanding the Spatially Differentiated Effects of the Belt and Road Initiative." *Journal of Development Economics* 146: 102496.

Lall, S. V., E. Schroeder, and E. Schmidt. 2014. "Identifying Spatial Efficiency–Equity Trade-Offs in Territorial Development Policies: Evidence from Uganda." *Journal of Development Studies* 50 (12): 1717–33.

Lall, S., S. Sinha-Roy, and F. Shilpi. 2022. "Trucking Costs and the Margins of Internal Trade: Evidence from a Trucking Portal in India." Policy Research Working Paper 10059, World Bank, Washington, DC.

Laird, J., and A.J. Venables. 2017. "Transport Investment and Economic Performance: A Framework for Project Appraisal." *Transport Policy* 56: 1–11.

Lau, H., V. Khosrawipour, P. Kocbach, A. Mikolajczyk, H. Ichii, M. Zacharski, J. Bania, and T. Khosrawipour. 2020. "The Association between International and Domestic Air Traffic and the Coronavirus (Covid-19) Outbreak." *Journal of Microbiology, Immunology and Infection* 53: 467–72.

Laurance, W.F., M. Goosem, and S.G.W. Laurance. 2009. "Impacts of Roads and Linear Clearings on Tropical Forests." *Trends in Ecology & Evolution* 24 (12): 659–69.

Lebrand, M. 2021. "Corridors without Borders in West Africa." Policy Research Working Paper 9855, World Bank, Washington, DC.

Li, H., G. Zhao, and Z. Teng. 2019. "Highway Access and Human Capital Investments in the Rural Regions of the People's Republic of China." Asian Development Bank Institute Working Paper Series. Beijing.

Lokshin, M., and R. Yemtsov. 2005. "Has Rural Infrastructure Rehabilitation in Georgia Helped the Poor?" *World Bank Economic Review* 19: 311–33.

Minten, B., and S. Kyle. 1999. "The Effect of Distance and Road Quality on Food Collection, Marketing Margins, and Traders' Wages: Evidence from the Former Zaire." *Journal of Development Economics* 60 (2): 467–95.

Moneke, N. 2020. "Can Big Push Infrastructure Unlock Development? Evidence from Ethiopia." Working paper. https://niclasmoneke.com/wp-content/uploads /Moneke-JMP-Big_Push_Infrastructure.pdf.

Mu, R., and D. van de Walle. 2011. "Rural Roads and Local Market Development in Vietnam." *Journal of Development Studies* 47 (5): 709–34.

Nakamura, S., T. Bundervoet, and M. Nuru. 2020. "Rural Roads, Poverty, and Resilience: Evidence from Ethiopia." *Journal of Development Studies* 56 (10): 1838–55.

Regondi, I., G. George, and N. Pillay. 2013. "HIV/AIDS in the Transport Sector of Southern Africa: Operational Challenges, Research Gaps and Policy Recommendations." *Development Southern Africa* 30 (4–5): 616–28.

Rizet, C., C. Cruz, and M. Mbacké. 2012. "Reducing Freight Transport CO_2 Emissions by Increasing the Load Factor." *Procedia–Social and Behavioral Sciences* 48: 184–95.

Roberts, M., U. Deichmann, B. Fingleton, and T. Shi. 2012. "Evaluating China's Road to Prosperity: A New Economic Geography Approach." *Regional Science and Urban Economics* 42 (4): 580–94.

Roberts, M., M. Melecky, T. Bougna, and Y. Xu. 2019. "Transport Corridors and Their Wider Economic Benefits: A Quantitative Review of the Literature." *Journal of Regional Science* 60: 207–48.

Rodríguez-Pose, A., V. Tselios, D. Winkler, and T. Farole. 2013. "Geography and the Determinants of Firm Exports in Indonesia." *World Development* 44 (April): 225–40.

Rothenberg, A. 2013. "Transport Infrastructure and Firm Location Choice in Equilibrium: Evidence from Indonesia's Highways." Working paper. https://www.dropbox.com/s/zul4ud9sc1ogzae/RoadsFirmLocations_JMP.pdf?raw=1.

Stifel, D., and B. Minten. 2017. "Market Access, Welfare, and Nutrition: Evidence from Ethiopia." *World Development* 90: 229–41.

Storeygard, A. 2016. "Farther on Down the Road: Transport Costs, Trade and Urban Growth in Sub-Saharan Africa." *Review of Economic Studies* 83 (3): 1263–95.

Vijil, M., L. Wagner, and M.T. Woldemichael. 2019. "Import Uncertainty and Export Dynamics." Policy Research Working Paper 8793, World Bank, Washington, DC.

Volpe Martincus, C., J. Carballo, and A. Cusolito. 2017. "Roads, Exports and Employment: Evidence from a Developing Country." *Journal of Development Economics* 125: 21–39.

Walnum, H.J., and M. Simonsen. 2015. "Does Driving Behavior Matter? An Analysis of Fuel Consumption Data from Heavy-Duty Trucks." *Transportation Research Part D: Transport and Environment* 36: 107–20.

WHO (World Health Organization). 2023. *Global Status Report on Road Safety*. Geneva.

World Bank. 2004. "Taming HIV/AIDS on Africa's Roads." Africa Transport Technical Note 35, Washington, DC.

World Bank. 2020. *World Development Report 2020: Trading for Development in the Age of Global Value Chains*. Washington, DC: World Bank.

Yang, J., S. Chen, P. Qin, F. Lu, and A. A. Liu. 2018. "The Effect of Subway Expansions on Vehicle Congestion: Evidence from Beijing." *Journal of Environmental Economics and Management* 88: 114–33.

Zhang, Y., A. Zhang, and J. Wang. 2020. "Exploring the Roles of High-Speed Train, Air and Coach Services in the Spread of Covid-19 in China." *Transport Policy* 94: 34–42.

APPENDIX A
Datasets

INTRODUCTION

The research for this report is based on several novel datasets, described in this appendix.

DATASET ON RETAIL PRICES IN AFRICA AND EASTERN EUROPE

Díaz de Astarloa and Pkhikidze (2024) use unit-level price data and apply the price differential methodology to estimate within-country trade costs in six low- and middle-income countries (Georgia, Kenya, Madagascar, Nigeria, Rwanda, and Tanzania). The dataset includes unit-level price data collected by countries' national statistical offices for consumer price index calculation purposes that include the monthly price quote, product description, in some cases the brand and presentation, the location where the price information was collected, and the locations where the product was produced or imported. Prices are at the town or city level, except for Rwanda, where prices are at the district level.

The number of products ranges from 9 in Madagascar to 43 in Rwanda. The number of locations at which the price was collected (markets, cities, or districts) ranges from 6 in Georgia to 38 in Nigeria. Except for the Nigerian sample, which starts in January 2001, all samples start after January 2010. The longest panel is for Madagascar (January 2010–April 2021); the shortest is for Kenya (October 2018–January 2022).

GLOBAL DATASET ON CONTRACTS FOR SHIPPING FOOD

Herrera Dappe, Lebrand, and others (2024) use a global dataset on contracts for shipping food to study the determinants of trucking rates, including shipment characteristics, distance, topography, economic geography, infrastructure, and conflict. It covers 60 low- and middle-income countries in which an international organization delivered food aid in 2019 and part of 2020 (refer to map A.1). The data span all World Bank regions but

MAP A.1 Countries included in the dataset on contracts for shipping food and number of routes connecting origins and destinations in each country

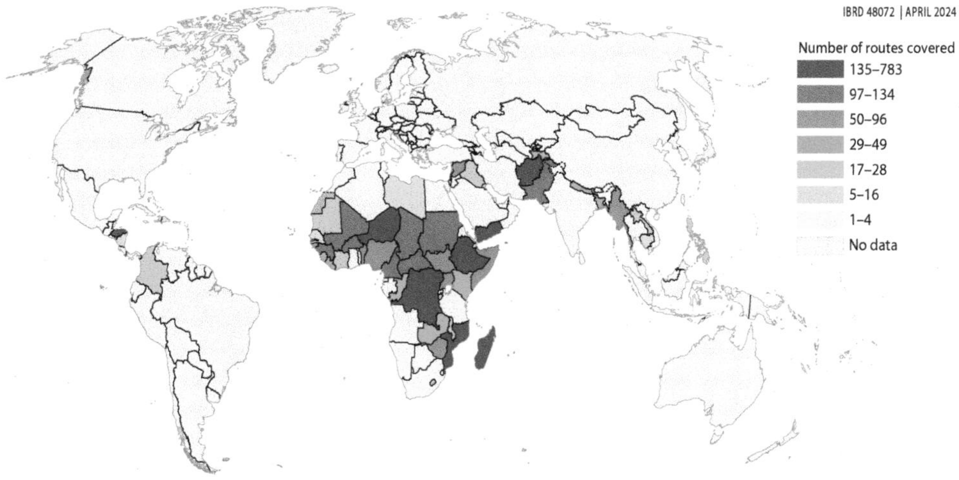

IBRD 48072 | APRIL 2024

Number of routes covered
- 135–783
- 97–134
- 50–96
- 29–49
- 17–28
- 5–16
- 1–4
- No data

Source: Original map for this publication.

has wider coverage of Africa. The data cover all 16 countries with high- or medium-intensity conflict according to the World Bank's 2020 List of Fragile and Conflict-Affected Situations as well as 10 countries with high institutional and social fragility.

The unit of observation is a shipment, where each shipment is associated with exactly one order. About 70 percent of all orders in the dataset deliver aid to destinations in Sub-Saharan Africa. Most of the analysis focuses on within-country shipments by road. The final sample consists of 53,106 domestic shipments and 6,750 shipments that cross an international land border.

The domestic shipments in the sample were transported between 600 origins and 2,856 destination cities. The destination city size ranges widely, with an interquartile range of 10,000–71,000 people. The origin and destination cities capture a wide variety in terms of economic activity, as proxied by nighttime lights intensity, food and nonfood crop production, mean precipitation, and other characteristics. About 38 percent of the destinations and 52 percent of the origins experienced conflict in their direct vicinity, based on Armed Conflict Location and Event Data (ACLED).

For each shipment, the least-cost route between its origin and destination was calculated using Mapbox Directions API, resulting in a total of 4,988 different routes, about 95 percent of which are between cities within the same country. A few countries, such as the Democratic Republic of Congo, Honduras, Mozambique, and the Republic of Yemen, have several hundred domestic routes. For each shipment, the database includes information on the first dispatch date, which indicates whether the shipment was transported during any part of the country's rainy season.

DATASETS ON INDIA

Molnar and Shilpi (2024) use a dataset of spot freight transactions and a dataset with road infrastructure characteristics from India to study the determinants of trucking rates, including shipment characteristics; distance; topography; urban congestion; road infrastructure characteristics, including whether roads are delivered by public-private partnerships (PPPs); and competition.

The freight transactions dataset consists of confidential transaction-level data on trucking from a logistics company in India for the period March 2017–March 2020. The almost 480,000 freight transactions records include the spot rate paid by shippers; the type of goods transported; truck characteristics, including length and capacity; and the coordinates for pick-up and drop-off. The data cover more than 8.7 million metric tons of cargo shipped over 70,300 (address-level) origin–destination pairs, with 6,889 unique origins and 8,932 unique destinations across all Indian states and union territories (except island territories).

The road infrastructure dataset consists of a spatial and routable inventory of major road projects in India that focuses on three major categories of roads: National Highways Development Project roads under the Golden Quadrilateral and North–South/East–West corridor programs, PPP roads, and access-controlled expressways. The dataset includes the locations and actual or estimated fees for 1,328 toll plazas.

The spatial inventory of PPP roads was built by merging the World Bank's Private Participation in Infrastructure (PPI) database with a database of PPP projects provided by the Department of Economic Affairs in the Ministry of Finance of the Government of India. The merging of the two data sources resulted in 667 road infrastructure PPPs constructed through January 1, 2018, of which 343 (45,777 km) were present in both databases, 245 (24,058 km) were present in the government of India database only, 64 (6,422 km) were present in the World Bank PPI database only, and 15 (1,712 km) were present in neither and were identified through supplementary research of government documentation.

DATASET ON PRICES PAID TO TRUCKERS IN COLOMBIA

Allen and others (2024) use a rich dataset of trucking prices paid to truckers to study the effect of market structure on trucking prices. It contains highly granular shipment-level data on the universe of legally registered nonagricultural shipments in Colombia between 2015 and 2021 (excluding 2018), which total 50 million trips. The dataset includes the complete history of shipments made by every truck in the country. For each individual shipment the data include the origin, destination, approximate start date, and truck's license plate. It includes truck characteristics and information on the truck owners from the National Registry of Trucks as well as data from the

Ministry of Transport on the average freight rate paid to the truck owner and the total quantity transported across these shipments, aggregated at the origin × destination × date × truck type (that is, number of axles) level. The data cover more than 590 million metric tons of cargo shipped over 112,469 origin–destination pairs, with 1,087 unique origins and 1,096 unique destinations across 1,122 municipalities (refer to map A.2).

MAP A.2 Number of trips by trucks in Colombia, by destination municipality, 2021

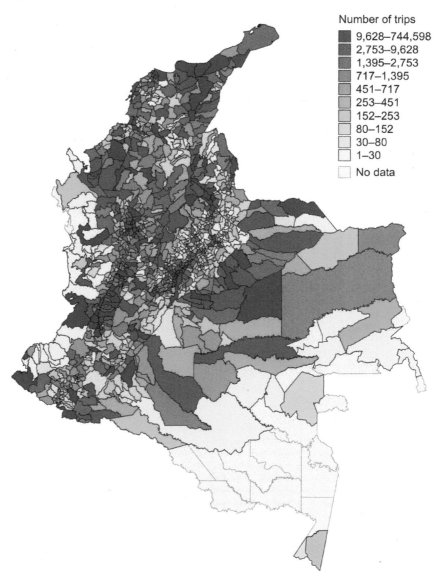

Source: Original map for this publication based on Allen and others 2024.

DATASET ON TRUCKING COSTS IN EASTERN EUROPE AND CENTRAL ASIA

Iimi (2023) studies the determinants of trucking (carrier) costs using a large dataset of shipments across Eastern European and Central Asian countries, looking at shipment characteristics, geography, infrastructure, economies of scale, and borders. The data come from the Central Asia Regional Economic Cooperation Corridor Performance Measurement and Monitoring database collected by the Asian Development Bank. The data used cover seven countries in Eastern Europe and Central Asia: Azerbaijan, Georgia, Kazakhstan, the Kyrgyz Republic, Tajikistan, Turkmenistan, and Uzbekistan. It contains 51,137 long-haul road shipments by 8,952 carriers across 397 locations.

The database, which is developed at the stop-by-stop level, includes distance, average speed, freight volume, and trucking costs for each shipment. Trucking costs include the vehicle operating cost—including the driver's wage, fuel cost, depreciation cost of the truck or trailer, repair and maintenance cost, and insurance—and (official and unofficial) payments made at intermediate stops, such as border-crossing and traffic police checkpoints.

The data cover wide variety of commodities and goods, which are classified into five groups in addition to empty cargo: agricultural commodities and food products; clothing, apparel and textile; consumption and other goods; equipment (including vehicles); and minerals, metals and materials.

GLOBAL DATASET ON TRAVEL SPEED AND TIME

Akbar and others (2024) investigate the speed and reliability of intercity road travel in 134 countries. They leverage a novel dataset of speed and travel time to compute indices of speed, reliability, congestion, and speed heterogeneity and relate them to attributes of the roads and local geography. The dataset covers nearly 15 million instances of trips connecting cities in 134 countries (refer to map A.3) of different income levels and across all World Bank regions. It includes 44 countries in Europe and Central Asia, 40 in Sub-Saharan Africa, 20 in Latin America and the Caribbean, 14 in the Middle East and North Africa, 11 in East Asia and Pacific, 4 in South Asia, and 1 in North America. The cities connected by the trips have populations of at least 50,000. The data cover 242,833 road segments in the 134 countries.

Akbar and others (2024) describe the sampling methodology and data collection methodology that was developed to create the database. The data collected were contrasted with GPS data from trucks in four low- and middle-income countries, as well as traffic sensors and web-mapping services in high-income countries.

MAP A.3 Countries included in the global dataset on travel speed and time

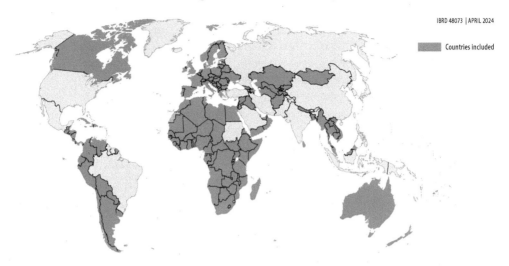

Source: Original map for this publication.

GLOBAL DATASETS ON CONTAINER PORTS AND MARITIME SHIPPING COSTS

Herrera Dappe, Serebrisky, and others (2024) study the role of port performance as a determinant of maritime shipping costs across the globe using various measures of performance, including the World Bank's Container Port Performance Index and a measure of technical efficiency estimated by the authors. Their study uses detailed data on over 250 container ports in 97 countries and close to 2 million observations on maritime shipping costs to the United States.

The container ports dataset includes data on port facilities (berths, cranes, terminal area); traffic; terminal operators; and maritime connectivity on 286 ports in 87 countries. The data come from S&P Global Market Intelligence; port authority and operator websites; trade and news publications; Google Earth; MDS Transmodal; and Notteboom, Pallis and Rodrigue (2022). They are complemented by the World Bank's Container Port Performance Index for 259 ports in 66 countries, bringing the coverage to 97 countries (refer to map A.4).

The data on container maritime shipping costs are from the US Census Bureau. The dataset includes almost 2 million observations on monthly maritime imports—including the shipping mode, cost, weight, and value—from each country to each district with a port in the United States at the Harmonized System 10 product level.

MAP A.4 Countries included in the dataset on port performance

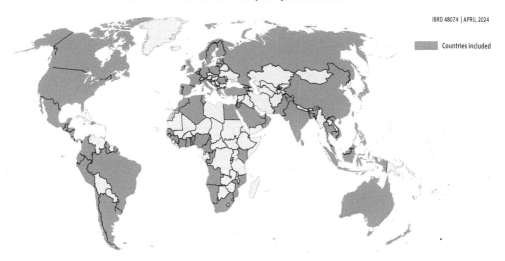

IBRD 48074 | APRIL 2024

Countries included

Source: Original map for this publication.

REFERENCES

Akbar, P.A., V. Couture, G. Duranton, L. Fan, and A. Storeygard. 2024. "Around the World in 24 Days? The Speed of Intercity Road Travel." World Bank, Washington, DC. Background paper prepared for this report.

Allen, T., D. Atkin, S. Cantillo Cleves, and C.E. Hernández. 2024. "Trucks." Background paper prepared for this report.

Díaz de Astarloa, B., and N. Pkhikidze. 2024. "Internal Trade Costs in Developing Countries." Policy Research Working Paper 10789, World Bank, Washington, DC. Background paper prepared for this report.

Herrera Dappe, M., M. Lebrand, B. Rowberry, and A. Stokenberga. 2024. "Moving Goods: Road Transport Costs in Developing Countries." World Bank, Washington, DC. Background paper prepared for this report.

Herrera Dappe, M., T. Serebrisky, A. Suárez-Alemán, and B. Turkgulu. 2024. "Being Efficient Pays Off: The Case of Ports and Maritime Transport Costs Worldwide." World Bank, Washington, DC. Background paper prepared for this report.

Iimi, A. 2023. "Estimating Road Freight Transport Costs in Eastern Europe and Central Asia Using Large Shipping Data." Policy Research Working Paper 10533, World Bank, Washington, DC. Background paper prepared for this report.

Molnar, A., and F. Shilpi. 2024. "Urban and Infrastructure Determinants of Freight Cost in India." World Bank, Washington, DC. Background paper prepared for this report.

Notteboom, T., A. Pallis, and J.-P. Rodrigue. 2022. *Port Economics, Management and Policy.* New York: Routledge.

Methods for Measuring Overland Transport Costs

INTRODUCTION

Transport cost measures should have three properties (Combes and Lafourcade 2005): Reflect the itinerary chosen between the origin and the destination; be specific to the mode of transport used; and be specific to commodity groups with distinct unit weight and volume characteristics.

Three methods are used to measure and quantify transport costs: survey-based methods, imputation-based methods, and estimation-based methods.[1]

SURVEY-BASED METHODS

The best method for measuring a phenomenon is to collect direct quantitative data about it. Collection of high-quality survey data requires well-established sampling and stratification procedures on the universe of shippers or carriers in a country. In Canada, the Trucking Commodity Origin and Destination Survey has collected information on the for-hire trucking industry since 1994, targeting trucking companies with at least one establishment and a minimum annual revenue of about $1 million. High-quality surveys like this one are rare. Examples of survey-based data on trucking costs in low- and middle-income countries include Teravaninthorn and Raballand (2009) for Africa; Herrera Dappe and others (2020) for Bangladesh; Osborne, Pachon, and Araya (2014) for international trade corridors in Central America; and Lam, Sriram, and Khera (2019) for Viet Nam. Practitioners and researchers often combine datasets on truck fleets and trade flows within countries to get a picture of road transportation.

IMPUTATION-BASED METHODS

Calculating unit costs for any economic activity is challenging when there are fixed and joint costs. Even if direct information on carriers' self-reported costs is available, one can be skeptical about the degree to which the information captures true underlying costs. It is therefore common practice in economics to estimate unit costs assuming that producers minimize costs. If there are data on key cost components such as driver wages (which can be proxied by other low-skilled occupational wages), fuel, and vehicle depreciation, a cost minimization routine can be used to impute optimal itineraries and associated costs.

The increased availability and diffusion of Geographic Information System (GIS) data have enabled researchers to calculate least-cost routing decisions and associated transit times. The starting point is a digitized transportation network. Information about travel speed along each link helps calculate fastest routes and associated travel times between nodes. Recent examples of studies that rely on GIS data include Bird, Lebrand, and Venables (2020); de Soyres and others (2019); and Lall and Lebrand (2020), who study the impacts of transport investments associated with the Belt and Road Initiative. Herrera Dappe, Lebrand, and Van Patten (2021) apply this methodology to regional trade between Bangladesh and India. Formulating the relevant cost minimization problem, however, requires making assumptions on how carriers operate. Do they choose the fastest or the shortest routes? How willing are they to pay tolls if doing so reduces travel distance and duration?

New GPS technologies allow actual itineraries and trip times to be observed, obviating the need to calculate routing and travel times. Hernández (2021) uses tracking data from GPS devices located in trucks operating in Colombia. Such GPS data may not be readily available for researchers and practitioners. Therefore, node-to-node least-cost path calculations remain the most viable option for a wide range of applications.

Allen and Arkolakis (2014) and Donaldson and Hornbeck (2016) impute domestic transport costs. Using the fast-marching algorithm on a detailed map of the transport network across continental US counties, together with information on trade flows from the Commodity Flow Survey, Allen and Arkolakis (2014) embed a mode-specific transport cost minimization to the estimation of general trade costs. Donaldson and Hornbeck (2016) focus on transportation costs alone to analyze the impact of railroads on the US economy in the 19th century.

ESTIMATION-BASED METHODS: THE GRAVITY APPROACH

Imputation-based methods can predict monetary shipping costs across hypothetical routes; they cannot reveal how these costs affect shipping demand and trade between locations. A gravity approach can be used to identify the impacts of distance, time, or costs on trade flows.

Empirical studies of trade have long established that bilateral exports between countries or regions within countries are proportional to their economic size and inversely proportional to the distance between them. The fundamental equation for estimating a gravity model to explain trade flows X_{od} between origin o and destination d is $\ln(X_{od}) = \gamma_o + \gamma_d + \sigma \cdot \ln(\tau_{od}) + \epsilon_o,$

where σ is the elasticity of trade-to-trade costs $\tau_{od} \geq 1$. Origin and destination fixed effects, γ, control for size and productivity differences across locations. If trade costs (TC_{od}) are already specified in monetary terms, one can directly use $\tau_{od} = TC_{od}$. Otherwise, a functional form should be used to transform travel distance or travel time to trade costs.

The minimal data needed for this estimation are trade flows between locations within a country. Ideally, these locations should be spatially disaggregated, so that most flows are across regions for which one can construct fine measures of distance or travel time. High-quality data on domestic trade flows typically exists in high- and some middle-income countries. These are compiled from various sources. Some are from specialized surveys, such as the Commodity Flow Survey in the United States or the *Encuesta Origen–Destino a Vehiculos de Carga* in Colombia. In most low- and middle-income countries, comprehensive domestic trade flow data may not be available. A number of countries have made available administrative databases that contain information about firm-to-firm transactions, however. Although such transactions are not direct evidence for cargo shipments, they inform researchers about trade flows between locations.

ESTIMATION-BASED METHODS: THE PRICE DIFFERENTIAL APPROACH

Spatial price gaps are informative about trade costs. Suppose the price of a good in location o is p_o, and its price in location d is p_d. Assuming that there is a competitive trading sector, researchers invoke the following condition to estimate transport costs between locations o and d, t_{od}: $p_d = p_o + t_{od}$.

The first challenge is obtaining prices of identical goods. The prevalence of bar-code level scanner price datasets has enabled researchers to circumvent this issue and use price datasets containing information for a large number of consumer goods. Such data, however, are typically available only for a handful of developed markets.

Another recent innovation is to scrape online prices, but this option remains limited to countries where online shopping has a nontrivial market share (Cavallo and Rigobon 2016). Atkin and Donaldson (2015) apply the price gaps methodology to estimate trade costs in Ethiopia and Nigeria by using data on prices of several staple consumer goods collected by statistical agencies for constructing the consumer price index. Díaz de Astarloa and Pkhikidze (2024) do so for Georgia, Kenya, Madagascar, Nigeria, Rwanda, and Tanzania.

NOTE

1. This appendix is based on Coşar (2022).

REFERENCES

Allen, T., and C. Arkolakis. 2014. "Trade and the Topography of the Spatial Economy." *Quarterly Journal of Economics* 129: 1085–140.

Atkin, D., and D. Donaldson. 2015. "Who's Getting Globalized? The Size and Implications of Intra-National Trade Costs." NBER Working Paper 21439, National Bureau of Economic Research, Cambridge, MA.

Bird, J., M. Lebrand, and A.J. Venables. 2020. "The Belt and Road Initiative: Reshaping Economic Geography in Central Asia?" *Journal of Development Economics* 144.

Cavallo, A., and R. Rigobon. 2016. "The Billion Prices Project: Using Online Prices for Measurement and Research." *Journal of Economic Perspectives* 30: 151–78.

Combes, P.-P., and M. Lafourcade. 2005. "Transport Costs: Measures, Determinants, and Regional Policy Implications for France." *Journal of Economic Geography* 5: 319–49.

Coşar, A.K. 2022. "Overland Transport Costs." Policy Research Working Paper 10156, World Bank, Washington, DC. Background paper prepared for this report.

de Soyres, F., A. Mulabdic, S. Murray, N. Rocha, and M. Ruta. 2019. "How Much Will the Belt and Road Initiative Reduce Trade Costs?" *International Economics* 159(C).

Díaz de Astarloa, B., and N. Pkhikidze. 2024. "Internal Trade Costs in Developing Countries." Policy Research Working Paper 10789, World Bank, Washington, DC. Background paper prepared for this report.

Donaldson, D., and R. Hornbeck. 2016. "Railroads and American Economic Growth: A 'Market Access' Approach. *Quarterly Journal of Economics* 131: 799–858.

Hernández, C. 2021. "Waits and Delays in Road Freight Transport." Research Department Working Paper 1724, CAF Development Bank of Latin America. Caracas. https://scioteca.caf.com/handle/123456789/1724.

Herrera Dappe, M., C. Kunaka, M. Lebrand, and N. Weisskopf. 2020. *Moving Forward: Connectivity and Logistics to Sustain Bangladesh's Success*. Washington, DC: World Bank.

Herrera Dappe, M., M. Lebrand, and D. Van Patten. 2021. "Bridging Bangladesh and India: Cross-Border Trade and the Motor Vehicles Agreement." Policy Research Working Paper 9592, World Bank, Washington, DC.

Lall, S., and M. Lebrand. 2020. "Who Wins, Who Loses? Understanding the Spatially Differentiated Effects of the Belt and Road Initiative." *Journal of Development Economics* 146.

Lam, Y.Y., K. Sriram, and N. Khera. 2019. "Strengthening Vietnam's Trucking Sector: Towards Lower Logistics Costs and Greenhouse Gas Emissions. Vietnam Transport Knowledge Series. Washington, DC: World Bank Group.

Osborne, T., M. Pachon, and G. Araya. 2014. "What Drives the High Price of Road Freight Transport in Central America?" Policy Research Working Paper 6844, World Bank, Washington, DC.

Teravaninthorn, S., and G. Raballand. 2009. *Transport Prices and Costs in Africa: A Review of the International Corridors*. Washington, DC: World Bank.